Constructing a Community of Thought

Critical Pedagogical Perspectives

Greg S. Goodman, *General Editor*

Vol. 22

The Educational Psychology series is part of the Peter Lang Education list.
Every volume is peer reviewed and meets
the highest quality standards for content and production.

PETER LANG
New York • Washington, D.C./Baltimore • Bern
Frankfurt • Berlin • Brussels • Vienna • Oxford

Constructing a Community of Thought

Letters on the
Scholarship, Teaching,
and Mentoring of
Vera John-Steiner

EDITED BY Robert Lake
& M. Cathrene Connery

PETER LANG
New York • Washington, D.C./Baltimore • Bern
Frankfurt • Berlin • Brussels • Vienna • Oxford

Library of Congress Cataloging-in-Publication Data

Constructing a community of thought: letters on the scholarship, teaching,
and mentoring of Vera John-Steiner / edited by Robert Lake, M. Cathrene Connery.
p. cm. — (Educational psychology: critical pedagogical perspectives; v. 22)
Includes bibliographical references.
1. John-Steiner, Vera, 1930–. 2. Educators—United States. 3. Educational psychology.
4. Learning. 5. Education—Study and teaching (Higher). 6. Creative thinking—
Study and teaching (Higher). 7. Linguistics—Study and
teaching (Higher). I. Lake, Robert. II. Connery, M. Cathrene.
LA2317.J58C66   370.92—dc23 [B]   2012032554
ISBN 978-1-4331-1917-0 (hardcover)
ISBN 978-1-4331-1916-3 (paperback)
ISBN 978-1-4539-0974-4 (e-book)
ISSN 1943-8109

Bibliographic information published by **Die Deutsche Nationalbibliothek**.
Die Deutsche Nationalbibliothek lists this publication in the "Deutsche
Nationalbibliografie"; detailed bibliographic data is available
on the Internet at http://dnb.d-nb.de/.

Cover photograph by Gretchen Garner

© 2013 Peter Lang Publishing, Inc., New York
29 Broadway, 18th floor, New York, NY 10006
www.peterlang.com

All rights reserved.
Reprint or reproduction, even partially, in all forms such as microfilm,
xerography, microfiche, microcard, and offset strictly prohibited.

This book is collectively dedicated to the genius, generosity, and vision of Lev Vygotsky, Paulo Freire, and all our students.

To my wife, Elizabeth, my children, and grandchildren from whom I have learned more about creativity, collaboration, imagination, and life itself than I could ever capture in writing in one lifetime. R.L.

To Michael, sage, succor, and the song in my heart. M.C.C.

Table of Contents

Acknowledgments — xi

PART ONE: THE SOCIAL CONSTRUCTION OF A THOUGHT COMMUNITY

1. Building Bridges: The Contribution of Dr. Vera John-Steiner's Work — 3
   M. Cathrene Connery
2. Constructing a Community of Thought: Access through Epistolary Understanding — 5
   Robert Lake and M. Cathrene Connery

PART TWO: LETTERS ON A LIFE

3. The Bold and Courageous Path of Vera John-Steiner — 13
   Peter Smagorinsky
4. Living Memory — 16
   Edward De Santis
5. My Life-Long Dialogue with Vera John-Steiner — 19
   Constance R. Sutton
6. Veronka, My Czardas Dancing, Creative Thinking Mother — 21
   Suki John
7. My Favorite Collaborator — 23
   Reuben Hersh
8. From Your House to My House — 25
   Anne Wiltshire
9. Above and Beyond Box Consciousness — 28
   Bernard Spolsky
10. Memories of a Long Conversation — 31
    Michael Cole
11. Networks in Life and in Science — 34
    Csaba Pléh and Ottilia Boross

PART THREE: LETTERS ON SCHOLARSHIP

12. The Remarkable Power of Bisociation — 41
    Susan Ervin-Tripp

13.	Young Children's Sociodramatic Play: Wellspring of Collaboration and Learning Laura E. Berk	44
14.	Discovering Self in Play Artin Göncü	50
15.	Vera Was a Vygotskian before She Knew Who Vygotsky Was Steven G. McCafferty	54
16.	Vera: Tribute and Tributary Maryhelen Snyder	57
17.	Revisiting an Interactive Approach to Advancing Literacy Linda Finlay	61
18.	Working Classroom: An Intergenerational Arts Community Nan Elsasser	65
19.	Resonance Henry Shonerd	73
20.	Water and Wine: Painting as the Emergence of Word Meanings from Images David Kellogg	76
21.	Applying a Functional Systems Approach to the Study of Language Development Teresa Meehan	81
22.	Vera John-Steiner's Influence on Creativity Research R. Keith Sawyer	86
23.	Who Knew? Being Part of a Thought Community on Creativity: An Essay in Honor of Vera John-Steiner David Henry Feldman	89
24.	Dignified Interdependence Patricia A. St. John	94
25.	Cognitive Pluralism and Creative Collaboration Kimberly Cotter-Lemus	99
26.	Reverberations Shirley Brice Heath	103
27.	The Influence of Vera John-Steiner's Work on Sabra Sowell-Lovejoy: Artist and Educator Sabra Sowell-Lovejoy	107
28.	Bridges are Made for Movement Robert Lake	111

29.	Tapestry: Interwoven Minds, Emerging Meanings *Seana Moran*	115
30.	Vera John-Steiner on Creativity and Collaboration: A Scholar Ahead of Her Time *Nancy J. Uscher*	119
31.	And Perhaps Our Research Leads Us Back to a World We Lost *Eleni Bastéa*	122
32.	Creative Collaboration as Revolutionary and Transformative *Robin Oppenheimer*	126
33.	Creativity in All of Us: A Dialogue with Vera John-Steiner *Anna Stetsenko*	129
34.	Collaboration Is at the Heart of the Human Condition *Andy Blunden*	133
35.	My Awakening *Patricia A. Richard-Amato*	136
36.	From Vygotsky to Vera to All of Us: The Mentoring Magnifies *LeAnn Putney and Joan Wink*	139
37.	A Researcher's Grail: A Search for an Alternative to Conventional Teacher–Student Discourse *Ronald Gallimore*	145
38.	Dr. Vera John-Steiner as a Key: Unlocking a Theory of Receptive Discourse *Laura Rychly*	149
39.	The Constellation, Maker *Robert Danberg*	153

PART FOUR: LETTERS ON TEACHING AND MENTORING

40.	You Will Meet Vera *Courtney Angermeier*	159
41.	Vera John-Steiner: Mentor and Collaborator *Christopher C. Shank*	161
42.	Creativity and Collaboration: A Student's Salvation? *Susan K. Metheny*	166
43.	Creative Collaboration in the Art Museum *Sara Otto-Diniz*	169

44.	Collaborative Recreation *Rod Parker-Rees*	172
45.	Coming into Being: Creative Collaboration as a Life-Long Gift *Judah Ronch*	176
46.	The Schools Have Failed the Poor *Carolyn Panofsky*	180
47.	My Noble Quest *Annalisa Aguilar*	184
48.	Grateful Recollections from Your Zone of Proximal Development *Kathryn (Kate) J. Miller*	188
49.	Vera and the Gift of Confidence *Holbrook Mahn*	192
50.	Vera: My Inspiration for Discovering the 'Invisibilities' in the Activity-Theoretical Studies of Innovation *Mervi Hasu*	195
51.	Finding Myself in Vera and Finding Vera in Me *Linney Wix*	201
52.	Creative Transformation through Mentorship and Intergenerational Collaboration *Sara Abercrombie*	205
53.	Enacting What We Sought to Understand *Michele Minnis*	208
54.	Being Community: Engaging Struggles, Constructing Academic Lives, and Effecting Social Change *Lois M. Meyer*	213
55.	Bridges Beyond Budapest *Valerie Clement*	217

PART FIVE: EXPANDING THE COMMUNITY OF THOUGHT

56.	A Blueprint for an Architecture of Accomplishment *M. Cathrene Connery & Robert Lake*	223

Acknowledgments

The publication of this text exemplifies both creative collaboration and collaborative creation. Therefore, several acknowledgments are in order. First, we want to thank our 54 contributors to this book. We are acutely aware that you took precious time away from other projects, deadlines, family responsibilities, and commitments to add to this collection of letters. Many of you have collaborated with Vera for several years, while others only recently identified the scholar as a distant mentor through her writings. Yet all of you have played a significant part in constructing this polyphonic expression of Vera's life and scholarship to complement not only her writing, but your own scholarship and teaching as well.

We also want to thank Chris Myers, Greg Goodman, and Shirley Steinberg at Peter Lang Publishing for their extraordinary vision of publishing that makes a project like this possible. We are deeply appreciative of the time, talents, and assistance of Amber Bryan, a graduate assistant at Georgia Southern University, for her amazing help proofreading the first drafts of the letters. Finally, we would like to express our gratitude to Dr. Vera John-Steiner for allowing us to edit this book. For those of you who have not met her, Vera is a very humble, quiet, and private person. We suspect the public expression of the text's contents sometimes went against the grain of such a modest and self-effacing individual. However, she has once again generously provided the context of her career where we, as her students, mentees, collaborators, and colleagues might have access to opportunities for growth. We are grateful to Vera for being the kind of scholar, mentor, and friend who inspires all of us to be creative, critical, and caring in these times of widespread apathy, standardized thinking, and depersonalization.

PART ONE

The Social Construction of a Thought Community

LETTER ONE

Building Bridges
The Contribution of Dr. Vera John-Steiner's Work

M. Cathrene Connery

Dear Veronka and Colleagues:
Night falls over the Danube
    Like a soft, blue velvet curtain.
A father
    Lifts his brown-eyed daughter into his arms
    Pointing to the emerging stars
    And lights of the capital below.
Together they stand
    On an architectural wonder
    Bridging the dialectics of
    East & West
    Physics & physicality
    Ingenuity & iron
    The ancient clans of Buda and Pest
    Neighbors who dared envision a future together.
After the war, the Széchenyi Chain Bridge was rebuilt
    By the determination of the Hungarian people.
    Today it stands
    A symbol of grace
    Exuding balance, dignity, and strength
    Like the girl who grew into a woman.
But not all bridges are cast of metal.
Morning swells over the Río Grande
    In a pink-lavender blanket of early light.
A brown-eyed professor
    Smiles at her nervous students
    Illuminating an academic legacy
    Based on human hope.
She has stood beside us

While constructing
An intellectual wonder
Bridging the dialectics of
    Thought & language
    Artist & partnership
    Cognition & emotion
    Self & society
Creating sociocultural arches requisite to the establishment of
    Respectful interdependence
    Social justice
    Lasting equity and
    The serenity of peace.
It is mid-day.
    The sun radiates with promise in the turquoise sky.
Her students
    Will continue to refine these bridges
    Responsible for returning the gift of confidence.
    For together we build our futures
    Uniquely universal
    We are diverse and
    We are one.

Adelante con la lucha / Best wishes as we move forward together,
Cathrene

DR. CATHRENE CONNERY is Assistant Professor of Education at Ithaca College where she teaches a course on interface between language, literacy, and sociocultural experience. Her most recent book, *Profiles in Emergent Biliteracy*, received the 2011 Peter Lang Publishing Educational Psychology Book of the Year Award.

LETTER TWO

Constructing a Community of Thought
Access through Epistolary Understanding

Robert Lake and M. Cathrene Connery

Dear Reader:

As editors of this collection of letters on the scholarship, teaching, and mentoring of Dr. Vera John-Steiner, we welcome you to our community of thought! You are invited to step into the center of this intergenerational and multidisciplinary community, where the value of relational ways of knowing and experiencing the known are exercised through shared dialogue, multi-modal interactions, and mutual interdependence. We are confident that, in traversing the series of circles represented in this text, you will discover intrapersonal and interpersonal spaces to help you sustain, create, and share in these crucial times.

This book project taught us many vital lessons about the immense value of collaboration and the need to reconsider traditional, academic formalities that often silence *perezhivanie*, or the lived experience. Like many diverse thinkers before us, we have experienced salient and powerful sources of knowledge that are often banished from or hidden behind formal norms of academic writing. Therefore, we begin this letter of introduction by providing a brief overview on the value of collaborative efforts, letters as a written genre, and their reciprocal relationship appropriate to this text. We first discuss the notion of a community of thought, derived from Vera's scholarship and professional experience. Second, we explain why we chose the epistolary genre or letter format for this particular edited volume. We end this letter with a strategy for you to navigate the structure of the larger book.

THOUGHT COMMUNITIES AND COLLABORATIVE CREATION

Vera defines a *thought community* as a group of "experienced thinkers who engage in intense interaction with each other while promoting a perspective shift in their discipline" (2000, p. 6). She adopted this term from the biologist/sociologist Ludwik Fleck (1935/1979), who viewed "cognition as the result of social activity" (ibid, p. 195).

The construction of a community of thought is characterized by its functional division of labor, cooperation, preparatory work, as well as the mutual and controversial exchange of ideas in which the whole is much greater than the sum of its individual parts. Many of us who are engaged in the social sciences, especially within the field of education, are keenly aware of the need for paradigmatic change and a shift to meaningful and dignified praxis. Our increasingly complex and diversified global context has outlived the mythical ideal associated with the rugged individualist. In reflecting on these outdated notions, Vera notes:

> Rodin's sculpture, *The Thinker*, dominates our collective imagination as the purest representation of human inquiry—the lone stoic thinker. But while the Western belief in individualism romanticizes this perception of the solitary creative process, the reality is that scientific and artistic forms emerge from joint thinking, passionate conversations, emotional connections, and shared struggles common in meaningful relationship (John-Steiner, 2000).

Of course, it was one of Vera's distant mentors, Lev S. Vygotsky, who strongly inspired her thinking in this direction. Through his short life, Vygotsky affirmed that "creative activities are social, that thinking is not confined to the individual brain/mind, and that the construction of knowledge is embedded in the cultural and historical milieu in which it arises" (John-Steiner, 2000, p. 5). Indeed, the serious challenges of the 21st century beckon us to come together, to cease viewing divergent thinking in a deficit manner, and to bring "to light the role of dialogue and the diversity of perspectives which, when linked to a common purpose, reveal the power of collaboration" (ibid, p. 192).

As you will discover in the letters of this volume, Vera's scholarship, teaching, and mentoring have had an enormous impact on the lives of her students and fellow collaborators. In addition to the collective efforts represented in her seminal work, *Creative Collaboration*, including Aaron Copeland and Leonard Bernstein, Will and Ariel Durant, and the Guarneri Quartet, Vera's professional practice involves the reciprocal, generative relationships active within communities of thought. Comments on her own classes and collaborations reveal that the scholar herself receives "new insights into this dense network of concepts and ideas, and as the students scaffold each other, I can witness as well as participate in the co-construction of knowledge" (John-Steiner, 2010, personal communication). As a central recurring theme of this volume, Vera's respect for, love of, and commitment to teaching, mentoring, and collaborating shines in her comments about what she has learned teaching a course called Language and Thought: "We think aloud together in these classes. The reaction papers and peer exam reaffirm for me…the powerful dialectics between spoken and written language, and social and individual processes that facilitate dialectics in learning.… Teaching these and other classes allows me to experience each semester anew, and reconnect to the grand, collective project of trying to understand ourselves as engaged, thinking beings" (ibid).

It is our hope that, as you read through this text, you will be inspired to take risks to adopt and create new methods of collaboration, including the promotion of interdisciplinarity. When you consider the diverse range of work of the contributors, the seamless convergence of this community of thought is even more amazing to witness. Vera's correspondents represent multiple funds of knowledge as well as a host of scholarly, pragmatic, and performative aspects within their respective disciplines. The testimonies of psychologists, dancers, graphic artists, mathematicians, anthropologists, architectural historians, musicians, and linguists powerfully support the rich possibilities that await those who are willing to explore collaborative and interdisciplinary endeavors to "transcend the constraints of biology, of time, of habit, and achieve a fuller self, beyond the limitations and the talents of the isolated individual"(John-Steiner, 2000, p. 188).

THE POWER OF THE EPISTOLARY GENRE: ACCESS INTO UNDERSTANDING

Initially, some of our contributors asked why we chose to use an epistolary genre for this text instead of a more traditional venue such as a book of essays or the standard Festschrift. Perhaps the dictionary definition of this term can provide us with a contrast of purposes: The *American Heritage Dictionary* (2009) defines the word *Festschrift* as a "volume of learned articles or essays by colleagues and admirers, serving as a tribute or memorial especially to a scholar." Possibly you have read or maybe even contributed to volume of this kind; we certainly recognize the value of such works. However, in this instance, a memorial is not appropriate. Despite her retirement, Vera continues to engage in vibrant, productive, and rigorous scholarship, teaching, mentoring, and collaboration. The dialogic nature of her work in creativity and shared ways of knowing call for a much more personal genre of writing.

The epistolary genre is as old as writing itself. As a means of research data or source of understanding, especially in educational biography and creativity studies where the self is not considered a contaminating taboo, there is much to learn about relationships, personal history, and intellectual and emotional impact. Therefore, the use of letters for this text is both functional and appropriate.

The letters in this volume invite you into circles of relationship to share intimate transactions of thought and practice that would otherwise not be accessed through standard academic writing. Sonia Nieto, the noted multicultural educationist, has worked in this genre for many years with her students and has this to say about the genre:

> The power of the epistolary genre resides in precisely this: it makes a private act public and it gives others access to insights and wisdom that might otherwise be inaccessible to them. In the process, it allows readers to see the interactions between two people who have a personal connection, one of whom has agreed to let others listen in on the conversation. While the private letters of many famous people have been published (although they might never have been meant to see the light of day), books such as *Dear Paulo* (Nieto, 2008) and *Dear Maxine* (Lake, 2010) are different in that they are meant, from the outset, to be public encounters that go beyond the writer and the addressee. These letters are meant to illuminate, teach, inspire, and to help us face life with some new meanings and motivations." (Nieto, 2010, p. xi)

In addition, we respectfully remind you that every day letters, texts, and e-mails are written beyond abstract or generic audiences with a very specific human recipient in mind. Such a venue constructs the context for shared epistemologies and relational aspects of understanding to be "frozen" on paper and in time. Because the entire body of Vera's interdisciplinary work in collaboration and creativity emphasizes the dynamic nature of language as an on-going social process, it is fitting to record this curriculum-as-conversation as an artifact of her larger thought community. In this manner, Vera's professional constructions, captured through the collaborative epistolary, strongly reflect Bakhtin's (1986) notion of the dialogic nature of utterance: "utterance is filled with *dialogic overtones*, and they must be taken into account in order to fully understand the style of the utterance. After all, our thought itself—philosophical, scientific, artistic—is born and shaped in the process of interaction and struggle with others' thought, and this cannot but be reflected in the forms that verbally express our thought as well" (p. 92).

NAVIGATING THE TEXT: TRAVERSING NESTED CIRCLES

In closing, we would like to present you with a strategy to navigate this text in a manner that allows you to move progressively from the stance of an external observer of Vera's professional life into the dynamic participation in your own reality. As you can see in Figure 1, we have organized this book into a series of nested circles that permit you to successively gain entrance into Vera's thought community. The first circle is comprised of biographical letters in which we introduce you to Vera as a woman of many roles. By reading the letters of the second circle, you can step into a sphere of thought reflecting the various themes of Vera's scholarship represented in a companion volume to this text, entitled *The Selected Works of Vera John-Steiner: Sculpting Mind and Meaning in Sociocultural Theory*. Within a third ring of letters, you are invited to experience a continuum of relationship from the *perezhivanija*, or lived experiences, of Vera's students, mentees, colleagues, and collaborators. This inward progression actively places you at the heart of our thought community.

Constructing a Community of Thought | 9

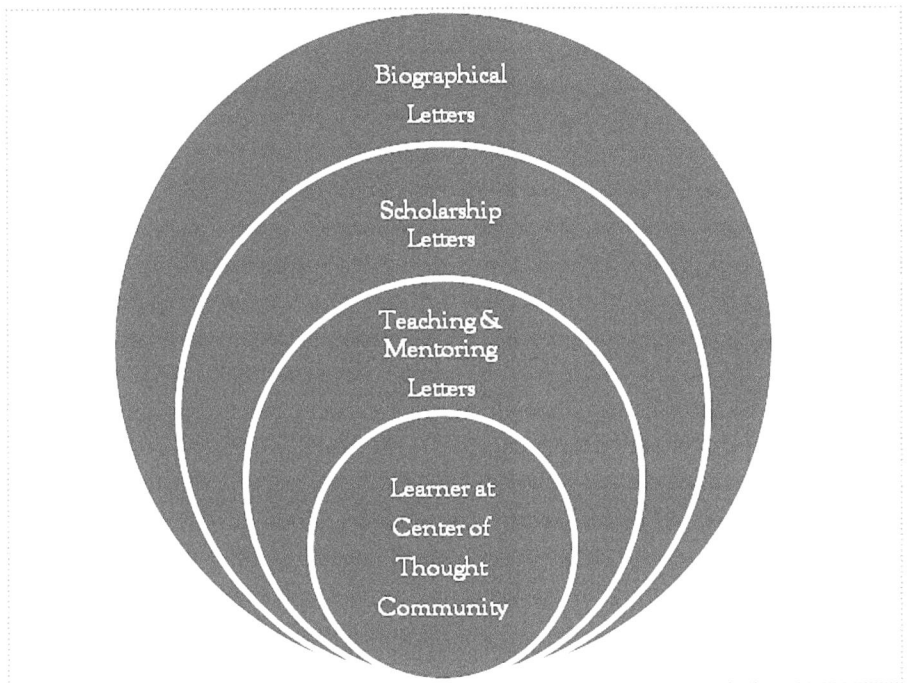

From this vantage point in the concluding chapter, we will request that you turn around to review the significance of each nested ring: the multidimensionality of Vera as a woman and a profound thinker; her interdisciplinary, balanced scholarship based on dialectical synthesis; her pedagogy rooted in praxis and an ethos of collegiality, rigor, and care. After progressing through these spherical zones, we promise to reconnect with you at the center, dear reader, to examine how you might assist in co-constructing the sustaining, transformative dynamic of a thought community based on a creativity of hope.

All our best wishes,
Robert and Cathrene

ROBERT LAKE, Ph.D., is Associate Professor in the Department of Curriculum, Foundations, and Reading at Georgia Southern University where he teaches both undergraduate and graduate courses in multicultural education from local and global perspectives. His expertise in music and English as a Second Language led to his investigation of imaginative curriculum for his doctoral dissertation. Dr. Lake has served as an academic advisor and cultural events facilitator for the U.S. Department of State's International Leadership in Education Program (ILEP). A frequent presenter at international conferences, he has recently completed *Vygotsky on Education* released by Peter Lang Publishers in 2012. Dr. Lake has also edited and contributed to two books of letters published by Teachers College Press titled, *Dear Maxine: Letters from the Unfinished Conversation with Maxine Greene* (2010) and *Letters to Nel Noddings: Circles of Care* (2012).

DR. M. CATHRENE CONNERY is Assistant Professor of Education at Ithaca College. A bilingual educator, researcher, and advocate, she has drawn on her visual arts education as a painter to inform her research and professional activities in language, literacy, and sociocultural studies. Dr. Connery has presented on theoretical, pedagogic, and programmatic concerns surrounding the education of culturally and linguistically diverse children in the United States for the past 25 years. Her current research interests include multicultural teacher education, biliteracy & the development of first & second languages, semiotics, sociopolitical issues in development, learning, and education as well as the social construction of feminist identities by female artists and teachers. She has utilized Vygotskian theory to articulate ethnographic accounts in *Profiles in Emergent Biliteracy: Children Making Meaning in a Chicano Community* (2011) and as an editor and contributor to *Vygotsky and Creativity: A Cultural-historical Approach to Play, Meaning-making, and the Arts* (2010) published by Peter Lang.

REFERENCES

Bakhtin, M. (1986). *Speech genres and other late essays*. C. Emerson & M. Holquist (Eds.). Translated by Vern W. McGee. Austin: University of Texas Press.

Festschrift. (2009). *American Heritage Dictionary online*. Retrieved from http://ahdictionary.com/word/search.html?q=Festschrift

Fleck, L. (1935/1979). *Genesis and development of scientific fact*. Chicago: University of Chicago Press.

John-Steiner, V. (2000). *Creative collaboration*. Oxford, UK. Oxford University Press.

Lake, R. (2010). *Dear Maxine: Letters from the unfinished conversation with Maxine Greene*. New York: Teachers College Press.

Nieto, S. (2008). *Dear Paulo: Letters from those who dare to teach*. Boulder: Paradigm Publishers.

Nieto, S. (2010). Foreword. In R. Lake (Ed.) *Dear Maxine: Letters from the unfinished conversation with Maxine Greene*. New York: Teachers College Press.

PART TWO

Letters on a Life

The Woman and Her Many Roles

LETTER THREE

The Bold and Courageous Path of Vera John-Steiner

Peter Smagorinsky

"It is quite a leap from Budapest to Rough Rock, Arizona, but the diversity of thought and the impact of culture as part of thought were vividly manifested in both places. For Navajos, the creating of beauty in paintings and ordinary artifacts has a life-sustaining power in the midst of harsh conditions they often face. Seeing this power, I asked myself: What sustains creative and intellectual endeavor?" (John-Steiner, 1985, p. xiv)

With this question, Vera John-Steiner launched her inquiry into the creative and intellectual processes of exceptionally talented and innovative people across a variety of disciplines. Budapest, Hungary, was her childhood home in the 1930s before she and thousands of other European Jews fled to the U.S. as Hitler began his systematic extermination of the Jewish Problem. English was not her first language, or second, or third; but her fourth. She used it in her U.S. studies in psychology at the University of Chicago, following which she relocated to the American Southwest where her remarkable career has unfolded. Her experiences under harsh conditions in Europe, and among those living harshly in the Southwest, have led her to understand how people think symbolically and construct textual worlds through which they make their lives meaningful. This work was pioneering in its inception and remains influential as the field of psychology catches up on the path she has cut through a thicket of opposition.

As the notion of cognitive pluralism has become mainstream thanks to the work of Howard Gardner and others, it's hard to remember—especially for those of us who were barely out of diapers at the time—just how courageous it was for Vera to work against the reigning orthodoxies of her day in undertaking these questions. If I may digress and briefly tell a family story: My sister Anne was an undergraduate psychology major at Princeton from 1969–1973, and for her senior thesis did a paper on what might be called the psychology of advertising. Now, here in the 21st century, this topic sounds like a reasonable idea, one that might help establish a career as, say, an advertising art director, which is what she did for many years. But in the 1970s, her thesis review committee took quite a dim view of her work because it wasn't carried out in a laboratory and was too grounded in mundane activity.

Anne did this work well over a decade after Vera had undertaken an even more radical departure from the clinical approaches to skull-bound cognition in her consideration not only of the multiple symbol systems through which people think but the cultural activity by means of which ways of thinking develop. Not only did she go against orthodoxy to consider this topic, she did so as one of the few women to work on a doctorate in the 1950s, as a Jew at a time when Jews were held to quotas in many universities and other institutions and were associated with communism through questionable attributions of the Bolshevik Revolution to Jewish leadership, and as an immigrant during a period of post-war xenophobia fueled by the anti-Semitism that, paradoxically, placed Jews as the third most hated ethnic group after the Germans and Japanese in mid-century America (Johnson, 1988). Virtually everything about Vera's profile suggested that she would be well-served by being obedient, fitting in, and following her professors' dicta. I imagine that if she had, the field of social-cultural-historical psychology would be less robust, more logocentric, and less advanced than it is today. Without question, Vera has been in the vanguard of our field's thinking for over a half-century now. I surely owe much of what I know about culture, communication, and cognition to her groundbreaking work in the field.

I first met Vera in 1994 at the International Conference on Lev Vygotsky and the Contemporary Human Sciences in the conference center in Golitsyna, about an hour from Moscow, an event I attended as a wide-eyed assistant professor who had just begun to incorporate Vygotsky's thinking into my own, without the benefit of any formal training in his research program. I knew of Vera through her role as co-editor of *Mind in Society* and as the author of *Notebooks of the Mind*, both among the essential readings in the Vygotskian canon. Meeting one's heroes can be a precarious undertaking, because too many turn out to be far too human to ultimately emulate: vain, aloof, uncaring, manipulative, unethical, hypocritical, and all manner of other disappointing traits. What I found in Vera, in contrast, was someone I wanted to grow up to be just like.

First, she carried herself with tremendous humility. Vera was clearly a star at a conference filled with notable Vygotskian scholars, yet was among the conference's most approachable people, especially for the young, tentative, and callow, among whom I surely numbered. She always made herself available to anyone who wanted time with her, and I suspect that I was one of many early-career "fourth-generation" Vygotskian researchers who felt that simply getting to know Vera was worth the trip to Russia.

Along with this humility came the graciousness for which Vera is so well known. She talked appreciatively with those whose papers she liked and professed to have learned much from them, a gesture that gave us a boost in confidence and the feeling that perhaps, on some small level, we actually belonged in this company. This is not to say that she uncritically spoke glowingly of every person or paper, for she has admirable standards for what elevates scholarship above the commonplace or misplaced. When she liked an idea, however, she went out of her way to get to know the person who presented it and learn a little more, no matter how much she already knew.

A final quality that impressed me then, and continues to earn my high regard, is the most difficult to pinpoint, that being Vera's great wisdom. Many in the field are smart, but are also petty, conceited, ambitious, mean, narcissistic, and otherwise lacking in the sort of qualities that separate the intelligent from those who are wise. I think that one reason that people gravitate to Vera is that she leads by the example she sets for how to conduct oneself in great company, or in the midst of overwhelming opposition. Perhaps this disposition was forged in her days as a Hungarian Jew during Hitler's orchestration of anti-Semitic hatred into a broad-based policy of ethnic extermination. Perhaps it was fostered in her adjustment to a new culture and language upon her arrival in the U.S. Perhaps her experiences in defying the orthodoxies of the field of psychology contributed to the resolute manner in which she pursues what she believes is right and does so with conviction and integrity. Perhaps the sum of her life's work has provided the accumulation of experiences that, combined with her native gifts and resilience, has enabled her to stand for what she believes in with such admirable honor that others inevitably see her as one whose example they hope someday to follow. Those of wisdom lead, whether they want to or not.

Perhaps it's the very paradoxes of Vera John-Steiner that make her such an admirable and exemplary scholar to those who make up the field. She is as tough as nails, yet gentle with others, particularly those who feel vulnerable. She is formidably intelligent yet eminently accessible to the meekest among us. She carries herself with dignity even though she has experienced the worst of humanity in Nazi-era Europe and has spent much of her life among indigenous Southwestern people to whom injustice is a way of life. She is one of my heroes, and has more than stood up to the scrutiny that such achievement invites. I'm honored to be part of this collection that helps to recognize her many contributions to the work and lives of so many people.

Peter Smagorinsky

PETER SMAGORINSKY, Ph.D., holds the rank of Distinguished Research Professor of English Education in the Department of Language and Literacy Education in the College of Education at the University of Georgia. He taught high school English in the Chicago area for many years and is the recipient of several national honors for his commitment to adolescents and their teachers.

REFERENCES

John-Steiner, V. (1985). *Notebooks of the mind: Explorations of thinking.* Albuquerque: University of New Mexico Press.

Johnson, P. (1988). *A history of the Jews.* New York: HarperPerennial.

Vygotsky, L. S. (1978). *Mind in society: The development of higher psychological processes* (M. Cole, V. John-Steiner, S. Scribner, & E. Souberman, Eds.). Cambridge, MA: Harvard University Press.

LETTER FOUR

Living Memory

Edward De Santis

"Immersing oneself in the works of a predecessor and retracing his or her path, yields a useful counterpoint to the cafeteria of school learning for the person preparing for a creative life."

(John-Steiner, 1997, p. 208)

Dear Vera,

Many years ago you visited one of my Honors program seminars, "Literature of the Holocaust". All but two of the students were women, ages from their early twenties to their late fifties. None had ever encountered a survivor, until that day. After you departed, all sat motionless for what seemed like hours. Finally, when one of the older women began to speak, she couldn't hold back her tears. She wasn't the only one. The next week we heard what the students wrote about the impact you had upon them. Your story of leaving home to buy milk, all the while knowing that you were being closely watched as you walked by German soldiers, called to mind the suspense and dread felt by Anne Frank. So close in age. No way out. Staying alive. Not to be noticed. Each step, or glance, or word could be the last. Against the greatest odds, to preserve one's life.

Anne Frank left us her diary. You have left us books that are ultimately about living, your life and those lives you have explored. *Loving and Hating Mathematics* struck me immediately as a dysfunctional family quarrel about life: a mathematical genius yields to absurd choices, has improbable points of view or unmasks bizarre behavior. Which reminded me of Wagner, whose Farewell and Magic Fire Music at the end of "Die Walkure" can take my soul deeply into the sublime love between Wotan and Brunhilde, yet he debased himself as an anti-semite.

In *Notebooks of the Mind*, you revealed with brilliance newer and different approaches toward an understanding of the manifold and ubiquitous phenomenon of creativity. You went directly to your sources, creative human beings, especially those living, to explicate the dynamics, the power of self-awareness, of intuition, imagination, and boldness. Living with the purpose of making something new again and again shows their steadfastness and hope, and with no assurance of success.

With *Creative Collaboration* you introduced many to humanity's timeless gift of collective creativity in recent memory. My ardent interest in antiquities led me to explore the age of monasticism and the development of towns, and beyond that into the Hebrew Scriptures, and the South Africans who manufactured materials, such as oils produced from animal bone marrow and ground stone for cave paintings over a hundred thousand years ago. Small groups of inspired and talented persons committed to a creative project, who work at their own pace and set their own parameters, learn how to yield to a better idea or direction for the sake of the collective creation.

Recently I read an articulate and illuminating book by Daniel Barenboim, *Music Quickens Time*. He wrote, "There has always been a tendency, in a certain line of Jewish thought, to adhere to the universality of human experience...Spinoza, Heinrich Heine, Martin Buber and Sigmund Freud among others...made no distinction between Jewishness and otherness." Barenboim (2009, p. 105). Ironically, nearly a century ago, Martin Buber envisaged a Jewish Renaissance. However, there was a problem. German Jews, for the most part, had assimilated into the German culture. Many tried to suppress their Jewish identity, to appear more Germanic. Buber, however, who had a firm belief in the importance of building and belonging to a dynamic and united community in which each citizen had a responsibility for his or her neighbors, saw Jews living in ghettos in the Slavic states, often without the basics of life. He expected the German Jews to acknowledge their kinship with the East European Jews, who shared with them a common origin and a bond of continuity. Unfortunately, they looked the other way. So, Buber turned to the east and discovered a powerful source of authentic Jewish culture in the treasure and wisdom that was Hasidic folklore. From this vast store of knowledge and talent you emerged with so many others, such as Leo Sheskov (Russia), Clara Haskil (Romania), and Gyorgy Ligeti (Hungary).

The Jews of the ghetto welcomed the free atmosphere of the Hasidic life. They preferred to hear from their Rabbis allegorical rather than literal and legalistic interpretations of the Bible. They could enjoy accessibility to the Divine in the most humble circumstances, especially those of the lower classes. Hasidic mysticism encouraged "tikkun," giving them the opportunity to restore justice and peace, and eliminate poverty. Buber's socialist communitarian perspective of a "dialogical community" was sustained by an interpersonal "dialogical relationship." Isn't this comparable to the learning environment you create for your students and colleagues?

As you know, Buber was an innovator, and at times, seen by some as controversial. He sought to foster a connection between Judaism and the modern world through Zionism. But Zionism didn't always comport with his understanding of it. For Buber, each cultural tradition should be kept alive and reborn when its artists, scientists, educators, and philosophers draw upon a bulwark of living memory. Also, it is this memory that joins people and cultures, even if there is enmity between them. Here begins the student's realization that he or she and the teacher are truly sharing in each other's life. Vera, this may be what defines you more than anything else, as a scholar and a mentor, in my memory of you.

There is more. Vera, your silence is a personal strength, which shows your reverence for others. When you speak, one stops to learn from you, and is, thus, inclined to respond by asking a question. Few of our contemporaries practice the virtue of silence. In conversation with you, one often doesn't draw conclusions. It is not about rendering judgments. There is, instead, passivity. Listening. Participation. Giving all present a chance to be heard. Little action, except dialogue. Clarifying. Sharing. Reconsidering. Seeking what to agree upon. Letting an opponent know that you want to listen to his or her side of an issue. Allowing moments of silence to prevail over clatter. This is not the absence of human communication, but a gradual process of engaging others, forming friendships, and eventually establishing a professional or personal relationship.

For decades I have had a special affinity to the music of Gustav Mahler and Richard Strauss. I have shared hundreds of hours listening to their works with friends and students. Before I began writing this letter, I listened yet again to compositions that I thought would inspire me. And they did. Strauss' "Four Last Songs," and Mahler's Second ("Resurrection"), Third, and his Eighth ("Symphony of a Thousand") symphonies, respectively, reflect the dedicated musicians and poets who were seized with wonder by the physical beauty of Nature, by every level of Love on the evolutionary spiral, and by the mystery of Life itself. These works represent some of my favorite Germanic and East European Jewish romanticism. In both Strauss and Mahler (especially the latter) there is a deep-felt expectation that life, although changing, will continue. Death may be a conclusion, but also a transfiguration to a higher and more beautiful form of existence.

A mutual friend of ours informed me that you regularly attend the concerts of the Tanglewood Music Festival in the Berkshires, where Strauss' and Mahler's works are frequently on the program. As you know, our memories are capable of awakening to the replay, as it were, of performances that once flooded our thoughts and emotions, and do so over and over. Such moments often remind us of others, such as that child, who walked in the sun one morning in Budapest a long time ago. She accepted both sorrow and joy; lives in tranquility; attained the light of wisdom; loves what is hers; will reach the pinnacle of consciousness; is forever free; and will live forever.

With gratitude and affection,
Edward De Santis

DR. EDWARD DESANTIS is Professor Emeritus of the University of New Mexico. The former Director of the University College's Honors Program, Dr. DeSantis served as an ardent advocate of student and faculty rights presiding as the President of the Faculty Senate for many years.

REFERENCE

Barenboim, D. (2009). *Music quickens time*. London: Verso.

LETTER FIVE

My Life-Long Dialogue with Vera John-Steiner

Constance R. Sutton

"The study of collaboration supports the following claim: productive interdependence is a critical resource for expanding the self throughout the life span." (John-Steiner, 2000, p. 191)

My dear Veruska, sister-friend,

I found it difficult to select a short quote from your work. I so wanted to quote the passage in which you describe the dual role of parenting/mentoring with its evolving and exciting benefits to my anthropologist son David (CC: 156–158). Here you quoted from my article "Motherhood Is Powerful" (1998): "Soon the balance of knowledge shifted, and I was learning as much as I was imparting. We had become colleagues." (Sutton, 1998; CC: 157). This is an experience I continue to have not only with my son but also with many of my former anthropology students.

Nonetheless, my title holds. We have been "life-long" friends who have been in constant dialogue ever since we met as graduate students at the University of Chicago in the early 1950s. You were studying social psychology and I was studying anthropology and both of our husbands, Roy John and Sam Sutton, were studying physiological psychology. Your name Vera was my Russian mother's name and as we came to be close friends I called you by the familiar Russian affectionate form.

We found that we shared a concern about the Nazi holocaust, which though it affected each of us differently had led to our similar involvement in US politics and its political movements over time. But more immediate was our shared concern about combining marriage and motherhood with a professional academic career. We were among the early women who faced these challenges in the 1950s, even with support from our husbands. These challenges included the types of research projects women were beginning to undertake, and the questioning of gender-biased received knowledge and the gender-based hierarchies encountered at every institutional level. Yes, there was much to dialogue about and our frequent discussions served to validate each other's perceptions and actions. It also gave support to new personal and intellectual undertakings (in my case undertaking anthropological field research in another country without my husband).

By the mid-fifties, we had all moved east, but to different cities. I and Sam Sutton moved to New York City which you would visit frequently and often stay for long periods, sometimes with us. Throughout the years we always stayed in touch. And when we would meet, we would catch up on all the key happenings in our lives, our children's lives, as well as the world at large. But most importantly, we always would discuss changes in our research and teaching—as I sought to know more about the beliefs, practices, and engagements of people living in the Caribbean and West Africa and you sought to learn more about "the life of the mind." And as we dialogued about these subjects—past and present—we both found that history and context were key to interpreting what we found. As close friends and professional educators in different universities we had much to teach and learn from each other, including the specific contexts that determined the social movements in which we each became engaged.

Yes, Veruska, we have been productively interdependent throughout our long lives together. Now in our eighties, we learn from our children and grandchildren who are creatively pursuing a range of activities, as we continue to dialogue about things both personal and global.

It is my special pleasure to contribute this brief statement to a book that honors you and your creative contributions to understanding "the workings of the mind."

Constance

CONSTANCE SUTTON, Ph.D., is Professor Emerita of Anthropology at New York University. A researcher of Caribbean and Yoruban cultures and active member of the international women's movement, she has published on issues concerning gender hierarchies, trans-national migrant identities, and post-colonial historical remembrances.

REFERENCES

Sutton, C. R. (1998). Motherhood is powerful: embodied knowledge from evolving field-based experiences. *Anthropology and Humanism*, 23(2), 139–145.

LETTER SIX

Veronka, My Czardas Dancing, Creative Thinking Mother

Suki John

Without my mother Veronka's help (in mid-life she finally insisted people call her by her given Hungarian name), I would not have graduated from Kindergarten. That may be true for most children, but in my case I believe it has been especially true. I admit to relying on my mother's brilliant mind as foil, stimulant, and translator, all the way through graduate school and into my first full-time academic position. My mother followed her own mother's example, becoming a teacher who changed students' lives. Like the women whose genes I carry, I was expected to do well in school. I was not on their scholarly level, but I held my own...thanks to their help.

My mother lives the "life of the mind," as she is fond of saying. As a dancer, I have always lived the life of the studio, learning experientially and following up with belated analysis. My mother had the inimitable gift of helping me decipher my observations and channel my impulsiveness; she always honored our basic metabolic differences. A dazzling beauty, she never indulged in that bizarre competition some women foist upon their daughters. She encouraged me to dress nicely but trust my own judgment, to keep my head neatly coiffed but filled with ideas, and to find my own expression, whether it was through dance or through words. She gave me an enormous advantage by marrying a writer who loved dance; my stepfather became my kindest and most honest critic while Veronka remained my ardent fan. Between the two of them I learned to assess my own work frankly while seeing the world as mine to conquer.

Veronka has the wonderful gift of insight, which allows her to put almost any situation into a larger context. She has helped me to make sense of everything from Balanchine to Bahktin, at the same time helping me to make sense of myself. She taught—by example—that mothers work hard, think deeply, and love generously. She also insisted I study my French. As a teen I was dismayed to learn that she was usually right.

My mother, being an educator, sent me to a progressive school in Greenwich Village while she taught a few blocks away at Yeshiva University. I think she has almost completed paying off my elementary school tuition. At the exclusive hippie school where Bob Dylan sent his children, I learned to sing and play baseball with the boys, to go to woodshop as well as art class, to handle a live snake, and to revere the ancient Greeks. I also learned a fair amount of reading, writing and arithmetic. But it wasn't until I was trying to conjugate the French verb *être* that my mother's European education kicked in. I have an indelible image of her sitting on my bed, forcing me to memorize, *je suis, tu es, il est*. It had never occurred to me that learning required that sort of effort, that you could not always study what or how you wanted, and that it was not, always, fun. That was an enlightening moment.

Through high school, college, graduate school, and the mysteries of the tenure process, my mother has offered feedback without being intrusive or superior, and certainly without ever doing the work for me. She read my papers when asked and responded as objectively as a professional Hungarian Jewish mother possibly could. When I was being intellectually lazy, she actually let me know! Now, as I struggle to turn the unpublished memoir that was a dissertation into a scholarly book, I can honestly say my mother has been the best reader imaginable. I am not the first to say that about her. It may be an unfair advantage, but one I'd be a fool to squander. Reading my chapters on Caribbean Dance—just as she read my brother's manuscript on Bolivian history and my husband's dissertation on Agricultural Economics— Veronka responds with amazing clarity on a conceptual and formal level. Once again I must admit she is usually right.

These days most of our conversations revolve around my young son, the object of her current research. She is fascinated by his use of language, his tart observations, and his ongoing experiments that have progressed from the role of gravity on toy trucks to the complexities of Lego robots. Only my mother could formulate the following phrase about a child: "He manipulates objects with great passion."

I have watched Veronka go kicking and screaming into retirement. She loves her life of the mind, and the community of thinkers and friends that she has cultivated over the years. I know that with her amazingly agile intellect she will continue to create and explore, disarming strangers and friends alike with her unmatched social grace. She once crashed a rental car into an art dealer on Madison Avenue and proceeded to make a new friend instead of a lawsuit. But that is another story.

It is my hope that Veronka gets to spend a lot more time in Paris, practicing her French and gently correcting the conjugations of her extended family.

Bisous,
Suki

SUKI JOHN, Ph.D., is Assistant Professor in the School for Classical and Contemporary Dance at Texas Christian University. She has danced, choreographed, and written extensively about dance in the U.S., Europe, and Cuba.

LETTER SEVEN

My Favorite Collaborator

Reuben Hersh

Veronka Dear,

In the first few years after you arrived in Santa Fe, I would meet you mainly at your New Year's Eve parties. Your life seemed somewhat glamorous, with celebrities crowding around. Being one of your guests was a bit of an adventure for me. Later on, you interviewed me for *Notebooks of the Mind*. An exciting woman, actually interested in my thoughts! And more than that, you forced me to pay attention to my own thinking process. With a life story so different from mine, and yet with interests and values so close. In you I found a deep interest in trying to understand what the universe is all about and an unbreakable commitment to trying to make this a better world. It was sad when the interviewing was over. I didn't want it to end. Years later, it turned out that we were able to share our lives. Under your influence, I became less of a head-in-the-clouds self-absorbed professor, more like a normal human being. But I still have a long way to go, in learning from your example of unfailing pure kindness. It was your daring suggestion, "Let's do something together!' that resulted, six years later, in our book, *Loving and Hating Mathematics*. Writing another book was something I would never have undertaken, with my 80th year approaching. Yet we have succeeded. We produced something worthwhile. We revealed the turbulent emotional inner life of mathematics, in youth and age, with its friendships and competitions, its anxieties and exaltations, "warts and all," as David Mumford said gratefully.

For me, it was easy to re-tell the stories and anecdotes that we found in the literature, along with my own recollections of mathematicians' involvements with mathematics and with each other. It was your psychological insight, your sympathetic imagination, your willingness to speculate about people's minds and hearts that gave depth and resonance to those recountings. Every chapter benefits from your insight and imagination. The deeper topics, such as the nature of the culture of mathematics, and the essential role of emotional involvement in teaching algebra, are your special contributions. Our publisher and our readers, as well as I, owe you gratitude, for your essential and unique share in our book.

Even while we worked on *Loving and Hating Mathematics*, we undertook another daring, risky project—jointly teaching an honors course on *Four Subversive Thinkers: Darwin, Marx, Freud and Einstein*. As to Freud, well, one of us is a psychologist. But a psychologist-mathematician team, daring to take on evolutionary biology, revolutionary political economy, and special relativity, all in one semester! What an adventure, for us even more than for our students.

In fact, *Loving and Hating Mathematics* was not our first collaboration. Twenty years earlier, we visited your home city Budapest together. American mathematicians knew about something they called "the Hungarian miracle"—the amazing number of first-class mathematicians that Hungary produced in the years after World War I. What was the explanation? Together, we interviewed all the mathematicians we could reach, even driving down from Budapest to the Balaton for Pal Erdos, and taking the train to Szeged for Bela Sz.-Nagy. We found out about the Eotvos competition, and the high-school math newspaper, and we heard tragic stories of the Holocaust in Hungary. The resulting article: *A Visit to Hungarian Mathematics* (Hersh & John-Steiner 1993) is something we can still be proud of, to this day. Even earlier, we wrote a joint book review, exposing the fallacies in a bad book about the male gender.

It wasn't always easy. We each had our own style, our own viewpoint. Reconciling them sometimes could be strenuous and exhausting. But in the end, gratifying and satisfying. Over the years, I have collaborated with a dozen or so co-authors. Yours is by far the most interesting and enjoyable collaboration of my life.

Reuben

REUBEN HERSH, Ph.D., is Professor Emeritus from the Department of Mathematics and Statistics at the University of New Mexico. He has authored and co-authored several books on the practice and philosophy of mathematics, as well as numerous papers in research, philosophical, and pedagogical journals.

REFERENCES

Hersh, R., & John-Steiner, V. (2011). *Loving and hating mathematics: Challenging the myths of mathematical life*. Princeton, NJ: Princeton University Press.

Hersh, R., & John-Steiner, V. (1993). A visit to Hungarian mathematics. *The Mathematical Intelligencer*, 15(2), 13–26.

LETTER EIGHT

From Your House to My House

Anne Wiltshire

"Sustained, productive work requires more than the mind for sheltering thought. It requires a well-organized and well-selected work space." (John-Steiner, 1985, p. 73)

Dear Véronka,

I first met you as a distant teacher when finding *Notebooks* in the Linguistics library when a new graduate student. Then you became teacher, mentor and friend. The most vivid and transformative phase of this relationship for me was the mentor period that I now call the 'expansion phase'. It was during this time I was able to move to Santa Fe and live in your guesthouse while a doctoral candidate. It is said that there are no accidents only synchronicities, which seemed to be happening then, given the complex web of events that made this arrangement possible. For me it was not just a beautiful place to live, it was actually a new life.

It was a magical place, situated on a hilltop with spacious grounds and no visible neighbours. It was in the historic part of Santa Fe where the approaching road was deliberately unpaved and without street lights, creating a tranquil, rustic setting for the property that was actually very close to the plaza in the centre of the old town.

The guesthouse that was originally designed and added as a writer's studio was compact, simple and light with windows on three sides. This had the effect of bringing the exterior inside so that the landscape of chamise, sagebrush and pinon was perfectly enhanced by whitewashed walls, brick floors and kiva fireplaces. The backdrop to this canvas was the mountain that seemed to change moods in different light and revealed details of trees and rocks if one gazed long enough. Every morning I would open the upper part of the Dutch door to appreciate this beauty and mutter words of gratitude—leaving the door open even when chilly. The garden was surrounded by a high, adobe wall that emphasised the unique quality of privacy and tranquillity, at the same time being open and expansive. Here it was possible to perch on a rock to eat a sandwich or drink coffee during the day, and on summer nights to take the sleeping bag outside and fall asleep watching the stars. The sky was usually clear and velvety, so that the stars shone brilliantly, undimmed by city lights. Sometimes I even felt a trifle guilty that I was able to enjoy this setting while you were busy commuting three times a week to UNM in Albuquerque.

In this glorious environment I began the work required for acceptance of a proposal, but I also breathed deeply of the pristine, high altitude atmosphere that opened my perceptions to all sorts of other unrelated pursuits—from African dance and drumming to jazz piano. Through all this apparent lack of focus and distraction from the major task at hand, you watched and listened with patience and interest. There was never any sense of approbation or reminders of what I was supposed to be doing; on the contrary, as a true mentor you were interested in the larger process that was taking place as I responded to a new and unusual degree of freedom.

We respected each other's space and privacy. There was little interchange between the houses, though we occasionally shared a sortie to the cinema or a concert. What did become a ritual was the half hour you granted me each Sunday afternoon when we would go down the Garcia St. hill to the coffee shop where your voluminous weekend edition of the *New York Times* awaited you. There you would sit and listen. I realised even then the extraordinary discipline with which you conducted your life, similar to the subjects of your research for *Notebooks* who you found consistently shared this trait. That was one of your challenges to the cliché that creative people such as artists are a disorganised, unruly lot. Your discipline was not overt as something imposed externally and therefore appearing forbidding and stern, not at all, the discipline was applied only to your mind and so was covert and did not intimidate those with whom you interacted. It was a classic case of teaching by example that I recognised but was incapable of emulating then. Your management of time was extremely disciplined and in itself a lesson in living and knowing how to use time and energy productively. Time is an under-estimated commodity that we are all given for an indeterminate period and rarely learn how to use effectively. In that precious half hour, you gave me your attention and listened closely. Ultimately time and attention are all that we can offer to one another and yet it is rare in human interaction. You allowed me to talk like a stream of consciousness that my broadening perceptions, nourished by the environment had not yet internalised, but sought through verbalisation to make some kind of sense. You were like a witness to a process that I did not understand at the time, but in retrospect I am sure that you knew what was happening and was critical for me then as it would become later. When we did talk about the project and ideas that came up, you would tell me to write it down, advising me to make notebooks of my own mind. That advice was not always taken, as I did not then recognise the fragility and random nature of thoughts arising. So I probably lost many unsown seeds that may have germinated, or perhaps they returned in a different guise—that is the problem, that there is no way of telling without a record of written notes.

"The development of self-knowledge—the realization of one's special talents and the best way to use them—does not necessarily follow a simple linear progression" (John-Steiner, 1985, p. 72). Life after the dissertation offered a different kind of challenge that left no time to relax and continue to enjoy the idyllic place in Santa Fe. There followed a trying time in Australia due to medical emergencies that took several months. After all that, I came back to pack up and leave the little apartment with indefinable emotions as I set out on the next 'phase of exploration' into uncertainty. The nomadic period began with some open questions and an open time frame. Within two years it became evident that the external journey was really an internal one. So I left behind cathedrals and art galleries and places familiar to you from where I could send a postcard. I drifted eastward to countries that were less comfortable, but where I would find interesting approaches to understanding the mind. I learned to distinguish between knowledge that is information-based and that which is actually experienced—a distinction that has been lost in the term 'knowledge' today as formerly it was only applied to the latter. In fact knowledge of self is by definition experience-based but is not typically included in classroom curricula alongside objective knowledge. As you point out, self-knowledge becomes a critical link to the realisation of one's talents and those who discussed their journey in your interviews had lots of help directly or indirectly in finding their way. The inner work is solitary, because it is internal, requiring careful and constant observation of the mind so as to understand how it works. Observation leads to an understanding of the fleeting nature of thoughts and the structure and texture of those that stay, in effect it is processing the stream of consciousness. However, the effort to arrive at this point of self-recognition requires the help and support of many people and appropriate conditions. Your contribution in providing both physical conditions and the role of mentor has been of inestimable value, which I cherished then and regard now as a benchmark in development. In your research you have also challenged the rather arrogant claim and myth of the self-made man that is still prevalent today, especially in the individualistic culture of North America.

Synchronicity was mentioned at the beginning of this letter. It is at work again, because by another set of extraordinary circumstances, the opportunity to join this project and write to you arose at an important moment. More than a decade ago you offered me a place of beauty and tranquility, a house that nurtured my freedom. After a period of searching and uncertainty, I began to crave a house of my own in which to assimilate the experience and knowledge of the exploratory phase to enter into the reflective phase. Now at this writing, I am literally and figuratively in the process of inhabiting a country cottage in rural SW France. The countryside is beautiful, and the house is being transformed into a luminous and organised space in which to build my thoughts. Being in an environment where I am not yet fluent in the ambient language, I have to choose words carefully, thus being conscious of every utterance. I also have to listen carefully—it is ideal.

Véronika, this relationship began as a distant one through the agency of *Notebooks*, now we are distant only by geography.

With love and gratitude,
Anne

DR. ANNE WILTSHIRE is an Independent Research Specialist living in France. Her research interests include the synchronicity between speech and non-verbal body language.

LETTER NINE

Above and Beyond Box Consciousness

Bernard Spolsky

"Integrating the two traditions [Vygotsky and Freire] was a challenging task, in theory as well as in practice, since our work included teaching students from disenfranchised groups to read." (John-Steiner, Panofsky, & Smith, 1994, p. 3)

Dear Vera,

In an age where Twitter-like text messages or informal e-mails are becoming established as a way of communicating, it is a challenge to be invited to write you a letter that is not only formal but will be published in hard copy, guaranteeing a wider readership and longer availability to a reading public. But as both of us consider literacy to be one of the most important of human inventions, I can be forgiven perhaps for this preliminary meta-analysis.

Of course I'd rather be able to sit down with you with a glass of wine some pleasant Southwestern or mid-Eastern evening. It reminds me that one of the photos I have of you sitting alongside Joshua Fishman in the garden of our Albuquerque house during the 1980 Linguistic Institute.

This reminds me further that one of the most successful administrative coups of my time at UNM was persuading you in the 1970s to leave Joshua Fishman and the Language and Behavior program at Yeshiva University, attracted as I was by the relevance of your work on early childhood bilingual education (John-Steiner, 1971) and your early book on language and education (John-Steiner, Cazden, & Hymes, 1972) which was my *vade mecum* in teaching and research, and join the burgeoning Educational Linguistics program in New Mexico. As I had hoped, you helped cement the link between Education and Humanities that was a rare feature of the program, and enabled us to aim at the integration of theory and practice that you found in Vygotsky and Freire and passed on to our students.

As a result of your move to the Southwest, for the next eight years I was privileged to have your backing in academic and bureaucratic functions (you also took on the direction of the Santa Graduate Program which came under my purview as Graduate Dean) and to share with you students and program planning.

More than anyone I can think of, you came to represent the best features and the full potential of Educational Linguistics which you continued to lead after I moved to Israel: the combining of theoretical findings of a number of related approaches to the study of language and literacy (anthropological, linguistic, educational, sociological, psychological) with the practical task of dealing with educational problems of the disenfranchised as well as the majority student, and appropriate localization of international learning.

As a researcher, you added new realms to our understanding of language and brain, with your daring exploration of non-linguistic as well as linguistic creativity (who else would ask how mathematicians or choreographers think?) and of collaboration (which you have continued to study and to demonstrate in your research and publications). As a teacher and mentor, you provided a role model of intellectual rigor and social responsibility that was passed to the best of your students.

As a faculty member, you took a larger than usual share in the building and maintenance of smooth administration within which learning and research could flourish. And as a person, you built a valuable bridge between your European intellectual past and the Southwestern US pioneer environment in which you chose to work. In this way, you continued to assert and exhibit the social and psychological advantages of plurilingual individuals in multilingual societies.

Your own plurilingual background and experience in multilingual contexts, something echoed in your choice of a Russian and a Brazilian as intellectual gurus, account for your early publications encouraging bilingual education of children. Once you recognized that the brain was not naturally monolingual, a common assumption among US psychologists who conducted research on white monolingual first year students, you were able to explore the burgeoning multilingualism of New York and the established multilingualism of New Mexico, going beyond the Texan approach in which "bilingual" was a polite word for Mexican. This freed you to look at non-linguistic aspects of brain activity and coding, such as the "languages" of mathematicians and artists and choreographers, and move beyond the cramping simplistic Whorfian hypothesis of thought constrained by a language to exploring creativity itself, and beyond the limitation to single minds to the understanding of the nature and possibilities of creative collaboration. In the work on creativity (John-Steiner & Moran, 2002), you add to your major academic enterprise, the successful spread of Vygotskian ideas in Western psychology. This Russian Jewish literary critic and schoolteacher turned psychologist, as you describe him, died young, his work suppressed by Stalin and unknown during the Cold War. You have done as much as anyone to rescue the gems of cognitive insight that might have been lost and to show how much he still has to contribute to education, linguistics and the understanding of the human mind.

Happy as I have been in Israel (where it was a special privilege to collaborate for many years with our friend Robert Cooper—our weekly coffee sessions monitored our own books and our joint research), I missed the opportunity to share students with you, giving them the benefit of your combination of psycholinguistic sophistication and empathy with indigenous peoples (something which you shared with your late husband Stan—I vividly recall a summer public lecture shortly after our arrival in New Mexico where he introduced us to the New Indians and later reading his work on La Raza).

Your integration of Vygotsky and Freire added a valuable richness to the UNM program in Educational Linguistics, just as your career has provided another major bridge between US and "foreign" research, a critically needed connection that maintains the internationalization of the intellect.

So I appreciate this opportunity to communicate with you again, even if at a distance of time and formality, and wish you continued productivity and happiness.

Bernard Spolsky

DR. BERNARD SPOLSKY is Professor Emeritus from Bar-Ilan University in Ramat Gan, Israel. He has published research in language testing, second language learning, computers in the humanities, applied linguistics, sociolinguistics, and language policy across the course of a highly distinguished career as a key figure in the field of sociolinguistics.

REFERENCES

John-Steiner, V. (1971). *Early childhood bilingual education.* New York: Modern Language Association.

John-Steiner, V., Cazden, C., & Hymes, D. (Eds.). (1972). *The functions of language in the classroom.* New York: Teachers College Press.

John-Steiner, V., & Moran, S. (Eds.). (2002). *Creativity in the making.* Oxford, UK: Oxford University Press.

John-Steiner, V., Panofsky, C. F., & Smith, L. (Eds.). (1994). *Sociocultural approaches to language and literacy: An interactionist approach.* Cambridge: Cambridge University Press.

LETTER TEN

Memories of a Long Conversation

Michael Cole

Hi Vera,

I do not recall the year that you and I first met. But we were in conversation well ahead of our first meeting. That early conversation revolved around issues of cultural differences in cognitive ability: Were such differences to be interpreted as qualitatively different forms of a universal ability to acquire cultural knowledge or did they indicate cognitive deficits, deficiencies?

If one chose to interpret the data as significant cognitive deficits, to what should this deficit be attributed? Was there something lacking in the culture that deprived children of sufficient environmental stimulation or did it reflect something fundamentally genetic, "innate" and unchangeable, innate that explained the continuing poor test performances and academic achievement of poor children and particularly poor African American children?

These arguments were being played out a decade after the *Brown vs. Board* decision. Moreover, they were no longer just academic debates. Those who took the view that ethnic & social class difference arose from environmental (cultural, but also social and political) causes were recruited, and volunteered for, a role in the War on Poverty.

This tangle of issues around the role of culture and socio-environmental factors in bringing about the "achievement gap" present when *Brown vs. Board* became law, provided on important arena in which we began my earliest conversations with you, mediated through academic journals. The other major, common concern was the work of Lev Vygotsky.

To the present generation it might come as a surprise that you drew inspiration from Vygotsky's ideas about language and thought to help explain the source of language difficulties encountered by poor, African American children. I, on the other hand, entered this conversation unhappy with the entire apparatus of psychological testing as a means for assessing intellectual abilities. Vygotsky figured in that discussion, along with Basil Bernstein, Oscar Lewis, and others as promoting the idea of cultural deprivation.

At present I can understand the sources of confusion; I even sometimes feel as if I have some of the issues sorted out. But at that early time, you and I appeared to be on opposite sides in our evaluation of Vygotsky. You were of course correct about the enormous generativity to be had from taking Vygotsky's ideas seriously. However, my insistence on taking a critical stance toward cultural deprivation theories and understanding deficits as politically organized manifestation of sociopolitical forces also seems, in retrospect, not a bad idea.

The project that brought us into close contact, of course, was the years-long effort to publish two of Vygotsky's books, *Tool and Symbol in Children Development*, and *The Development of Higher Psychological Functions*. The project was undertaken at the request of Arthur Rosenthal, then head of Harvard University Press, and Alexander Luria, who had been my postdoctoral mentor. Luria was anxious to see as many books by Vygotsky and his colleagues as possible, and this pair of books were to kick off a series. (Rosenthal had already published a good deal of Luria's work, and they struck up a personal relationship.)

I was, initially, to play no more than the role of messenger. I arranged for the translation of one of the books, the other having been given to me in English by Luria. I had read both manuscripts, and while I could find some of the experiments interesting, I had a great deal of difficulty with the argumentation focused as it was on controversies extant in the 1920's and the previous 50 years of (largely) European psychology. Moreover the work clearly required someone familiar with Marxism as well as world psychology. To my great good luck, Sylvia Scribner had joined my laboratory at Rockefeller University. She suggested that you would be just the person to act as editor. That was great by me, because I was already deeply involved in trying to understand Alexander Luria's autobiography and his work in Central Asia, never mind the Lab's active empirical research program on culture and cognitive development.

You and your colleague, Ellen Souberman, graciously accepted the project. It seemed like "problem solved" so I could put the matter out of my mind. The project came to an abrupt halt when I received the manuscripts back from you. Your editorial work was just fine. The difficulty was my own continuing inability to understand Vygotsky's text. Personally unsure of what to do I sent the texts to Rosenthal. It was his agreement with Luria, not my business that determined what to do next.

Rosenthal flatly refused the texts, which he had read as he did all the books considered for publication by Harvard University Press at the time. He found it incomprehensible and asked, rhetorically, "Who would buy this book?" I was unprepared either to explain to him what made the book so important or so difficult to read. I was then handed the task of coming up with a text that would fulfill the promise to Luria. A Vygotsky text that Rosenthal would approve of and send on to his board of syndics.

The result, after a long series of back and forth letters between Albuquerque and New York, was the collection of essays gathered in *Mind and Society*. It consisted of parts of *Tool and Symbol*, to which we added sections from *History of Higher Psychological Functions*. Because we were being challenged to come up with a book that others would want to read, we added essays taken from a posthumously published volume on learning and development, play, and early writing. Quite contrary to my expectations, the book had an unusually broad impact when Steven Toulmin used it to trumpet Vygotsky as the "Mozart of Psychology." We are still living with the consequences of that "Vygotsky boom." One of those consequences has been a lot of attention paid to Vygotsky while Luria fades into the background. That is precisely what Luria had set out to accomplish. For that I am genuinely pleased.

What was important in all of this for me personally was that, in the process of our discussions about the texts and their meaning and their contemporary relevance, supplemented by multiple iterative written and spoken discussions, I became deeply committed to Vygotsky and Luria, even as I struggled to deal with the cultural difference/cultural deficit issue that to my mind, they had fully come to grips with. For that alone, all of the difficulties of producing the book were fully justified.

In the process of producing *Mind in Society* we found a new topic for conversation: your involvement with the Native American peoples of the Southwest. We were able to converse around cross-cultural research because of your involvement with the Native American community. Stories of these children differed little in length, but the content uncovered two distinct cultural patterns. The Plains Indian Sioux children, whose cultural tradition includes a strong emphasis on activities which exhibit bravery, retold stories stressing action. The Navajo children, whose tradition emphasizes nature, beauty, and harmony, retold stories which included many more verbalized visual elements and their versions were quieter and more contemplative. Central to this work was the concept of cognitive pluralism, the idea that that people's cognitive processes are formed through patterned uses of semiotic means acquired and deployed in different cultural practices. More or less in parallel, Sylvia Scribner and I were arriving at the same unit of analysis in our research on Vai literacy. So we all had plenty to converse about!

For a number of years our research programs diverged. As we at the Laboratory of Comparative Human Cognition in San Diego were delving into the problem of ecological validity and beginning to design activities using Vygotskian ideas as a key resource, you were on your voyage with Darwin's notebooks and the entire range of incredibly interesting examples of externalized internal speech that become semiotic means for future development. Somewhere in there you began to write about creativity. Preoccupied as I was with implementing our model systems, for years I did not look up from the trenches long enough to know exactly when this happened.

Recently I have felt myself drawn to questions of imagination and creativity and particularly to Vygotsky's ideas on this subject. And of course, there you were, ready with a lifetime of thought and research on this very topic.

Blessed are those who are privileged to have such a long and satisfying conversation.

DR. MICHAEL COLE is Distinguished Professor of Communication, Psychology, and Human Development at the University of California, San Diego, where he is Berman Chair of Language and Communication. His primary research field is the study of the role of culture in cognitive development.

LETTER ELEVEN

Networks in Life and in Science

Csaba Pléh and Ottilia Boross

Drága Vera,

Thanks to this frequently cursed, but actually "awesome" internet, whenever we miss someone, who is very special to us but is just at the other side of our otherwise shrinking planet, we just strike some keys and send a message to her. In fact, just as we're doing at the moment.

There are at least two reasons why we're doing this right now, dear Vera. One and the very first of those is that your exceptional personality, your inspiring but calm and reassuring presence have always had a deep impact on us, and it is still there, indeed still there.

All right, we'll stop embarrassing both you and ourselves. So let us get on to the second subject, which—though deeply professional—has personal connotations, too. So get ready, dear Vera J.... We turn to some role playing, to please you and to commemorate your Protean personality.

AN INTERLUDE TO INTRODUCE AN AUNTIE

Vera John-Steiner, alias Polgár Vera, was born in Hungary and has kept certain parts of her Hungarian identity long after she had to leave the country.

Even today she speaks beautiful and eloquent Hungarian, the stylistic roots of which were laid and cultivated in the 17th century by Kelemen Mikes. The talented writer and essayist Mikes was also a loyal companion of II. Rákóczi Ferenc, a Hungarian prince, who, because of organizing and leading an uprising against the Habsburg Monarchy, was sent to exile to Rodosto (Tekirdag), Turkey. Mikes, the "Hungarian Goethe", wrote 207 letters to E.P., a fictitious baroness (my dearest Auntie), which he never published or sent to anyone in his life. In these little masterpieces of short novels he gave an authentic description of contemporary Turkey, the conspiratorial tricks of Turkish diplomacy, or the everyday trifles of the emigrants. He was also very personal in his epistolary confessions, revealing his deepest feelings, wishes, or desires in an informal manner to this sweet and understanding auntie.

Now we would like to turn back to this 300-year-old way of telling things that are a mixture of facts, opinions and feelings.

DEAR AUNTIE, A FEW WORDS ABOUT VERA

Here, under this shining treasure of the sun, we have come across someone who has an incredible ability to combine the personal and the scientific. She is leading an open house in Santa Fe, welcoming all sorts of people from all around the world. She is open in sharing and caring.

At the same time she is an excellent psychologist, linguist and education researcher who combines an interest in personal relationships with the role of her mediating notebooks in intellectual life. She has been not only influenced by the Russian scholar Vygotsky but also contributed to the Vygotsky scholarship. She has elaborated the 'mediation' into modern theory about the role of external mediating media as outlined in her *Notebooks of the Mind* (John-Steiner, 1997). The important point is that in her version of mediation, theory mediating notes not only regulate behavior but also help to create novel ideas. That relates to one of her other leading ideas: the role of cooperative creation of knowledge. Social and individuated personal relations are crucial in bringing new ideas about, in the form of *Creative Collaboration* (John-Steiner, 2000). She has been highly critical in pointing out this creativity inducing nature of collaboration (John-Steiner, Weber, & Minnis, 1998).

Vera's methods in a way precede and foresee the new network theories of human relations and knowledge dissemination. There certainly is a growing new network theory around the social sciences at large (Borgatti, Mehra, Brass, & Labianca, 2009), and in an even broader 'scale free sense' regarding all sorts biological and social networks as in the works of Laci Barabási (2002).

For psychologists, the new interest towards network ideas is a reemergence of mid-twentieth century ideas. The Ego centered network issue entered psychology with a strong emotional component, as Vera had shown regarding Vygotsky. But this was true for other classical stars such as Moreno (1953), and in Hungary Mérei (1971). They had shown the importance of emotional involvement in networks. Few in present day network research recognize this heritage, with Borgatti et al. (2009) being among them. But this is only a side issue of historical interest. The reason for this neglect was the fact that it was mainly dealing with small networks involving intense emotional investment, that is so dear to Vera, and so much of a problem for techno based network theories.

Dear Auntie, it would be great if you directly provoke Vera with some questions. A first question you may want to consider relates to the issue of the relationships between small nets—ego centered networks, if you like—and the large nets. It is a triviality in recent network research that there are have and 'have nots' in networks. Following Lotka's law (1926), and Zipf's law (1949) they find density points named hubs (Barabási, 2002) all around the place. The power law is true for scientific productivity, for social relations, but as well for the spread of diseases and for the distribution of frequent and rare words. Our first puzzlement relates to this. One has the impression that the elegant mathematical laws are in fact hiding an interesting diversity of networks. In social contacts, as well as in scientific productivity the dense, high productive and highly connected somehow are central and important. In other domains, however, such as language the frequent and dominant (as the article, the conjunctions, pronouns) units are the ones that have very little meaning. *And, the, are* do not constitute the Einsteins or Neumans of language. How can one resolve this apparent contradiction? That would be a nice query towards Vera.

Our second issue relates to the much emphasized idea proposed by Granovetter (1973) about the importance of weak ties. Granovetter has emphasized that weak ties are important in creating connections between ideas coming from different domains. The interesting issue is whether one can relate this to the problem of the internal, mental network issue. It would be interesting to entertain the idea that weak social ties are responsible for creating weakly connected loose mental networks coming from sources in different domains. In this way one could find an isomorphy between social openness and mental openness.

This brings us to the last issue. There is growing awareness about the importance of bilingualism in increasing mental flexibility, in taking different perspectives, both socially and intellectually (Kovács, 2009). When we first met Vera, both in Hungary and in New Mexico, the amazing feature was that how she could still be the Hungarian girl, Vera Polgár, after living far away from her native culture for half a century.

Dear Auntie, meeting Vera you may want to say that bilingualism and multiculturalism is not only important in creating flexibility in babies and youngsters, but it might also be the key, or one of the keys for preserving freshness and creativity over the life span.

Dear Auntie! You should try to bring Vera back home to discuss all these issues with her in person. Her variety of visions, her eternal sense of connectedness is a clue for both of us in maintaining intellectual openness and social creativity. She may be able to tell you the secret of how to combine happiness, wisdom and freshness.

Otti and Csaba

CSABA PLÉH, Ph.D., is a Hungarian psycholinguist and Professor in the Department of Cognitive Science at Budapest University of Technology and Economics. He serves as the chief editor of the *Hungarian Review of Psychology*.

OTTILIA BOROSS teaches courses on introductory, developmental, educational and health psychology at several institutions of higher learning in Hungary. A trained psychologist, she has implemented multiple forms of therapies in the clinical field and conducted a host of teacher-training courses.

REFERENCES

Barabási, A. (2002). *Linked: How everything is connected to everything else and what it means for business, science, and everyday life.* New York: Penguin Group.

Borgatti, S. P., Mehra, A., Brass, D., & Labianca, G. (2009). Network analysis in the social sciences. *Science, 323,* 892–895.

Granovetter, M. (1973). The strength of weak ties. *American Journal of Sociology, 78*, 1360–1380.

John-Steiner, V. (1997). *Notebooks of the mind: Explorations of thinking.* New York: Oxford University Press.

John-Steiner, V. (2000). *Creative collaboration.* New York: Oxford University Press.

John-Steiner, V., Weber, R. J., & Minnis, M. (1998). The challenge of studying collaboration. *American Educational Research Journal, 35*(4), 773–783.

Kovács, Á. M. (2009): Early bilingualism enhances mechanisms of false-belief reasoning. *Developmental Science, 12* (1), 48–54.

Lotka, A.J. (1926): The frequency distribution of scientific productivity. *Journal of the Washington Academy of Sciences, 16,* 317–323.

Mérei Ferenc. *(1971/2006): Közösségek rejtett hálózata.* [The hidden network of communities] Budapest: Osiris Kiadó.

Zipf, G. K. (1949). *Human behavior and the principle of least effort.* New York: Wiley.

PART THREE

Letters on Scholarship

A Sphere of Thought

LETTER TWELVE

The Remarkable Power of Bisociation

Susan Ervin-Tripp

"Generative ideas emerge from joint thinking, from significant conversations, and from sustained, shared struggles to achieve new insights by partners in thought" (John-Steiner, 2000, p. 3)

Vera came from an intellectual family of achievement, so it is not surprising that she understood how thinking and collaboration are related. One of the earliest places I saw Vera's work was in the *Study of Spontaneous Talk* published with William Soskin in 1963. A young couple carried a radio transmitter connected to a receiver and recorder. When I read that work, I was fascinated by the everyday talk, and by how the pragmatics of asking and telling got done. I have been doing that ever since.

But Vera saw something very different. She was interested in how talk helps people solve problems, and how outer talk to others connects to inner talk to the self. So we see here the germ of her work on inner speech, *Notebooks of the Mind*, and on collaboration. Her fundamental interest has been in creativity.

The work she has done in the Southwest in particular has been informed by her interest in cultural variation in how creativity is accomplished. Vera has been examining variation, not just between individuals, of the sort she found in talking to mathematicians and novelists, but also cultural variation. She has found that Navajo children have vivid visual recall, which may be related to their exceptional abilities in painting. She proposed that educators create realistic functions for language in the classroom, and that they build from cultural variations. One name for this is cognitive pluralism.

Vera is concerned that there can be mismatches between the practices of teachers and of parents. A school can use or overlook the reliance on peer collaboration that children experience in the family and in the playground. Much of her work in education has been a search for how to create varied educational environments that nurture children's creativity.

Early western researchers on language looked at mothers and children, rarely at siblings and peers, rarely at interaction in daily life. Russian researchers spoke of the zone of proximal development, the distance between what is possible alone and what is possible with a mentor's guidance or peer interaction to aid in pursuing problems. They saw there is a kind of collaboration between children or between teacher and child in the development of ideas.

Vygotsky pointed out that reading and writing shouldn't be taught just for passing a test, but because they are needed for the functioning of the child in valued group activities. We find these views in Vera's work.

In her curiosity about how creativity is nurtured, Vera has interviewed creative scientists, artists, and writers. Her work on collaboration includes the relation between equals as well as mentors as sources of creative growth.

She began by reading the reports on great collaborations, like the Curies and Joliot-Curies. Many of these have been reported in memoirs or biographies. She found that Russian researchers shared a thought community, traveling together, co-constructing their ideas. Over the years Vera has sought out cultural leaders and co-authors and developed an interview program. On the basis of her first work it was possible to identify many dimensions of collaboration.

In the collaborations of men and women she found some differences. Men used more visual metaphors, and energetic, aggressive imagery in their descriptions, seeing clear paths and stages in their work, and negotiation and dialogue with their colleague. Women were more verbal, and were more concerned with surface and depth and off-path issues. Women were less concerned with negotiation than with trust and interdependence. Thus men were more often complementary and dialectic, women more often integrative and similar.

Gradually, this research has been building knowledge about how collaboration works. The people who collaborate have to have a strong belief in the capabilities of the other, but they don't have to be alike, often having complementary working styles or temperaments. Nobel Prize winners Watson and Crick talked about using each other to close off blind alleys. Having a collaborator also helps promote the persistence needed to bring work to fruition.

It turns out that people who have complementary roles in a collaboration and those who work integratively use language differently. It looks as if the people who collaborate with someone from a different field may require more explicit clarification of ideas, and cannot deal as well intuitively with inexplicit inner speech or abbreviated suggestions. Some collaborators—women more often than men—finish each other's sentences and speak briefly but still work together successfully. Elinor Ochs and Bambi Schieffelin, who wrote books together on child language and culture in other societies, used to sit down at a typewriter and alternate typing lines in joint manuscripts.

Vera's work on topics like this reminds me of the great 19th century naturalists. She observes, collects the widest range of the phenomenon, in order to find out what the major dimensions are that will deserve study. Above all, she is a great listener.

One of her most remarkable contributions has been the work in *Notebooks of the Mind*, where she wrote on the varieties of mental experience.

Vygotsky, Luria and other Russian researchers reported that creative innovations within the mind take the form of predicative inner speech, like the quick notes we write ourselves which presuppose what the topic is. Vera has studied children's inner speech and found that at each grade level, relevant private speech is related to future achievement gains.

But there is something extra from connecting private to vocalized speech. In speaking with others, one is obliged to be explicit, to anticipate the misunderstandings of the listener. A great deal of the work on education has been concerned with helping children learn how to communicate with others who don't share their inner experiences, helping them to become explicit. Writing usually is intended for displacements in time and space, so that the reader has to guess a lot if the writer isn't explicit. Vygotsky had a social and functional perspective on language and saw a relation between outer and inner speech, transforming one into the other.

The idea that thought is verbal is a common one among social scientists. It has led to research on verbal mediation in memory and problem solving, and a rich range of research on verbal thinking. But in *Notebooks of the Mind*, Vera showed that music notations, diagrams and maps as well as words can be communicative systems. They are used like talk to collaborate, to teach and to conventionalize by social use.

As the mother of a dancer, Vera knew that other modalities besides speech and words generate creative activity. She found that images, kinesthesia, music, all play a role for different creative individuals. As in the collaboration studies, she found journals in which creative persons had reported how their work developed, and how they envisioned the issues.

She found wonderfully vivid examples. On the whole, about 15% of people are purely verbal in their thinking, 15% purely visual and the rest mixed. Many examples were both kinesthetic and visual. For instance Einstein imagined riding through space on a light wave and looking behind himself at the next wave. Crick and Watson when they were working on DNA kept building TinkerToy models of genes, putting into three dimensions a kind of visualization that must have been in their minds. The objectification of the model allowed easier discussion with each other, and easier evidence of what was a problem.

The poet Spender said that poetry depends on strong recall of sense impressions that are relived during the writing process. Anais Nin and D.H. Lawrence drew on visual memory too. Gauguin could clearly recall specific visual experiences, in analogy to running a movie again.

Somewhat different modes of thinking appeared for emotive and scientific experience than for visual and verbal. Biologists and physical scientists are often quite visual and use visual means to share ideas. Darwin, for example, drew irregular branching trees when concentrating on his evolutionary models.

As she interviewed creative people in many fields she was amazed to find the variety of means of organizing and manipulating experience mentally—a mathematician mentioned pictures, geometrical images, music, maps, spheres, which remained in his memory and returned when he took up the same theoretical problem years later. It is surprising to find how many creative thinkers keep notebooks and sketchbooks and use them as a way to keep in persistent touch with their own ideas.

In tracing the epigenesis of important contributions, the trail may lead across visual experiences and kinesthetic inventions. It turns out that it even makes a difference what kind of mathematics one does; some ideas call for analogic imagery, some for analysis. So here we are with cognitive pluralism again.

But in creative work, certain themes recur, such as bisociation, the bringing together of unrelated knowledge; having two minds may work better than one. Creative thinkers used analogy a lot. Many had had apprenticeships and they emphasized the value of encouragement in their playful engagement with ideas.

What Vera John-Steiner has done is not to find final answers and put issues away, but to open new issues and make extraordinarily rich observations that will lead to new research on mental processes in relation to collaboration and creativity. Her work is foundational.

REFERENCES

John-Steiner, V. (2000). *Creative collaboration.* Oxford, UK: Oxford University Press.

Soskin, W. ,& John-Steiner, V. (1963). The study of spontaneous talk. In G. Barker (Ed.), *The stream of behavior: Explorations of its structure and content.* Cambridge, MA: MIT Press.

DR. SUSAN ERVIN-TRIPP assisted in the development of the field of psycholinguistics in the early stages of her career. A lecturer at Harvard and Professor at the University of California, her research interests have spanned bilingualism, child language, sociolinguistics, and pragmatics.

LETTER THIRTEEN

Young Children's Sociodramatic Play
Wellspring of Collaboration and Learning

Laura E. Berk

"An individual learns, creates, and achieves mastery in and through his or her relationships with other individuals. Ideas, tools, and processes that emerge from joint activity are appropriated, or internalized, by the individual and become the basis of the individual's subsequent development." (John-Steiner, 2000, p. 5)

Vera, we have not been face-to-face for nearly two decades, since conversing in the early 1990s at an international conference in Madrid, Spain. But I recall that occasion well. Your work has captivated and influenced me as, over the past decade and a half, I turned my attention to the significance of make-believe play in young children's learning and development.

My empirical research and writings on make-believe play, as with my sojourn into children's private speech, have been deeply inspired by Vygotsky. In your essays on education, you mention Vygotsky's profoundly insightful ideas on the role of symbolic play in child development. You note, in particular, Vygotsky's (1966) view of imaginative play—in which the child assigns new meanings to objects through gestures and words—as vital preparation for mastering the symbol systems of culture, including written language.

In this way and in others, play provides a supportive foundation for the formal learning children will encounter after entering elementary school. Indeed, Vygotsky (1978) regarded make-believe play as a paramount early childhood learning context, granting it the status of a leading factor in development. He saw joint pretense as a unique, broadly influential zone of proximal development (ZPD) in which children advance themselves, experimenting with a wide array of challenging skills and, thus, acquiring diverse, culturally valued competencies.

Play, like private speech, does not begin (as Piaget believed) as an autonomous, egocentric activity. Pretense—like other complex mental functions—originates in social experience. As Vygotskian scholars have documented, children first learn to engage in make-believe through the sensitive guidance of expert players (El'konin, 1978; Fiese, 1990; Haight & Miller, 1993). As soon as toddlers have the basic representational capacities to participate, parents and older siblings scaffold their make-believe. From these interactions, young children appropriate many skills that enhance their play with peers and their competencies in other contexts.

In addition to imaginative play's symbolic features, Vygotsky (1966) highlighted its rule-oriented nature. This pair of distinctive qualities, Vygotsky explained, endows pretense with special power to contribute to the development of self-regulation. Make-believe assists children in using symbols, especially language, as tools for overcoming impulse and managing their own behavior. At the same time, because children's imaginary scenarios require them to follow social rules, imaginative play continuously demands that they act in socially desirable and responsible ways (Berk, 2001; Berk, Mann, & Ogan, 2006). Subordinating impulse to the rules of make-believe becomes for children "a new form of desire"—one that responds to their need for acceptance by and participation in their cultural community (Vygotsky, 1978, p. 100). Informal observations reveal that the negotiations preschoolers engage in to create play scenes—and the settings, actions, and dialogues of those scenes—repeatedly draw on cultural models and conventions of cooperation (as cited in Ortega, 2003).

Vera, you have written insightfully and eloquently about collaboration as crucial for meaningful learning. Sociodramatic play is the child's first and formative "community of learners." It lays the developmental groundwork for future "coparticipation, cooperative learning, and joint discovery" and for "negotiated values" arrived at through resolving differences of opinion, sharing ideas, and working together in pursuit of common goals (John-Steiner & Mahn, 1996, p. 202). Sociodramatic play exemplifies, in preliminary form, vital ingredients of the sociocultural approach to educational practice.

As predicted by Vygotsky's insights, social pretense engages and motivates children in ways that foster myriad complex mental abilities. A burgeoning literature—using diverse research designs, from correlational to experimental/intervention strategies—reveals benefits for general intellectual development, sustained attention, deliberate memory, self-regulation, logical reasoning, language and literacy, imagination, divergent thinking, understanding of emotions, ability to reflect on one's own thinking and take another's perspective, and social skills (see, for example, Bergen & Mauer, 2000; Berk, 2001; Elias & Berk, 2002; Hirsh-Pasek, Golinkoff, Berk, & Singer, 2009; Lindsey & Colwell, 2003; Ogan & Berk, 2009; Ruff & Capozzoli, 2003). The centrality of pretense in development can also be seen in children's near-universal drive to engage in it, even in the most distressing and demoralizing situations, such as hospitals and war zones.

Moreover, fundamental ingredients of mature creativity likely have roots in the pretend scenarios of early childhood. The drive to fantasize, Vygotsky maintained, does not fade away with childhood. Rather, he asserted, the imagination of later years is an internalized, condensed form of early childhood pretense that can be considered play without action. When adults apply analytical, adaptive thinking to this inner playfulness, the result may be the beginnings of a creative idea or product.

Additionally, your description, Vera, of the collaborative context that gives rise to creativity—"a mutual zone of proximal development where participants can increase their repertory of cognitive and emotional expression" (John-Steiner, 2000, p. 187)—bears striking similarity to Vygotsky's notion of the ZPD inherent in joint pretense. My own explorations of the biographies and autobiographies of a dozen or so eminent writers, artists, and scientists—for example, Sylvia Plath, Charlie Chaplin, and Marie Curie—reveal that sociodramatic play was a highly influential dimension of their early childhoods (see Berk, 2001, pp. 130–131).

Yet despite play's powerful role in all domains of psychological development, in recent years it has come under siege. Suppression of the rich, playful mentality that young children naturally bring to the classroom has even extended down to U.S. preschools and kindergartens, though the trend is antithetical to early childhood education's vast historic and current knowledge base. As one set of experts noted, "Play has become a four-letter word" (Hirsh-Pasek et al., 2009, p. 3). Play-based curricula have been supplanted by academic drill and practice, out of fear by both parents and teachers that otherwise, children won't be prepared for the academic demands of today's kindergartens and for the atomized, test-based measures of child "success" that now permeate U.S. public education. In American homes, children's play spaces are being overloaded with devices promising to "educate," including unifunctional electronic toys and DVDs that replace adult–child dialogue and playful engagement.

Clearly, a false dichotomy has arisen between play and learning, largely stemming from two sources. The first is widespread anxiety over U.S. young people's long-standing mediocre academic achievement in international comparisons, which has fueled societal misconceptions about what children actually need for optimum brain growth and psychologically healthy development during the sensitive period of early childhood. The second relates to the persistently large achievement gap between children from economically disadvantaged and advantaged families (Hirsh-Pasek et al., 2009). Underprivileged preschoolers and kindergartners are especially likely to be exposed to training in fragmented academic skills, and they are also the most harmed by it. Young children who spend much time filling in worksheets, as opposed to being actively engaged in play-based learning centers, show reduced motivation and developmental progress in motor, cognitive, language, and social domains (Marcon, 1999; Stipek, Feiler, Daniels, & Milburn, 1995). These negative outcomes translate into poorer study habits and academic achievement during the elementary school years, with stronger effects for children from low-SES homes (Stipek, 2004; Stipek & Byler, 1997).

A decade-and-half ago, you wrote, "Because [sociocultural] theory is complex and breaks radically from the traditional American educational model in which teachers were schooled, it is hard to appropriate" (John-Steiner & Mahn, 1996, p. 204). The educational gulf to which you referred is more pronounced today, ten years since the U.S. No Child Left Behind Act formally narrowed the national definition of effective teaching and learning to year-end scores on standardized tests. Yet your writings on education express great optimism, forecasting that as educators become more aware of sociocultural theory, they will devise applications that broaden and strengthen it.

Consistent with that prophecy, grass-roots reforms in early childhood education are currently under way. Though not yet a groundswell enroute to system-wide change, they are promising trends that, with dissemination of the documented favorable impact of play on development, are increasingly likely to gain momentum. For example, a 2009 report by the Alliance for Childhood termed the suppression of early childhood play an educational "crisis." It argued persuasively, on the basis of research evidence, for play's restoration to kindergarten curricula, calling particular attention to the benefits of sociodramatic play:

> The common misconceptions about young children's play fall apart when we look closely at what is really going on. We begin to be able to differentiate between superficial play and the complex make-believe play that can engage five-year-olds for an hour or more, fueled by their own original ideas and rich use of language.... Young children work hard at play. They invent scenes and stories, solve problems, and negotiate their way through social roadblocks. They know what they want to do and work diligently to do it. Because their motivation comes from within, they learn the powerful lesson of pursuing their own ideas to a successful conclusion. (Miller & Almon, 2009, p. 7).

Spurred by such messages, prominent media outlets, including the *New York Times* and *National Public Radio*, have collaborated with researchers on editorials addressing the power of play and how to reinstate it in children's lives (Bartlett, 2011; Spiegel, 2008; Stout, 2011). Prominent play researchers are also striving to energize a national play movement. In 2010, they took evidence on play-based learning to New York City's Central Park in the Ultimate Block Party, a day of hands-on play exhibits that attracted over 40,000 parents and children. The following year, block parties sprung up in scores of cities and towns across the county.

New early childhood curricula have also emerged. The best-known of these, Tools of the Mind, translates Vygotsky's view of mature, intentional make-believe play as a leading activity of early childhood into classroom practice (Bodrova & Leong, 2007). A randomized control trial confirmed that the Tools curriculum substantially augments self-regulation in preschoolers from low-income families (Diamond, Barnett, Thomas, & Munro, 2007). Another program, Jumpstart for Young Children, provides supplementary intervention to 3- to 5-year-olds in Head Start and child-care centers through adult–child storybook reading and dialogues, in a 1 to 3 ratio, followed by related, individualized playful learning activities. Jumpstart's curriculum, though less explicitly based on Vygotsky's theory than Tools of the Mind, is nevertheless highly consistent with it. Once again, a randomized control trial revealed substantial advantages for preschoolers exposed to Jumpstart in year-end language, literacy, and social skills (Harris & Berk, 2011). Currently, both Tools of the Mind and Jumpstart are vigorously extending their reach to increasing numbers of at-risk children.

Sociocultural voices in American early childhood education are alive and well and continue to make themselves heard. Nevertheless, in a broad contemporary climate that eschews child playfulness as key in promoting the reasoning, problem-solving, and socioemotional capacities essential for succeeding in the twenty-first century world, much remains to be done. The clarity and incisiveness of your educational vision, Vera, offer justification and inspiration for these efforts.

Laura

LAURA BERK, Ph.D., is Distinguished Professor of Psychology Emerita at Illinois State University. The author of multiple publications on child and human development, her research has focused on the effects of school environments, development of private speech, and contributions of make-believe play to self-regulation.

REFERENCES

Bartlett, T. (2011, February 20). The case for play. *Chronicle of Higher Education.* Retrieved from: http://chronicle.com/article/The-Case-for-Play/126382/

Bergen, D., & Mauer, D. (2000). Symbolic play, phonological awareness, and literacy skills at three age levels. In K. A. Roskos & J. F. Christie (Eds.), *Play and literacy in early childhood: Research from multiple perspectives* (pp. 45–62). Mahwah, NJ: Erlbaum.

Berk, L. E. (2001). *Awakening children's minds: How parents and teachers can make a difference.* New York: Oxford University Press.

Berk, L. E., Mann, T. D., & Ogan, A. T. (2006). Make-believe play: Wellspring for development of self-regulation. In D. G. Singer, R. M. Golinkoff, & K. Hirsh-Pasek (Eds.), *Play=learning* (pp. 74–100). New York: Oxford University Press.

Bodrova, E., & Leong, D. J. (2007). *Tools of the mind: The Vygotskian approach to early childhood education* (2nd ed.). Upper Saddle River, NJ: Merrill Prentice Hall.

Diamond, A., Barnett, W. S., Thomas, J., & Munroe, S. (2007). Preschool program improves cognitive control. *Science, 318,* 1387–1388.

Elias, C. L., & Berk, L. E. (2002). Self-regulation in young children: Is there a role for sociodramatic play? *Early Childhood Research Quarterly, 17,* 1–17.

El'konin, D. (1978). *Psikhologia igri* [The psychology of play]. Moscow: Izdatel'stvo Pedagogika.

Fiese, B. (1990). Playful relationships: A contextual analysis of mother–toddler interaction and symbolic play. *Child Development, 61,* 1648–1656.

Haight, W. L., & Miller, P. J. (1993). *Pretending at home: Early development in a sociocultural context.* Albany, NY: State University of New York Press.

Harris, S., & Berk, L. E. (March, 2011). *Impact of individualized, supplementary preschool intervention on literacy, school readiness, and socioemotional skills.* Poster presented at the biennial meeting of the Society for Research in Child Development, Montreal, Canada.

Hirsh-Pasek, K., Golinkoff, R. M., Berk, L. E., & Singer, D. G. (2009). *A mandate for playful learning in preschool: Presenting the evidence.* New York: Oxford University Press.

John-Steiner, V. (2000). *Creative collaboration.* New York: Oxford University Press.

John-Steiner, V., & Mahn, H. (1996). Sociocultural approaches to learning and development: A Vygotskian framework. *Educational Psychologist, 31,* 191–206.

Lindsey, E. W., & Colwell, M. J. (2003). Preschoolers' emotional competence: Links to pretend and physical play. *Child Study Journal, 33,* 39–52.

Marcon, R. A. (1999). Differential impact of preschool models on development and early learning of inner-city children: A three-cohort study. *Developmental Psychology, 35,* 358–375.

Miller, E., & Almon, J. (2009). *Crisis in the kindergarten: Why children need to play in school.* College Park, MD: Alliance for Childhood.

Ogan, A., & Berk, L. E. (2009, April). *Effects of two approaches to make-believe play training on self-regulation in Head Start children.* Paper presented at the biennial meeting of the Society for Research in Child Development, Denver, CO.

Ortega, R. (2003). Play, activity, and thought: Reflections on Piaget's and Vygotsky's theories. In E. E. Lytle (Ed.), *Play and educational theory and practice* (pp. 99–115). Westport, CT: Praeger.

Ruff, H. A., & Capozzoli, M. C. (2003). Development of attention and distractibility in the first 4 years of life. *Developmental Psychology, 39,* 877–890.

Spiegel, S. (2008, January 5). Old-fashioned play builds serious skills. National Public Radio. *Morning Edition.* Retrieved from: http://www.npr.org/templates/story/story.php?storyId=19212514

Stipek, D. J. (2004). Teaching practices in kindergarten and first grade: Different strokes for different folks. *Early Childhood Research Quarterly, 19,* 548–568.

Stipek, D. J., & Byler, P. (1997). Early childhood education teachers: Do they practice what they preach? *Early Childhood Research Quarterly, 12,* 305–326.

Stipek, D. J., Feiler, R., Daniels, D., & Milburn, S. (1995). Effects of different instructional approaches on young children's achievement and motivation. *Child Development, 66,* 209–223.

Stout, H. (2011, January 5). *Effort to restore children's play gains momentum.* Retrieved from: http://www.nytimes.com/2011/01/06/garden/06play.html?pagewanted=all

Vygotsky, L. S. (1933). Fragment from notes for lectures on the psychology of preschool children. In D. B. El'konin, *Psicología del juego* [Psychology of play] (pp. 269–282). Madrid: Pablo del Rio.

Vygotsky, L. S. (1966). Play and its role in the mental development of the child. *Soviet Psychology, 12*(6), 62–76. (Original work published 1933)

Vygotsky, L. S. (1978). *Mind in society: The development of higher mental processes* (eds. & trans. M. Cole, V. John-Steiner, S. Scribner, & E. Souberman). Cambridge, MA: Harvard University Press. (Original works published 1930, 1933, and 1935)

LETTER FOURTEEN

Discovering Self in Play

Artin Göncü

"The earliest sources that creative individuals draw upon are linked to childhood play: to the many hours they have spent entranced by nature, by the play of lights, or by a book." (John-Steiner, 1997, p. 37)

Madame,

As you state in *Notebooks of the Mind*, perhaps one of the greatest beauties of life is the presence of "distant teachers," who guide one's work like those who are working with you elbow-to-elbow. Your presence in my life began as a distant teacher with the publication of *Mind in Society* when I was a doctoral student in the late 70s. However, as luck would have it, the distance between us lessened in many senses over the years. An intellectual contact that started with an introduction to Vygotsky became deeper with the publication of *Notebooks*, and gained interpersonal dimensions after having met you in person in the late 80s. Since then I enjoyed a friendly, empowering, and a humor-filled interaction with you as well as benefitting from your scholarly guidance.

With my passion to understand human play and its influence on development, reading *Notebooks* was like an ointment, healing a wound caused by poor treatment of this complex activity in highly controlled experimental research that took the passion out of it. In contrast, based on the personal experiences of the gifted, *Notebooks* provided examples of childhood play in its richness and its relation to adult play and creativity in different domains of art and science. Thereafter, this powerful evidence presented in a fluid and warm narrative became a model for me illustrating how one can defy dry disciplinary boundaries in the effort to remain loyal to human existence.

In getting ready for this letter, I re-read *Notebooks*. Almost overwhelmed by the thoughts evoked (and sometimes provoked!) by this work, I left it aside many times, took deep breaths, and then continued reading. Your examples led me to reflect, yet again, on my own childhood experiences, and I was drawn into imaginary conversations with you about the questions I found myself asking. Yes, indeed, as you aptly illustrate in the book, these initial conversations were internal and abbreviated as I was having them privately, on my own. I shall, however, unpack them here and make them public.

One question is how in imaginative play do we discover and create our selves in relation to but apart from the craft that interests us? To put it more forcefully, when the medium and the object of inquiry is one's own self, how does one go about discovering and transforming it?

As a corollary, I wonder how children create play space for themselves when the phenomenon of interest is not sanctioned by the community. What do children do when their communities prohibit their search for meaning in play due to many reasons including morality?

Finally, these questions about childhood play become all the more layered when we inquire into the continuity that I believe exists between childhood and adulthood play. In my view, the need to play imaginatively (along with the need to be attached) is ever-present throughout our lives but it gets fulfilled in different relational contexts at different stages of development. Childhood play gives way not only to creative activities such as writing but also continues to provide an arena for the exploration of self and meaning. We have this claim under scrutiny looking to see if adults report that they pretend all throughout their lives. If this is, indeed, the case, the next and more challenging question will be what kinds of transformations does such pretend lead to?

Existing evidence provides limited information that is related to the first two of these questions only about childhood play. We know that children bring to play those experiences of affective significance in their effort to make sense of them. We also know that this effort is often a shared one: children engage in sequences of negotiations with their peers in their effort to make those experiences public. However, we don't know much about the intra- and inter-psychological processes involved in children's effort to make sense of their experiences re-created or anticipated in play. It remains as a mystery to me how powerful but partially understood phenomena take children to the illusory world of play and provide guidance for them to appropriate meaning from their own imaginations under varying circumstances of support. And, an even greater mystery is how such transformations of meaning take place all throughout life.

I turned to my own childhood play in forming some tentative hypotheses about these questions. Growing up in Turkey as an Armenian minority, as the neighborhood sissy who never got accepted into the boys' club, as one of the rejects of the extended family because of being a child of the daughter-in-law who was an outsider, my life started as a struggle against alienation. Play was my solace, my only life saver. Only in my solitary play when there was nobody around, could I explore my questions about my developing gender and ethnic identity, my looks with darker features like my mother's, and my desire for power and release from "bondage." Then, I could put my sisters' frilly taffeta dresses on, wear makeup, and sing at the top of my lungs giving concerts to my in(visible) audience. Only in play, could I seek salvation as a child priest by conducting mass in an empty house, lighting candles, burning incense, and chanting. As such, I tried to cleanse myself from the guilt that was inflicted on me. But, how and to what end? To where does such play activities lead one later in life?

I feel that a beginning effort to address these questions requires three kinds of inquiry: First, I maintain that regardless of whether play is social or solitary, it is always conducted with certain audiences and "distant teachers" in mind, teachers who are adopted at varying degrees of consciousness. However, as of yet, we have very little knowledge about who these teachers are, what motivates children to choose them, and whether their guidance occurs in support of children or in opposition to them.

Second, it remains to be explored how appropriations of meaning under different circumstances of support or constraint occur with the guidance of such teachers. If my childhood experiences have any validity whatsoever, the "sacred" may be shared with others while the "profane" is likely to occur in private. As well, depending on the play agenda and the audience, appropriations are likely to involve "cognitive pluralism" of varying complexity, e.g., a sermon would rely on verbal talent while dance will embody movement.

Third and finally, we need to look into how meanings appropriated in play are integrated and externalized in a self-narrative with increasing degree of coherence throughout development. Play appropriations lead to trials not only in play but also those outside of play resulting in transformations of self. Also, during these trials, we discover that there are other distant teachers who are available outside of play. Empowered by my distant teachers in play, when I stepped into "real" life, I discovered many others who are ready to guide. I will never forget the day when I learned that Simone de Beauvoir and her sister also dealt with questions of gender and faith as little girls in their play. Since then, just like play teachers of childhood, de Beauvoir became a distant teacher, shedding light in a life-course.

All of these remain to be explored, but I would like to emphasize that these issues do not lend themselves to examination in experimental research. Rather, they require longitudinal and interpretive work with a focus on substantive play texts such as those exemplified in *Notebooks*.

You see, Madame, notwithstanding the cultural differences, I see play as a self-generative activity that enables growth for as long as we live. As such, every child and adult has a right to play. When people are deprived of play opportunities, their growth and creativity are arrested. Therefore, as it has become a common practice in the US these days, taking play opportunities away from children should be questioned in research on social justice. And, I hope that this issue will also be picked up in future work.

Alors, Madame, now I have reached my word limit. If you remember, when you excused yourself from dinner a bit earlier than the rest of us in one of the recent AERA meetings, I objected to your request because I did not want to continue the evening without you. In response, you said "I am an old lady" to which I replied "so am I." It is preciously these kinds of playful exchanges that free us from limitations imposed on us, allowing us to grow together. As I write these lines, I see that you are closer to me now than before. While I cherish this connection, I could not begin this letter by saying Dear Vera or Chérie, but Madame which in my opinion expresses more fully the intellectual sophistication and personal elegance you bring to our field.

So, here's to you, Madame!

DR. ARTIN GÖNCÜ is Professor in the Department of Educational Psychology at the University of Illinois in Chicago. An avid writer and editor, his research focuses on the development of imaginative play during childhood, parents' and teachers' roles in child development, the professional development of early childhood teachers as well as the role of play in adult education and development.

REFERENCES

John-Steiner, V. (1997). *Notebooks of the mind*. New York: Oxford University Press.

LETTER FIFTEEN

Vera Was a Vygotskian before She Knew Who Vygotsky Was

Steven G. McCafferty

I was one of Vera's doctoral students at the University of New Mexico, and the work that I did there under her mentorship as my advisor and the Chair of my dissertation committee has influenced virtually all of my subsequent professional publications, having followed a neo-Vygotskian path of scholarship. I had been living in Japan teaching English before moving to New Mexico, and while there I was informed by Merly Segal, who had taken a class with Vera, about her wonderful insights as a leading Vygotskian scholar. I was immediately intrigued, read some of the Vygotskian literature, applied to UNM and was accepted, graduating with a degree in Educational Linguistics in 1995 after spending three years as a lecturer at Cornell University.

I had spent a number of years overseas before attending UNM, not only in Japan but as an international student in Nigeria, a Peace Corps Volunteer in Thailand, and an English language teacher in Malaysia. As a result of those experiences, particularly as a volunteer in Thailand where I had a chance to gain some success as a language learner, I had become interested in how the experience of living in a new language and culture changes one's understandings, beliefs, and ways of being and doing in the world. I got a chance to study this matter through a course, Thought and Language, I took with Vera my first semester at UNM.

During the class Vera had us focus on private and inner speech as seminal to Vygotsky's perspective of the development of consciousness. This immediately captured my interest, which moreover was inspired by Vera's own scholarship in the area of private speech and its metacognitive functions in relation to planning and guiding activities as well as its affective role (always the final "why" for Vygotsky). I also had a chance to read *Notebooks of the Mind* (John-Steiner, 1985) at the same time, which impressed on me just how critical the intertwining of thought and language is, forming a new modality that becomes central not only to cognition/affect but to ontology as well in relation to culture.

Thinking that the study of private and inner speech might help me better understand how people change with exposure to a new language and culture, and with Vera's encouragement, I decided to focus on the use of private speech and its application to the learning of a second language for the required class project. In doing research leading to a study, I read Vera's chapter, "The Road to Competence in an Alien Land: A Vygotskian Perspective on Bilingualism" (John-Steiner, 1985). There were many things I found important in this chapter (below), but with regard to private and inner speech, I relied in large part as a guiding parameter the following question Vera posed:

> The relationship of language to thought is not one of static connections; it changes with the shifting lines of development of the two languages. Central to the examination of bilingualism is the question: how do speakers of two or more languages achieve a separation of them at the production level while uniting them internally at the level of verbal meaning and thought? (John-Steiner, 1985, pp. 357–358)

Indeed, the latter part of this question, particularly the uniting of two languages in terms of meaning making as an aspect of using a second language in naturalistic contexts (where the language is spoken on an everyday basis) and how this changes consciousness has been a focus of my research over the years. Also, while researching the project study, I came across the work of James P. Lantolf and William Frawley, who a few years earlier had conducted the only research at that time taking a Vygotskian approach to second language private speech, suggesting its importance to gaining self-regulation in the new language. Jim Lantolf would later become one of my most important colleagues, after first being introduced to me by Vera.

As I suggested above, there were other things about Vera's 1985 chapter that struck me. The study was basically of adult Europeans, who, although in the U.S., at the time of the study, relied on the use of grammar books, that is, preferring a school-based orientation in addition to naturalistic interaction to learn the language. For them, formal study was a necessary component of the process, not unlike learning other subject matter. However, interpersonally, these same participants demanded recognition of their learner status when interacting with American native speakers, otherwise they would break off engagement. I have cited this aspect of the study a number of times as it emphasizes the importance of context and orientation in relation to learning and development. Contexts and orientation should never be ignored, something that has not at all been kept in mind in the mainstream approach to second language acquisition, in which "subjects" are often treated as objects and orientation to the task is sidelined along with individual differences.

Vera imparted many explanations and examples over the semester, many of which were aimed at the intellectual "ripening fruit" of class members, and for years afterwards I would find myself remembering what she had said about a topic, coming to a fuller comprehension of her meaning over time. For example the idea of "ascending to the concrete." I came across this term a number of times, remembering what Vera had said, a phenomena that only disappeared once I had grasped her meaning more fully as a form of extended prolepsis. I also certainly noted just how Vygotskian this process was, using it with my own students as an analogy to how word (sign) meanings develop over time in a second language.

I went on to take more classes with Vera and work with her in her capacity as the Chair of my dissertation committee. I chose to continue my work on private speech from my first class with her. At one point she cautioned me that although taking a Vygotskian point of view was her choice, that I should consider that such a perspective was still not particularly popular at the time (something a good mentor should do). However, I had become convinced that Vygotsky had things "right" and that his work was important to understanding second language development, and should find a niche within the field of applied linguistics. For the dissertation I expanded the study of private speech into gesture, following the work of one of Vera's colleagues from the University of Chicago, David McNeill, and later in my career came back to this area of research, applying it more broadly in relation to Vygotskian theory. It was wonderful to have Vera's guidance and support in first getting started.

After finishing my degree, I had occasion to see Vera at conferences a number of times over the years, and had the pleasure of introducing her as part of an invited panel at a conference for the American Association for Applied Linguistics. By that time I had come to learn more about her dissertation work at the University of Chicago on private speech and so introduced her as "being a Vygotskian before she knew who Vygotsky was," a fact I still find quite stunning. When her book *Creative Collaborations* (John-Steiner, 2000) came out, we arranged for her to be a guest speaker at my university. It is still the only such event in the College of Education where I remember so many faculty from across campus attending. Vera is a profound person and scholar, and I will forever feel grateful to her for being a mentor and my doctoral advisor.

DR. STEVE MCCAFFERTY is Professor in the Department of Educational Research, Cognition, and Development at the University of Nevada–Las Vegas. His teaching and research include expertise in the areas of applied linguistics, second language acquisition, as well as learning, curriculum, and assessment.

REFERENCES

John-Steiner, V. (2000). *Creative collaboration*. Oxford, UK: Oxford University Press.

John-Steiner, V. (1985). *Notebooks of the mind*. Albuquerque: University of New Mexico Press.

John-Steiner, V. (1985). The road to competence in an alien land: a Vygotskian perspective on bilingualism. In J. V. Wertsch (Ed.), *Culture communication and cognition*. Cambridge: Cambridge University Press.

LETTER SIXTEEN

Vera: Tribute and Tributary

Maryhelen Snyder

To think, it seems to me, is to hold an idea long enough to unlock and shape its power in the varied contexts of shared human knowledge (John-Steiner, 1985, p. 9).

I celebrate Vera in three interwoven aspects of our relationship: our personal friendship; the unique contributions of her research and thought; her manner of living and teaching that witnesses to the marvels of mind as a dynamic, dialogic interflow of intelligence.

The influence of one human being on another, the effect of the interweaving of two (or more) hearts and minds, can scarcely be described except in poetry, but Vera John Steiner has undertaken that task more passionately than any contemporary I know. She has honored me with a place inside her circle of "collaborators." Hundreds have been so honored. And have reciprocally honored her with their own work. As just one example from my own circle of close relationships, one of her students and dissertation advisees had an opportunity under Vera's tutelage to effectively impact the public school system's willingness and capacity to mainstream children who are physically and mentally impaired. His doctoral dissertation documents his amazing journey as a father and advocate and documents the beauty of his son's mind and spirit. Vera's scholarly and evolving grounding in Vygotskian theory and methodology has been repeatedly inspiring to me in many domains of my own vocational life as a psychotherapist and educator. We are contemporaries and thus we share our vocational beginnings in the exciting intellectual climate of social constructionism and all the various expressions of the "co-creation of meaning" that emerged from its early beginnings with such pioneers as Lev Vygotsky, George Herbert Mead, William James, Mikhail Bakhtin and Gregory Bateson.

I want to explore the significance of Vera's words above in the two most significant domains of my work life: psychotherapy and poetry.

PSYCHOTHERAPY AS "MOVEMENT-IN-RELATION" BECOMING EACH OTHER, BECOMING OURSELVES, BECOMING

Carl and I had been engaged in intense conversation as we drove in Carl's truck along the winding roads in the foothills of Albuquerque's Sandia Mountains. Carl said "X," I said "Y" (I cannot actually remember the subject). Then Carl said, "I don't agree with you at all." I remember thinking, "That's not possible." Only later did it occur to me that this sense of the impossibility of disagreement arose out of my subjective sense that we were each speaking of lived experience, not of belief or opinion abstracted from experience.

So I suggested that we slow down our dialogue and make sure that each of us fully understood the other. I asked his permission to speak as though I were him with the understanding that he would interrupt and correct me if I was not attuned to his experience and meaning. We were both skilled in this methodology as practitioners, and particpant-designers, of "Relationship Enhancement Therapy." This role-reversal went well, and so I asked him to "become" me in the same way. As I recall, he needed me to repeat what I had said earlier when he thought he had disagreed with me. Then he spoke *as* me and did it well, accurately reflecting the feelings and meanings. Out of that shared activity of "becoming" me, more experience sharing and thinking of his own emerged. We went back and forth like this for over an hour with increasing clarity and delight. The shared thinking/feeling seemed to continually move forward into new openings, new insights, new meanings for each of us. A colleague (Kaethe Weingarten) wrote that "intimacy is the co-creation of shared meaning." We felt the intimacy of dialogue-as-intercourse. There was no necessary ownership, or even identification, of our "own ideas." We lost the ability to distinguish which ideas "belonged" to self and which to other. The idea of self as "movement-in-relation" is explored in John Steiner's "Creative Collaboration." We were in that movement: a dynamic flow of co-creation.

The full title of our mutual discovery that day emerged as: Becoming each other becoming ourselves becoming each other becoming ourselves ad infinitum. It is a "tool" I apply often in my work as a psychotherapist and facilitator of dialogue.

There is something mysterious and seemingly magical about the way in which this methodology transforms dialogue into its true etymological meaning. It becomes neither argument, nor even discussion, but rather a "flowing" together "through" language [διά (diá,through) + λόγος (logos, word, speech). "Dialogue" emphasizes listening and understanding. Buber, Bakhtin, and Vygotsky are among those who have developed their philosophy on the dialogical nature of human existence. Vera is passionately committed to this tradition.

The "magic" we experience and frequently observe in those to whom we teach this methodology is the freshness of perspective that keeps emerging from the brave entrance of one human being into the "lifeworld" of another. The concept of "lifeworld" from the phenomenological tradition connotes that experience is the foundation. The bravery required to do this is noted by Buber who used the phrase "the deepest stirring of one's own being."

An important aspect of this tool of "becoming the other" is the way in which the body language of emotions is integral to the process. Thought is never separate from feeling. They are seamless. In recent decades, we have learned more about how much our brains are "hard-wired" to attune empathically to the embodied meaning of what the other is communicating. To reflect thought accurately without reflecting feeling is not only virtually impossible, but is a violation of the richness and complexity of human meaning-making which is grounded in living. With this, I would like to segue into poetry, the second (or first) major calling of my life.

THE EMERGENCE OF THE POEM "TO HOLD AN IDEA LONG ENOUGH"

The House Was Quiet and the World Was Calm
Wallace Stevens

The house was quiet and the world was calm.
The reader became the book; and summer night
Was like the conscious being of the book.
The house was quiet and the world was calm.
The words were spoken as if there was no book,
Except that the reader leaned above the page,
Wanted to lean, wanted much to be
The scholar to whom his book is true, to whom
The summer night is like a perfection of thought.
The house was quiet because it had to be.
The quiet was part of the meaning, part of the mind:
The access of perfection to the page.
And the world was calm. The truth in a calm world,
In which there is no other meaning, itself
Is calm, itself is summer and night, itself

Is the reader leaning late and reading there.

The poet, Stevens, is sitting in his house on a summer night (or imagining/recollecting this). A thought appears in words, just as thought always does, seemingly "out of nowhere" and without a "thinker" separate from that thought.

Also, there is the book; thus the thought emerges out of shared knowledge—and will speak into and expand that shared language. As the poet holds it long enough "to unlock and shape its power." It is awesome to me how much this poem precisely illustrates how creative thought works. It is equally awesome how precisely John-Steiner describes the work of the poem. It is no accident that Vygotsky loved poetry, that Wittgenstein saw poetry as the only way in which language can ultimately touch meaning and simultaneously discard the ladder of its logic and leave the writer/reader with no capacity or motivation to paraphrase its meaning. What does this poem mean? It says what it means. Nothing more, nothing less. That is its perfection.

The words come to Stevens as he leans above the page, *wants* to lean, *wants* to experience the "perfection of thought." He "holds" the spoken words loyally, not changing them, accepting their reality without resistance long enough "to unlock and shape their power."

The house was quiet because it had to be. The poet is allowing the experience of meaning, the experience of mind, the experience of truth to dwell in consciousness as it shapes itself and is moved to the page (to the listener, to the audience, to the shared dialogue).

In her chapter on "Verbal Thinking" in *Notebook of the Mind*, John-Steiner explores in great depth the implications of Vygotsky's insights into "inner speech." "Language and thought are neither identical nor totally independent processes." There is a process of "dissolving" language into its felt meaning as we turn inward thought outward. "It is through making explicit not only what is new inside one's mind, but also what is the implicit background of ideas, knowledge, and beliefs that novelty and insight arises" (1985, p. 139).

Thus it is that great poetry can at times appear to be not only the preferred way to express a truth, but the only way.

Maryhelen (Mel) Snyder

MARYHELEN SNYDER is a poet, writer, and clinical psychologist in private practice. She specializes in the social construction of empowering relationships, grief resolution, and development of healthy conscience by children.

LETTER SEVENTEEN

Revisiting an Interactive Approach to Advancing Literacy

Linda Finlay

"The model we have presented and are committed to developing further evolves from the theories of both Freire and Vygotsky. They argue that language is developed, extended, and modified through the constant interaction of individuals and their social contexts." (Elsasser & John-Steiner, p. 368)

Dear Vera,

I met you in 1979 at the University of New Mexico. After reading the article quoted above by Nan Elsasser and you, I realized that you could teach me things I wanted to learn. So I spent my first sabbatical year studying with you and getting to know you. Your generous welcome made that year a delight for me, and I took from it research and teaching approaches that deeply influenced me.

This article was an important piece falling into place in the puzzle I was trying to solve: how to teach college students to write and think clearly in the early 70's—the exciting years of Open Admissions. My students seemed passive about their education; they seemed to experience themselves as powerless and disinterested. Graduate education had not prepared me to teach these alienated students. I began looking for help, and help came, first, in the person and ideas of Paulo Freire who, along with Jesuit priest and activist, Father Dan Berrigan, offered a seminar on education in the summer of 1974, to twenty-five young teachers. I was fortunate to be one of them.

I began using Freire's ideas in my approach to teaching, and then, in 1977, you and Nan Elsasser came along in this Harvard Education Review article and provided a psychological and developmental foundation, grounded in L. S. Vygotsky's interactionist approach to learning, for Freire's epistemological and educational theories and practices. As you wrote, "Vygotsky and Freire shared approaches that emphasized the crucial intertwining of social and educational change. While Vygotsky focuses on the psychological dynamics, Freire concentrated on developing appropriate pedagogical strategies" (Elsasser & John Steiner, p. 362).

Freire conceived of knowledge, not as a reflection of reality, but as an interactive co-construction of social reality by subjects cooperating in the essentially human work of "naming the world" (Freire, 1970, p. 11). He saw every word as a generalization of experience from some particular perspective; the perspective embodied in our language shapes the way we see and act in the world. Our culture reflects the dominant perspective. Genuine psychological, intellectual, and social development occurs as people are able to distinguish culture from nature and to understand culture as experience coded by language from particular perspectives that support particular ways of life.

L. S. Vygotsky's idea that "cognitive processes are jointly constructed, in interaction with others and with cultural artifacts which allow for historically shaped knowledge to be shared, applied and transformed" (p. 170) dovetails with Freire's theory of knowledge and education. Freire believes that good communication is not a matter of correct word use alone, but entails an understanding of the perspective from which words are assigned meaning in one's culture. He believed that when students and teachers together engage in analysis of language that expresses the dominant perspective of their culture, they can come to understand their own place in that culture, and to participate with others in sharing and/or transforming it.

When I arrived in New Mexico in the Fall of 1979, you offered warmth and friendship as well as exciting ideas and opportunities. You invited me to explore with you the way educators in the Navajo Nation were thinking about schools. You were working with Navajo leaders who had contracted to take over some schools in the Navajo Nation from the Bureau of Indian Affairs, and you took me along with you to a meeting in Rough Rock with Navajo school administrators and parents. Their agenda was to consider which aspects of traditional Navajo culture to affirm and maintain and which to let go in educating children for the future. What impressed me was the *consciousness* with which this question was addressed. Of course, decisions with you consequences for culture are made all the time, but often without awareness. I wondered if my culture could *consciously* make such an effort? One of the Navajo leaders said, "Your time will come. Your culture will have to make these choices too—what to save and pass on in the education of students, and what to let go."

I think often of his words. Has our time come? What is the process of education by which students will develop socially and intellectually and by which society will be transformed and developed by their knowledge?

The invitation to write this letter led me back to your 1977 article. Re-reading it 34 years after it was written, I had the same sense of excitement and discovery. The article spoke to the future in 1977, and it is still speaking to the future. What you and Elsasser offered was an educational process, inclusive and participatory, for individual and social growth and development. Problems were recognized and named, and approaches to them suggested. The problems are still with us. Our culture is being shaped by forces which very often drive events without the awareness or participation of those who are affected, and educational programs increasingly convey technical information, while the essential role of the interaction between teacher and student and between the quality and values of the culture and the development of knowledge are overlooked. Not so surprisingly, many students on all levels are bored and alienated, and many teachers are demoralized. The insights of Freire and Vygotsky to which you brought attention are still timely and vital.

Although the *Harvard Educational Review* article focuses on teaching students how to write, the principles invoked apply in many educational contexts. The essay begins with a discussion of what constitutes "basic literacy" and moves immediately to a recognition that there are "cognitive and social dynamics that produce incoherent writing" (Elsasser & John-Steiner, p. 356). Literacy is not simply about grammar and word use; it is about this incoherence that has both cognitive and social roots. In it, following Vygotsky, you recognize that educators and students together must examine the language

> by which children (and adults) systematize their perceptions.... These words, the fragile bridges upon which our thoughts must travel, are sociohistorically determined and therefore shaped, limited, or expanded through individual and collective experience" (Elsasser & John-Steiner, p.359).

Freire saw that, since words are the carriers of meaning,

> literacy can itself be the focal point for transformation of consciousness. When socially significant, "generative" words are employed in literacy programs, they permit learners to reflect on their experience, to critically examine it. In this way, teaching adults to read and write is not longer an inconsequential matter of memorizing alienated words, but a difficult apprenticeship in 'naming the world.' (Freire, 1970, p.11)

Vygotsky has made the same point:

> in this process, 'it is not merely the content of a word that changes, but the way in which reality is generalized and reflected in a word.' (Vygotsky, 1934/1962, pp. 121–122)

For Freire, naming is the fundamental social act because it gives meaning, and meaning governs human action. In the process of learning an individual internalizes the meaning of words, and then participates in shaping the social world by giving names to collective experience. If education does not enable the young to participate in naming the world, it will be named for them from perspectives that may not respect or value their experience or lives. We are still in the process of "naming the world" and of inviting students at all levels to join consciously and critically in their own self-development and in the development of society.

For you, educational theory begins with the fact that persons are not abstract, ideal entities, but flesh and blood people, who live in a real, particular social world. In your work over the years you have tried to understand and describe this dialectical process of mutual transformation as it occurs in infants, in older students, in professional colleagues, in creative thinkers, and artists. By your teaching as well as by your scholarship, you have consistently invited students and colleagues to share in this work, and you've highlighted the importance of understanding the process by which people learn, and the significance of both the personal interaction between educators and learners and of the shape of the social world they inhabit.

The intellectual and moral commitments implicit in this sort of education are present in your life as well as your work: in your consistent collaboration with other scholars, and in the deep courtesy manifest in your attention to Navajo children, to young people struggling to communicate their insights in writing, and to me as a young and very "green" scholar.

For all these reasons, I thank you and I salute you as a beloved teacher, as a scholar, and as a person who has added great shine to the world.

Linda Finlay

DR. LINDA FINLAY retired from Ithaca College as an Associate Professor after twenty-seven years to work as a professional mediator. Her scholarship into the new epistemologies influenced by Freire and Vygotsky led to a position teaching critical thinking at Cornell University's Weill Medical School in Quatar.

REFERENCES

Ellsasser, N., & John-Steiner, V. P. (1977). An interactive approach to advancing literacy. *Harvard Educational Review*, 47(3).

Freire, P. (1970). *Pedagogy of the oppressed*. New York: Seabury.

John-Steiner,V; Shank, C; Meehan, T. (2005). The role of metaphor in the narrative co-construction of collaborative experience. In U. M. Quashthoff & T. Becker, (Eds.) *Narrative interaction/studies in narrative 5*. Philadelphia: John Benjamins.

Vygotsky, L. S. (1962). *Language and thought*. Cambridge, MA: MIT Press.

LETTER EIGHTEEN

Working Classroom
An Intergenerational Arts Community

Nan Elsasser

Dear Vera,

I was a classic 60's activist when I entered graduate school, searching for an academic foundation to supplement and inform what had been a visceral response to the movement for racial equality and against the war in Vietnam. I spent time with anthropology, visited sociology and completed an MA in ESL, so I could earn a living while traveling. I spent several years flirting without committing to an academic career. Then I met you; you introduced me to L.S. Vygotsky and interactionist (CHAP) theory, and I found the praxis I had been seeking. My academic career as well as our fruitful collaboration ended when I left the University of the Virgin Islands in 1987. My new career—unexpected and unsought—resulted from visiting Nicaragua during a civil war and coming home to a country transformed by Ronald Reagan's successful revolution.

While preparing to leave the U.S. Virgin Islands, I noticed a request for volunteers to accompany a group of M.I.T. linguists to the English Creole speaking Atlantic Coast of Nicaragua. They were supporting the Sandinista government's efforts to promote literacy and bilingual education in a remote, culturally and linguistically isolated region of the country. Intrigued by the opportunity to compare language attitudes in a progressive political climate to those I'd experienced in the colonial Creole-speaking islands of the eastern Caribbean, I signed on.

While the literacy was a priority of the Sandinista government, in actuality, the war against the U.S.-funded *contras* usurped almost all available human and financial resources. In Bluefields, the small town and commercial hub of the Atlantic Coast, we found schools with no books, paper, pens or pencils and teachers with an average 4–5 years of formal education. The were few available materials, like the following sample.

After five years in the West Indies and two weeks in Nicaragua, I returned to a country transformed by Reagan-inspired conspicuous consumption and to college and university writing programs that had replaced affirmative admissions, remediation and critical inquiry with high-level vocational training and the vapid five-paragraph essay.

Unemployed and still processing my first exposure to war, I accepted an invitation to share my experiences at an inner city middle school where most students were recent immigrants or native New Mexican Hispanics. That encounter resulted in Books for Bluefields, a student-to-student educational project.

The middle school students who participated in Books for Bluefields were learning English—a process requiring them to express their thoughts through the narrow channel of what was essentially a foreign language. In other words, at an age of rapid

> *Water is a liquid.*
>
> *It is very useful.*
>
> *We must learn to use it well.*

cognitive development, these students lacked the vocabulary and syntax in English or Spanish to articulate increasingly complex communicative intent. In a school comprised primarily of Spanish speakers and a society offering scant opportunities to engage with native English speakers, there was little incentive to become proficient in English or acquire the vocabulary and syntax of Spanish academic registers.

Books for Bluefields provided both. The Albuquerque students assumed responsibility for creating educational materials for children on Nicaragua's Atlantic Coast, who were struggling to acquire basic literacy skills in two essentially foreign languages—Spanish and standard English.

To provide assistance, the young Albuquerque authors studied the geography and culture of Nicaragua and the language patterns of basic readers, then wrote and illustrated almost 30 chapter books, like these samples:

I dived deeper and deeper to escape from the powerful current. A million thoughts were going through my head. I wondered if I'd ever see my family again. Had my pod survived? Would I suffocate? Would I live? I was very tired and hungry. I couldn't swim anymore. Remembering the good times we'd had, I calmed down and fell asleep.

Twenty-five minutes later I woke up. I could tell how long it had been because I can only hold my breath a little more than twenty-five minutes. I began to surface for air. The closer I got, the harder it became to swim. I was only a few feet from the surface when a huge wave crashed on my back, sending me tumbling. My lungs ached for air. I put all my strength into my tail and gave it a few flaps which sent me looping into the air. Powerful winds of at least 150 miles per hour hit me

Dinosaurs were similar to lizards, just bigger. They lived a long long time ago. Some dinosaurs were taller than a house. Some were as small as a chicken. Some were as mean as a lion and some were as gentle as a rabbit.

Many were larger than the largest house in Bluefields but their brains were as small as a kitten's.

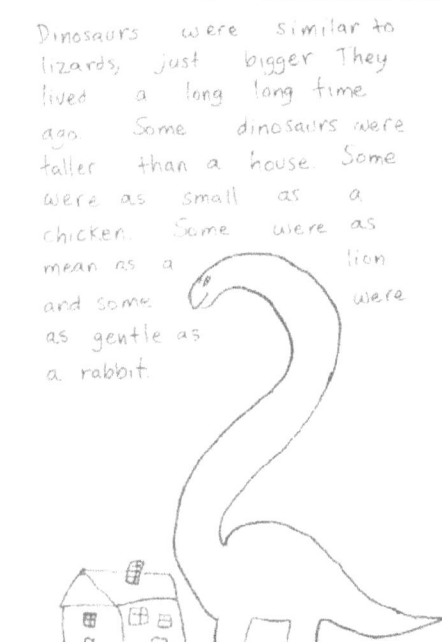

Below is the story of two dinosaurs that had a great adventure.

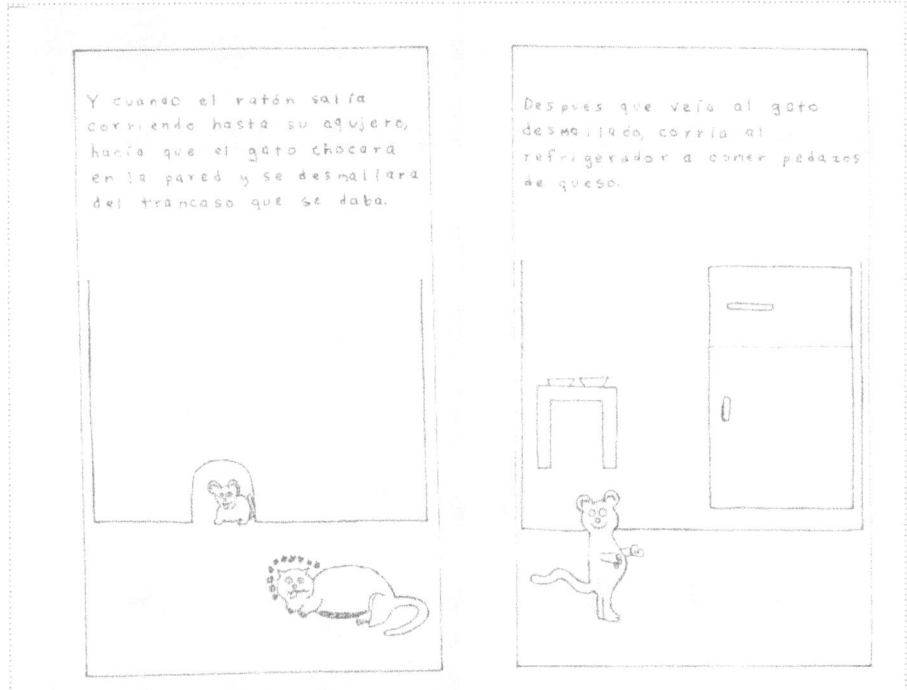

published by a local newspaper and distributed to schools in and around Bluefields. Teachers risked travel through war zones to obtain these books for children in their villages and wrote letters, like the ones on the next page, to the student authors.

The letters from Nicaraguan teachers and their pupils reinforced the young authors' commitment. They began participating in readings at local bookstores and libraries, appeared on radio and television and gave interviews to local reporters.

After reading about Books for Bluefields, psychologists and educators from George Washington University and the D.C. Children's Hospital invited the Albuquerque students to Washington, D.C. The psychologists wondered if a similar project could help Salvadoran refugee children experiencing a form of survivors' guilt remain connected with their families caught in the civil war back home. With new social and communicative opportunities, the student authors' social networks expanded: They wrote fundraising and thank you letters like the following to finance their trip, shared their project model with university professors and attended a reception in their honor at the Nicaraguan Embassy. Concomitantly, they acquired new vocabulary, added new registers to their communicative repertoire and increased fluency in both Spanish and English. Two students sold their stories to Leamos La Literatura, a bilingual reading series published by Houghton Mifflin. Collaboratively they wrote *Sueños Sin Fronteras/Borderless Dreams*, a fictionalized play about their

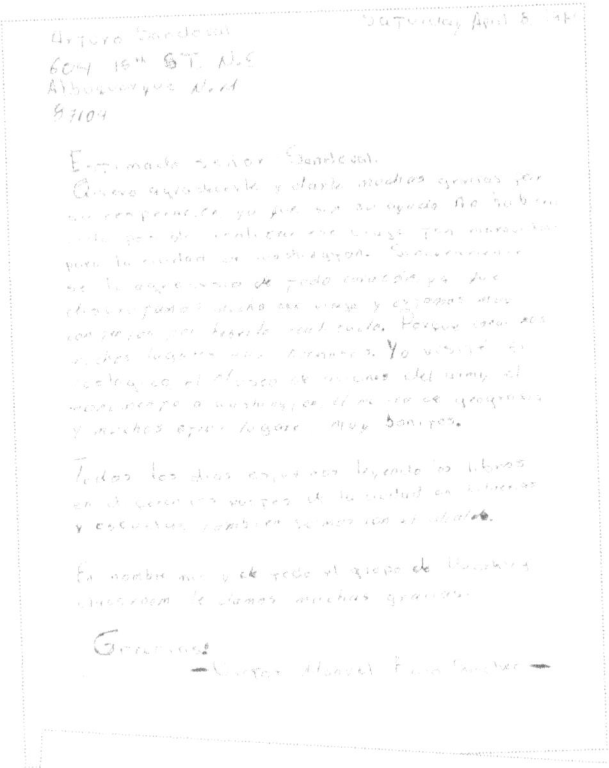

Saturday April 8, [illegible]

Arturo Sandoval
604 15th ST. N.E
Albuquerque N.M.
87104

Estimado señor Sandoval.
Quiero agradecerle y darle muchas gracias por su compresión, ya que sin su ayuda no hubiera sido posible realizar ese viaje tan maravilloso para la ciudad de washington. Sinceramente se lo agradezco de todo corazón ya que disfrutamos mucho ese viaje y estamos muy contentos por haberlo realizado. Porque conocimos muchos lugares muy hermosos. Yo visité el zoologico el Museo de [illegible] del army, el monumento a washington, el museo de geografía y muchos otros lugares muy bonitos.

Todos los días estamos leyendo los libros en el [illegible] de la ciudad en [illegible] y escuelas también [illegible] el [illegible].

En nombre mío y de todo el grupo de [illegible] classroom le damos muchas gracias.

Gracias!
—[illegible] Manuel [illegible] Sanchez—

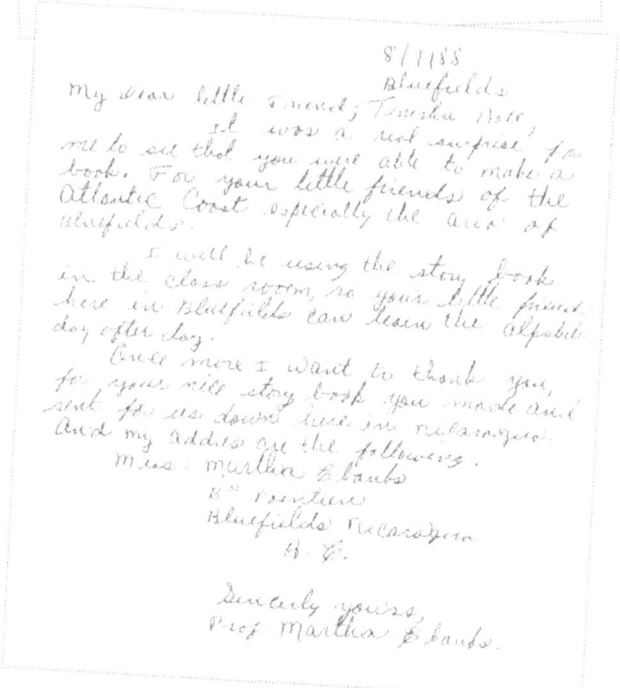

8/1/88
Bluefields

My dear little friend; Timothy Neir,
It was a real surprise for me to see that you were able to make a book. For your little friends of the Atlantic Coast especially the area of Bluefields.

I will be using the story book in the class room, so your little friends here in Bluefields can learn the alphabet day after day.

Once more I want to thank you for your nice story book you made and sent for us down here in Nicaragua.
And my address are the following.
Miss. Martha Ebanks
Bº Pointeen
Bluefields Nicaragua
A. C.

Sincerely yours,
Prof Martha Ebanks.

Hellow Tenesha Hall:

    This one who participating in the Bilingue Education, here in Nicaragua, for our isenifisation for our children here in our comunite of Rama Cay Nicaragua.

    And I love your book, which Title: My A B C Book. This will helps me a lot, also to my sch children. And Thank you very much for sending book for our Education process. we needs more helps

Thank you.

This is one who writting:

My name is

Bickwell Omier Omier
Rama Cay Nic.
Central America

actual and projected life experiences and performed locally, in community venues in the Bronx and Off-Broadway. The original student authors graduated from high school and have children of their own.

Their legacy is Working Classroom, an intergenerational arts community that evolved from Books for Bluefields and has grown into an internationally recognized model of arts-based individual and social transformation. Over 24 years, Working Classroom students have challenged and inspired me—writing, producing and touring *The Rubber Band*, an original play inspired by *Lysistrata* that provoked a statewide discussion about AIDS education plus plays on local land grant struggles, the politics of family violence and the crypto-Jewish legacy of the Inquisition; traveling to El Salvador to help community activists create an educational theater company for war-traumatized children, to Toronto to work with local artists interested in adapting Working Classroom's community mural program and to Rio de Janeiro to represent the United States at the VII International Festival of Theatre of the Oppressed.

Although my work is no longer academic, it is infused with the praxis I absorbed over the years of our collaboration. Specifically, Working Classroom's success derives from what you taught me about the inextricable interactions between internal cognitive development and external social context. Engaging in meaningful research, struggling with the conceptual challenges of artistic expression and participating in expanded social networks profoundly changes how Working Classroom students see themselves, and view the world. The scaffolding supporting this community is a formula I acquired as your graduate student, and its provenance and power will always be yours.

Thank you,
Nan Elsasser

NAN ELASSASER, Ph.D., is Founder and Executive Director of Working Classrooms in Albuquerque, New Mexico. Her independent, educational enterprise promotes a love of the arts and theatre for culturally, linguistically, and economically diverse homes.

LETTER NINETEEN

Resonance

Henry Shonerd

"It is this synthesis that most concerns me in this discussion: the joining of rapid bursts of thought with a regime of disciplined work." (John-Steiner, 1985, pp. 77–78) "While inner speech has been studied by others...*condensed thought across several modalities* has not been noted before." (p. 215)

Dear Vera,

Your influence on my work and thinking has been profound, partly because of the power of the ideas that you have encouraged me to explore, partly because of your generosity as a mentor and friend. As I have been jotting ideas for a letter, I find that you have influenced me by connecting who I am as a person with your generative thinking. Your mentoring has been both nurturing and demanding.

I wrote you a letter of thanks thirty years ago, less than a year after starting my doctoral work at University of New Mexico in the Educational Linguistics program, a program founded by you and Bernard Spolsky. I never sent the letter, realizing that it naively framed your mentoring almost entirely as that of a nurturer. Five years later you wrote on the inside cover of my copy of your recently published *Notebooks of the Mind*, "To Henry—a companion in many tasks and struggles." Now, twenty-five years on, I see that your mentoring, nurturing though it was, challenged me to challenge others to live a meaningful and committed life.

"Henry, you are a teacher," I remember you telling me, perhaps halfway through my doctoral work. Then and now, I feel out of my depth with researchers and academics who publish regularly...people like yourself. Yet, in my work as a teacher educator, I share with you the need to use and explain ideas that infuse scholarly work. You would often say in your courses that ideas have power. I learned about power of ideas, not as markers of academic status but as a means of simultaneously meeting life's challenges and creating a life of the mind. Of course, I came to the task with (I thought) a prepared mind. Yet I struggled with a sense of being indoctrinated into a world view. Now I see that I was looking for simple answers, while your view of the world required struggle and discipline, not simple acceptance. Even now I go through periods of doubt about the path I have taken and the tools I have chosen to take with me. It is the constant testing of ideas in the world that gives them power.

You are a generous and intimate thinker, in crediting other thinkers and seeing their work as resonating with yours. I met a number, thanks to you: Jerome Bruner, Shirley Brice Heath, Courtney Cazden and Howard Gardner. Their work became personal to me as a result. By personal I mean that their writing (and talking) became related directly to my research on language acquisition and cognition and has since become directly related to my work as a teacher educator. But their ideas are also personal, because they come from living, breathing people, people not entirely unlike me, however bright their star burns. It is that combination of power and humanity that I have tried to pass on to my own students. Your nurture and challenge, face to face and through your writing, has been fundamental to what I think and do in the world. To a world of mindless power, you have spoken the power of ideas. I take those ideas very personally. They save me every day from alienation and despair. To connect with you, a living, breathing person, those powerful ideas, gives hope, energy, and commitment.

As well and in kind, I came to see Vygotsky as a *distant teacher* (a term you use in *Notebooks*), a passionate thinker and mentor, who, like you, has influenced my work and that of so many others. For me, Vygotsky has not been entirely transparent. In reading him, I have looked to your interpretation of his work in extracting three ideas that constantly inform my work as a teacher educator: The Zone of Proximal Development, the nature of language and its relation to cognition, and scientific thinking.

The ZPD is the most powerful conceptual tool for me as a teacher of teachers. In my work, I typically preface my discussion of the ZPD with Gardner's idea that we should get away from measures of intelligence through testing and correlations of tests and look instead at how people around the world solve problems in domains of importance in varied cultural and community settings. (Gardner, 1993). At that point, I state the definition of the ZPD, verbatim from *Mind in Society* (p. 78) and relate it to the metaphor of scaffolding. This metaphor captures, on the one hand, the importance of expertise in domain-specific problem solving on the part of the teacher and/or more experienced peers and, on the other, the need for self-direction on the part of the learner. In the ZPD, effective assessment of learning involves the teacher or mentor suggesting to the learner the use of particular tools for solving the problems. This involvement of the teacher I take to be formative assessment, in contrast to the paradigm of hands-off, summative assessment that dominates test-driven curriculum today.

The ZPD is, in effect, a metaphor of teaching-as-scaffolding, hence a powerful illustration of the link between language and cognition. This provides me a chance to link Vygotskian thinking to the work of Lakoff, Langacker, and other researchers in the cognitive grammar enterprise, for whom metaphor is a focus of much research.

And here a flashback: Thirty years ago, when I was first learning from you about Vygotsky, I was introduced by your colleague in the UNM Linguistics Department, Larry Gorbet, to cognitive grammar, a budding enterprise that contrasted language as a manifestation of broad conceptual, discourse-based processes, with the dominant Chomskian paradigm of language as an autonomous, syntax-based capacity. I remember sitting at my desk in ancient Marron Hall (still standing!) and journaling and doodling connections between cognitive grammar and Vygotsky. I was coming to see that these enterprises were generative and complementary and would have a profound impact on views of language and learning, therefore on my own work as a teacher.

It is in scientific thinking where I struggle the most with Vygotsky. I have worked hard at understanding what he says about it in *Thought and Language*. What makes a concept scientific? Certainly, it must be grounded in data, but what kind of data? I have no problem with quantitative research, but don't think that measuring and counting is the last word in data. In fact, I believe that the hegemony of standardized testing in education has corrupted the educational enterprise in this country. I suspect that precisely where Vygotsky has captured the imagination and stimulated research is not in his efforts to be quantitatively scientific (in fact, he has been criticized for the lack of quantitative data) but in his willingness to engage in experiments that provide a humane narrative of learning and development.

I don't find credible the idea of "research-based" teaching strategies, as one reads in phonics-based literacy curricula, largely because it pretends an objectively and quantitatively determined way—a "teacher proof" way—to implement and assess learning and teaching. It lacks a sense of context, culture, and history. In its place, I favor what has been variously called "action research" and "practitioner research." This is not original thinking. It is formative assessment, which I think should be a primary driver of curriculum and instruction. It requires that the teacher constantly think as a learner, absolutely essential for teaching in the ZPD. It constantly addresses the question, "Why is this worth learning?", addressing the issues of motivation, relevance, and rigor head on.

Finally, I find I need to make explicit the quotes from *Notebooks* at the beginning of my letter. In making sense of my life and my work as a teacher of teachers, I have found two things to be essential. One is that I have had to work long and hard at being both credible and creative. The other is that, in this hard and continuous work, coherence in my thinking and doing has been scaffolded by words in your writing that resonate across varied domains of knowledge…words like "dialogue" and "enterprise," words packed with meaning, with power, with lived experience. I have been privileged and fortunate to have engaged in an extended dialog with you and your magic circle as I have taken on my network of enterprises.

Henry

DR. HENRY SHONERD is currently teaching at the University of New Mexico. A teacher educator for over thirty years, Dr. Shonerd's interest in educational linguistics and second language learning helped him to forge his expertise in classroom language functions and the application of Vygotskian theory to teaching and learning.

REFERENCES

Gardner, H. (1993). *Multiple intelligences: The theory in practice.* New York: Basic Books.

John-Steiner, V. (1985). *Notebooks of the mind: Explorations of thinking.* Albuquerque: University of New Mexico Press.

Vygotsky, L. S., (1978). *Mind in society.* Cambridge, MA: Harvard University Press

LETTER TWENTY

Water and Wine

Painting as the Emergence of Word Meanings from Images

David Kellogg

"Language is a bridge between individuals who wish to overcome divisions born of the diversity of human experience. It is also a bridge between inner thought and shared understanding; the past and the present, the world of the senses and the realm of thought." (John-Steiner, 1985, p. 111)

Dear Vera:

A good letter should be newsy, and looking uneasily over the vast interests we share (in defiance of the diversity of experience!), I find only narrow nooks where I know things that will be any news to you. But looking back, more calmly, over the very vastness of the field, I think that there must always be hidden links, like little prairie dog tunnels, connecting two perfectly familiar areas of the common terrain we share in some newsy way. Perhaps the tunnel that I poke my snout into here will not be perfectly new to you. It is the underground passage that connects the esthetic and the ethical dimension of a good Renaissance painting.

On p. 138 of *Notebooks*, you draw attention to curious fact that critics like Arnheim, who seek to convey ideas we get from paintings, often rely on the written word to claim that language is a basically conservative, consolidating, assimilatory force rather than a creative one. Piaget turns this artistic prejudice into something very like a science. You ask, *"Is language then, an afterthought in thinking?"*; "I do not think so," you reply.

Not even graphic, visual, painterly thinking? In Chapter Two of *Tool and Sign in Child Development*, Vygotsky and Luria remark that speech communication, reading, writing, calculation, and also drawing and painting can be seen as the "extra-mental" lines of development which correspond to, and even precede, the "intra-mental" lines of development which form verbalized perception, verbalized attention, and verbalized memory (which I think of as really just another name for vocabulary, but vocabulary conceived of as word meaning-memory rather than just a dictionary of sounds and spellings).

Verbalized perception, verbalized attention, and verbalized memory are not, of course, separate skills like pronunciation or handwriting. On the contrary, it is almost as if each psychological function has a lower end which interfaces with the environment (like a spoon, a knife, and a fork) and which therefore differs from all the others, and then a higher end which interfaces with volition, where the functions are all the same, or at least very similar (again, like a spoon, a knife, or a fork, except that the handle is mind-shaped or meaning-shaped rather than hand-shaped).

So is painting that tells a story a separate skill, like pronunciation or calligraphy, or is it more mind-shaped and meaning-shaped, more like vocabulary and grammar? If painting is language-laden in this latter, lexicogrammatical, way, then it should exemplify:

a) the key FUNCTIONAL difference between (on the one hand) tools which aid the adaptation of humans and other animals to the real, material environment and (on the other) signs which have the potential of creating an ideal environment adapted to human free will and even, with the aid of tools, realizing it, at least as a form of the "real ideal", e.g., as artwork.

b) the key STRUCTURAL difference by which this function is realized, namely, the necessity of looking at a sign and imaginatively, even empathetically, reconstructing the aim, the purpose, and even the mind of the sign-maker.

c) the key genetic SIMILARITY between tools and signs: how, as you say, they are born of the necessity to sublate the rich diversity of human experience and to build bridges between past and present and perhaps even a crude ferry into the future, which by the very fact that it is the future must necessarily be even more free of the purely graphic, visual element of painting.

On p. 8 of *Notebooks*, you remind us that when any experienced thinker at first stumbles on his or her peculiar "inner symbol system" it is "embodied in the history

VERONESE, *THE WEDDING AT CANA* (1563)

of an individual, beginning with his or her efforts at reflection that first developed in childhood." Maybe that explains why Vygotsky, in both his writings on ethics and esthetics in *Educational Psychology* and his dissertation on *The Psychology of Art*, chooses to illustrate the power of art with two Jewish jokes, both taken from the Gospels.

The first is the story of Christ feeding the four thousand with a few loaves and a few fishes. Vygotsky remarks that from the point of view of each individual down amongst the multitudes there isn't anything on offer except what we get in everyday life: more bread and more fish. One can imagine the great unwashed complaining "Is that all you got?" and looking ruefully over each other's shoulders to see if their neighbors have bigger loaves or plumper sardines.

The second Jewish joke is the wedding at Cana (John, 2: 6–9). Christ goes to a wedding, and the wine runs out. The mother of the bride is having a fit. Christ directs the servants to fill some empty jugs with plain water and we inwardly groan that he's going to do the same old loaf and sardine trick and send everybody home with a glass of water and a couple of parched anchovies.

But lo! The water changes into wine. In this painting by Paolo Veronese, *The Wedding at Cana* (1563), the blue of water and the red of wine are both linked and distinct in almost every corner of the complex painting (see, for example, Christ's dress). Yet as the eye travels from background to foreground, the overall impression

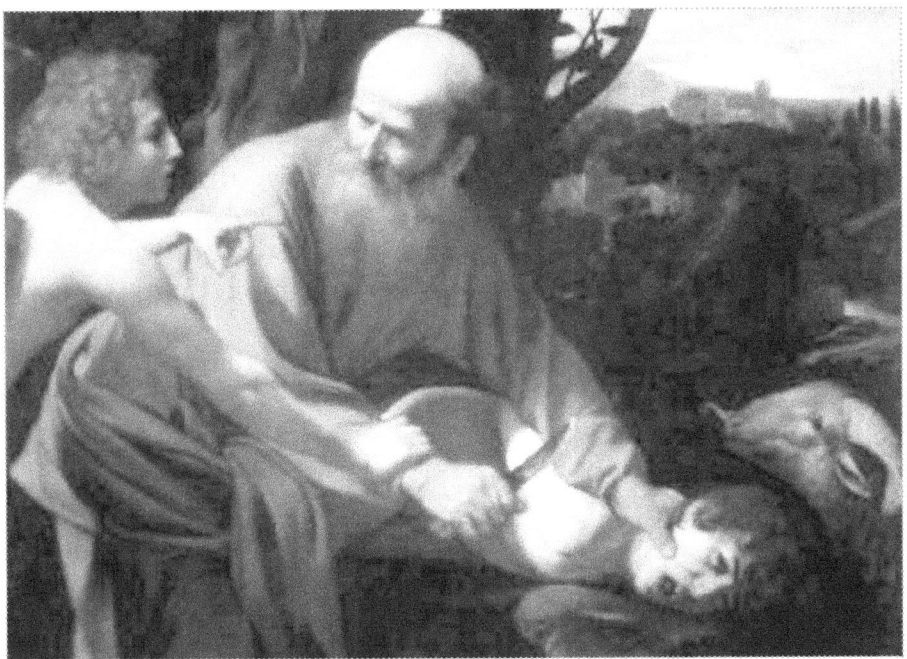

CARAVAGGIO, *THE SACRIFICE OF ISAAC*, (1603)

is that blue changes into red, and as our eye travels to the lower right hand corner, we see water being poured into jugs and observe a cranky sommelier critically, nay, incredulously, sampling the result. "Every man at the beginning doth set forth good wine; and when men have well drunk, then that which is worse: but thou hast kept the good wine until now." What kind of a Jewish wedding is this anyway?"

Notice that although there are over a hundred people at this wedding, nobody is talking. The painting was originally produced for a Benedictine monastery where speech was forbidden. One wonders, then, how many monks really understood the working, as well as the meaning, of the painting. My guess is that if any of them really did, they did not remain Benedictines for very long.

Vygotsky tells us that the miracle of art is not the paltry multiplication of fish (the "socialization" of an individual emotion). Instead, it's the instantiation of an emotion that is already thoroughly (but from the child's view objectively rather than subjectively) social. How does this happen, or rather, what does it actually feel like? I suspect it is not always as pleasant an experience as a glass of good wine at a wedding or a good splash of red on blue.

This painting on the previous page, which is in a way as much an example of written speech as, say, *Thinking and Speech*, or *Notebooks of the Mind*, is now four hundred years old. But let us pretend, just for a moment, that we are looking at it with the poor eyesight of a newborn infant. We might see a dark rectangle nearly slashed into two right triangles by a line of bright light that descends from roughly the upper left hand corner and culminates near the lower right hand corner.

Somewhere near the middle of the long warm line there is a kind of knot (look closely, with adult eyes, at the knot and you will see that Caravaggio has not actually bothered to paint in Isaac's twisted arm). A short, stubby cold glint seems to stick out of the knot at an angle perpendicular to the long line of warm light. Perhaps beneath the cold glint we discern a face, and it is crying. We too begin to cry, without really understanding why.

Now imagine that we are looking at this picture through rheumy old eyes nearly occluded by cataracts. Once again, we see a dark rectangle bisected by a line of bright light, but it means something quite different now. We read the painting from left to right and from top to bottom, like a text. The line itself descends inexorably like a sentence ("subject-verb-object").

But if it were a written sentence (e.g., "man kills boy") we would have to say that it is not a grammatical one, for there appear to be two different subjects vying for a single verb. Beneath the cold glint of that verb we can, if we draw closer to the canvas, make out two possible grammatical objects. Perhaps (if the reproduction in this book is good enough) we may notice that the second object, near the border of the canvas, appears to bear a faintly human (i.e., hopeful) smile.

All this suggests (to me, at any rate) that the verbal dimension to art that you kept finding in your *Notebooks* interviews is more than an artifact of the interview. But it also suggests (to me, at any rate) a specifically moral verbal dimension: that esthetic pleasure is (like other forms of pleasure), just as Spinoza said, intrinsically good in an ethical sense (Ethics, Part IV, Prop. 41).

Every good painting is in some sense about the "good life" even if the "good life" is only etched there as a negative, an ideal to be imaginatively contrasted with the real. So a painting is never merely itself; and never entirely something else either. Water is not wine, but even the purest wine still contains water.

David Kellogg

DR. DAVID KELLOGG is an applied linguist who teaches at Hankuk University of Foreign Studies in Seoul. A longtime enthusiast of the arts, languages, and cultural-historical theory, he is currently translating Vygotsky's works into Korean.

REFERENCES

John-Steiner, V. (1997). *Notebooks of the mind*. New York: Oxford University Press.
Spinoza, B. (1992). *The ethics*. Indianapolis, IN: Hackett.

LETTER TWENTY-ONE

Applying a Functional Systems Approach to the Study of Language Development

Teresa Meehan

"The prolonged dependence of young children on their caretakers is a basic condition of human life. The adult-child interactions during this period of dependency form the primary social sources for the development of linguistic and cognitive processes. The subsequent mastery of language, extending the meaning and scope of these early reciprocal exchanges, enables growing children to internalize the cultural knowledge of their communities and to reflect on their experiences. There is both receptivity to others and self-initiated exploration in the behavioral repertoire of very young children. The tension between these two highly adaptive tendencies contributes to the processes of individuation and enculturation." (John-Steiner & Tatter, 1983, p. 86)

Sociocultural theory is grounded in the notion that "human activities take place in cultural contexts, are mediated by language and other symbol systems, and can be best understood when investigated in their historical development" (John-Steiner & Mahn, 1996, p. 191). These concepts have become integrated into my thought processes as the result of countless conversations and several intense, joint writing sessions I've had the opportunity to share with my teacher, mentor, and collaborator, Dr. Vera John-Steiner.

Vera John-Steiner, who was motivated by her own mentors—those who faced the devastation of World War II in the concentration camps—has devoted her life to continuing what her mentors could not by contributing to a community of thought that views human evolution as a product of socio-historical development. Her many areas of study reflect her dedication to expanding our collective knowledge base and the application of sociocultural theory to education, language, and literacy (Gallimore, Tharp, & John-Steiner, 1992; Hersh & John-Steiner, 2011; John-Steiner, 1971; John-Steiner, 1985; John-Steiner, Cazden, & Hymes, 1972; John-Steiner & Mahn, 1996; John-Steiner, Panofsky, & Smith, 1994; John-Steiner & Tatter, 1983; Panofsky, John-Steiner, & Blackwell, 1990); cognitive pluralism (John-Steiner, 1995; Meehan, John-

Steiner, & Kennedy, 1995); functional systems (John-Steiner, Meehan, & Mahn, 1998); and possibly most dear to her heart, the development of complex collaborations (John-Steiner, 1996; John-Steiner, Shank, & Meehan 2005; John-Steiner, Weber, & Minnis, 1998; Mahn & John-Steiner, 2002), and how joint thinking in a creative environment can lead to powerful shifts in the conceptualization and understanding of complex problems (John-Steiner, 1989; John-Steiner, 1997; John-Steiner, 2000; John-Steiner & Meehan, 2000).

As a graduate student at the University of New Mexico, I had the wonderful experience of collaborating with Dr. John-Steiner on several joint projects. Her expertise and insight shared in the context of some of our collaborative experiences helped shape some of the ideas expressed in my doctoral dissertation (Meehan, 1999) and continues to influence my work in the field of substance use and human development.

The main challenge of my research over a decade ago was to outline a theoretical approach that was dynamic enough to embody the biological effects of drug exposure on the brain, the behavioral and environmental consequences of such exposure, and the interaction between the neurophysiological, psychological, and socio-cultural-historical planes of development (Meehan, 1999) in the context of dyadic interactions between mothers and their children when prenatal substance exposure to alcohol and other drugs (AOD) was a confounding factor. The dyadic interactions provided the social context for observing differences that could influence language development.

> Within a sociocultural framework, Vygotsky (1978) described the concept of development as a rejection of the frequently held view that cognitive development results from the gradual accumulation of separate changes.... [Rather] child development is a complex dialectical process characterized by periodicity, unevenness in the development of different functions, metamorphosis or qualitative transformation of one form into the other, intertwining of external and internal factors, and adaptive processes that overcome impediments that the child encounters." (p. 73)

Vygotsky (1978) theorized that a person appropriates the artifacts, tools, signs and meanings of his or her culture from others, and brings them under increasing self-control. At first, the person needs external objects to help regulate his or her behavior, but later can do so using only internal operations. Of all the psychological tools identified by Vygotsky (1978, 1986), language is the semiotic system humans rely on most for communicating desires, intentions, and feelings to others and for internalizing, regulating, and transforming thought processes. Because Vygotsky regarded language as a "critical bridge" between the sociocultural world and individual mental functioning, he viewed the acquisition of language as the most significant milestone in children's cognitive development (Berk & Winsler, 1995, p. 12).

John-Steiner (2000) provided an excellent example of this process:

Verbal discourse between individuals, particularly between young and mature speakers, is transformed into inner speech and further into verbal thinking. Young speakers appropriate socially elaborated symbol systems which form the basis of their own representational systems. Individual and social processes are unified through a dialectical synthesis, frequently referred to as the *zone of proximal development*. (p. 56)

In contrast to a dialectical method, reductionists and dualistic approaches depend on the separation of natural processes into isolable parts for individual study. In reference to the limitations of these approaches, Biddell (1998) writes: "They have provided a rich repertoire of information about the world, but they systematically ignore the aspects of reality that involve relations between the separated processes" (p. 330). This methodological approach can be seen quite clearly in most of the literature concerning the impact of prenatal exposure to toxigenic substances on developmental outcomes. Research regarding this special population continues to overlook the interconnectedness of biological, social, and cultural processes as they apply to cognitive development. A functional systems approach, however, provides a solid framework for investigating the complex interrelationships between individuals and their social, material, and psychological worlds (John-Steiner et al., 1998).

In his groundbreaking work on the neuropsychology and cerebral localization of functions in brain-damaged patients, A. R. Luria (1973) argued that during the course of development, not only do "functional structures of the processes" change, but the organization of such processes in the cerebral cortex are modified to accommodate the change (p. 32). A functional systems approach, therefore, presented me with the opportunity to study the dynamic internal and external processes of dyadic interaction while embedded within the sociocultural context of substance-using mothers. The strength of this approach is grounded in the notion that various processes within the system can be analyzed, but only as they relate to the other interdependent functions (John-Steiner & Meehan, 2000). It allows for simultaneous consideration of both a fully developed system and a system in the process of development (John-Steiner et al., 1998).

In my doctoral study, observations of dynamic interactions showed subtle differences in scaffolding behavior that could contribute to the language delays that often occur in children prenatally exposed to alcohol and other drugs (Meehan, 1999), as well as other children with learning disabilities (Berk & Landau, 1993). For instance, the biological mothers of prenatally exposed children were less likely than foster care mothers or mothers in the control group to allow their children to pursue their own interests during play sessions. The biological mothers were also less responsive to their child's needs, failed to interact or facilitate achievement, were more limited in their repertoire of play behaviors, and were less successful at gaining the child's attention and cooperation to participate in joint play activities.

Concurrently, the biological and foster dyads spent proportionally more time in parallel play than they spent jointly attending to or playing with a common object. The implications of this pattern could be serious with regard to the development of joint problem solving. The less time the members of the dyad spends attending to a common object during play, the less likely it is that the adult member is providing the scaffolding the child needs to solve problems in his or her zone of proximal development.

These are just a few findings from my research, but they are adequate to show that, unlike static models where development is viewed as unidirectional, a functional systems approach provides a conceptual framework in which development is viewed as multi-directional. This approach allows for the simultaneous observation of multiple levels of complexity that are continuously developing and thereby, dynamic in nature. As pointed out by John-Steiner et al., (1998), complexity theorists describe developing systems as being "stable enough to contain information and evanescent enough to be spontaneous, and adaptive" (p. 129).

As we continue to co-construct our community of thought and further expand our understanding of functional systems, inevitably we will turn to the insightful work of Dr. Vera John-Steiner for guidance, interpretation, and the pure joy of participating in a community of shared ideas. In her book on *Creative Collaboration*, John-Steiner (2000) brilliantly notes, "The co-construction of ideas is helped by a listening ear" (p. 127). Thus, in addition to our quest to jointly characterize the complexity of dynamic, functional systems, we will also develop our emotional abilities for successful collaboration. "By joining with others we accept their gift of confidence, and through interdependence, we achieve competence and connection" (p. 204).

TERESA MEEHAN, Ph.D., is CEO, President, and Senior Development Officer of ASPECTS Treatment & Learning Center, a non-profit, community-based mental health agency in Grants, New Mexico. She additionally teaches as an adjunct professor in the Social Sciences Department at New Mexico State University.

REFERENCES

Berk, L. E., & Landau, S. (1993). Private speech of learning disabled and normally achieving children in classroom academic and laboratory contexts. *Child Development, 64,* 556–571.

Berk, L. E., & Winsler, A. (1995). *Scaffolding children's learning: Vygotsky and early childhood education*. (Vol. 7). Washington, DC: National Association for the Education of Young Children.

Biddell, T. (1988). Vygotsky, Piaget and the dialectic of development. *Human Development, 31,* 329–348.

Gallimore, R., Tharp, R. G., & John-Steiner, V. (1992). *The development and socio-historical foundations of mentoring* (ERIC Document).

Hersh, R., & John-Steiner, V. (2011). *Loving & hating mathematics: Challenging the myths of mathematical life*. Princeton, NJ: Princeton University Press.

John-Steiner, V. (1971). *Early childhood bilingual education.* New York: Modern Language Association.

John-Steiner, V. (1985). The road to competence in an alien land: A Vygotskian perspective on bilingualism. In J. Wertsch (Ed.), *Culture, cognition, and communication* (pp. 348–372). Cambridge: Cambridge University Press.

John-Steiner, V. (1989). Beyond the transmission of knowledge: A Vygotskian perspective on creativity. In R. Bjorson & M. R. Waldman (Eds.), *The university of the future* (pp. 51–68). Columbus: Center for Comparative Studies in the Humanities, Ohio State University.

John-Steiner, V. (1995). Cognitive pluralism: A sociocultural approach. *Mind, Culture, and Activity, 2*(1), 2–11.

John-Steiner, V. (1996). Women's collaborative interactions. In D. I. Slobin, J. Gerhardt, A. Kyratzis, & J. Guo (Eds.), *Social interaction, social context, and language: Essays in honor of Susan Ervin-Tripp* (pp. 545–553). Hillsdale, NJ: Erlbaum.

John-Steiner, V. (1997). *Notebooks of the mind: Explorations of thinking* (2nd ed.). New York: Oxford University Press.

John-Steiner, V. (2000). *Creative collaboration.* New York: Oxford University Press.

John-Steiner, V., & Mahn, H. (1996). Sociocultural approaches to learning and development: A Vygotskian framework. *Educational Psychologist, 31,* 191–206.

John-Steiner, V., Cazden, C., & Hymes, D. (Eds.). (1972). *The functions of language in the classroom.* New York: Teachers College Press.

John-Steiner, V., & Meehan, T. M. (2000). Creativity and collaboration in knowledge construction. In C. D. Lee & P. Smagorinsky (Eds.), *Vygotskian perspectives on literacy research: Constructing meaning through collaborative inquiry,* (pp. 31–48). Cambridge: Cambridge University Press.

John-Steiner, V. Meehan, T. M., & Mahn, H. (1998). A functional systems approach to concept development. *Mind, Culture, and Activity, 5,* 127–134.

John-Steiner, V., Panofsky C., & Smith, L. (Eds.), (1994). *Sociocultural approaches to language & literacy: An interactionist perspective.* Cambridge, MA: Cambridge University Press.

John-Steiner, V., Shank, C., & Meehan, T. (2005). The role of metaphor in the narrative co-construction of collaborative experience. In U. M. Quastoff & T. Becker (Eds.), *Narrative interaction* (pp. 169–195). John Benjamins.

John-Steiner, V., & Tatter, P. (1983). An interactionist model of language development. In B. Bain (Ed.), *The sociogenesis of language and human conduct* (pp. 79–97). New York: Plenum.

John-Steiner, V., Weber, R. J., & Minnis, M. (1998). The challenge of studying collaboration. *American Educational Research Journal, 34*(4), 773–784.

Luria, A. R. (1973). *The working brain: An introduction to neuropsychology* (Basil Haigh, Trans.). New York: Basic Books.

Mahn, H., & John-Steiner, V. (2002). The gift of confidence: A Vygotskian view of emotions. In G. Wells & G. Claxton (Eds.), *Learning for life in the 21st century: Sociocultural perspectives on the future of education* (pp. 46–58). Oxford, UK: Blackwell.

Meehan, T. M. (1999). *Prenatal substance use: Effects on dyadic communication.* Unpublished doctoral dissertation. University of New Mexico.

Meehan, T. M., John-Steiner, V., & Kennedy, C. (1995). The implications of "First Language Acquisition as a Guide for Theories of Learning and Pedagogy" in a pluralistic world. *Linguistics and Education, 7,* 369–378.

Panofsky, C. P., John-Steiner, V., & Blackwell, P. J. (1990). The development of scientific concepts and discourse. In. L. C. Moll (Ed.), *Vygotsky and education: Instructional implications and applications of sociohistorical psychology* (pp. 251–267). Cambridge: Cambridge University Press.

Vygotsky, L. S. (1978). *Mind in society: The development of higher psychological processes.* Cambridge, MA: Harvard University Press.

Vygotsky, L. S. (1986). *Thought and language* (A. Kozulin, Trans.) Cambridge, MA: MIT Press.

LETTER TWENTY-TWO

Vera John-Steiner's Influence on Creativity Research

R. Keith Sawyer

"We have come to a new understanding of the life of the mind. The notion of the solitary thinker still appeals to those molded by the Western belief in individualism. However, a careful scrutiny of how knowledge is constructed and artistic forms are shaped reveals a different reality. Generative ideas emerge from joint thinking, from significant conversations, and from sustained, shared struggles to achieve new insights by partners in thought." (John-Steiner, 2000, p. 3)

Dear Vera,

I first became aware of your scholarship when I read your 1985 book *Notebooks of the Mind.* This book was important for its insight into the creative processes of exceptional creators. When it was published in 1985, psychologists who studied creativity had been almost exclusively focused on the internal mental processes that accompanied creativity. This was important research, but unfortunately, as a result of its decontextualized laboratory perspective, it tended to neglect an essential aspect of real-world creativity—that it always takes place with tangible materials and externally represented symbol systems.

In *Notebooks*, you used interviews and biographical material to demonstrate that creators depend on external representations of their unfolding thought. These external representations included scientific hypotheses and observations written in notebooks (as with Charles Darwin and the famous analyses of his notebooks by Howard Gruber, 1974); daily observations and short character studies, kept in notebooks by fiction writers; and visual sketches and even three-dimensional prototypes developed by designers and artists.

What I found even more profound was that your book captured the ways that creators use these external representations. They interact with them, as a sort of dialogic partner. For example, artists interact with their notebooks constantly, turning back to their old notes and sketches for inspiration. Writers and scientists reinterpret old ideas through their ever-changing current perspectives.

Those who are familiar with Vygotsky's writings can easily see the influence of Vygotsky on your ideas—his argument that thought is first external and then becomes internalized, that social interactions and dialogue then become internalized as thought. These social precursors to internal mental processes are visible in daily human encounters. No doubt, your early studies of Vygotsky led you to be sensitized to this important aspect of the creative process, one that had been neglected by creativity researchers. In spite of the rich theoretical grounding of the book, it is clear and accessible—in no way a mere academic exercise in Vygotskian theory. This is your trademark: your ability to draw on profound and substantial theories to gain insight and to aid in your interpretations, but then to communicate your findings clearly and reach a broad audience.

In your 2000 book *Creative Collaboration*, you again addressed an aspect of creativity that had been neglected by psychologists: the role of collaboration and conversation in creativity. Your book was part of a broad turn in creativity research in the 1990s toward what I call a "sociocultural approach"—a focus on contexts, groups, cultures, and societies, in contrast to an earlier focus on individual cognitive processes (Sawyer, 2011). As with *Notebooks*, this new book also drew its power from your close analysis of real-world creators and the processes that resulted in their breakthrough creations. In contrast to laboratory studies that reduce creativity to its small, cognitive components, *Creative Collaboration* studied creativity in its rich complexity.

While I was writing *Explaining Creativity* (Sawyer, 2006, 2011), I had an opportunity to review the full span of scholarly studies on creativity, extending back to J. P. Guilford's legendary 1950 address to the APA titled "Creativity." Through the 1950s and 1960s, psychologists focused on the creative personality. In the 1970s and 1980s, psychologists focused on the cognitive processes associated with creativity—yet again, the focus was on the creative individual, and creative groups and contexts were neglected.

When you began your studies of creative collaboration, there was no precedent for a sociocultural approach to creativity. You showed true vision by being one of the very first scholars to perceive that the focus on the creative individual was missing the collaborative, active, and embodied reality of creativity.

I had an opportunity to collaborate with you when I was approached by Phil Laughlin, then the psychology editor at Oxford University Press. Phil was the editor responsible for the *Counterpoints* series of edited volumes, and he was excited about the idea of bringing together a senior scholar (you) and a junior scholar (me) to do a book somehow related to creativity. Because my own research touched on both creativity and development, I had been thinking about the various links between developmental psychology and creativity research. Your research also straddled both of these fields—with your Vygotsky scholarship addressing developmental theory, and your two books focused on creativity. I too had published research in both areas—with a 1997 book on children's pretend play (Sawyer, 1997b), and my published studies of jazz and theater improvisation (e.g., Sawyer, 1997a, 1998). So I proposed a book to be titled *Creativity and Development*, and you enthusiastically agreed to work with me. Published in 2003 (Sawyer, John-Steiner, et al., 2003), the book brought together five psychologists whose work had touched on both developmental themes and creativity. This project was an important experience in my career, in that it gave me the opportunity to work with the top scholars I most respect—not only you, but also Mike Csikszentmihalyi, Bob Sternberg, and David Henry Feldman (and two other junior scholars as co-authors, Seana Moran and Jeanne Nakamura).

I admire you for your vision and insight in leading the field of creativity research toward a focus on real-world creativity—collaborative, situated, and embodied. Your writing is clear, and always focuses directly on the most important issues. I also admire you for your leadership in the field, and your willingness to work with junior scholars and mentor them.

Sincerely,
Keith Sawyer

DR. KEITH SAWYER is a professor at Washington University in St. Louis. He studies creativity, collaboration, and learning. He has published over 80 scholarly articles and 11 books, including *Explaining Creativity: The Science of Human Innovation* (Oxford) and *Group Genius: The Creative Power of Collaboration* (Basic Books). In 2003, he co-authored a book with Vera John-Steiner and others titled *Creativity and Development* (Oxford).

REFERENCES

Gruber, H. E. (1974). *Darwin on man: A psychological study of scientific creativity.* Chicago: University of Chicago Press.

John-Steiner, V. (1985). *Notebooks of the mind: Explorations of thinking.* Albuquerque: University of New Mexico Press.

John-Steiner, V. (2000). *Creative collaboration,* Oxford, UK: Oxford University Press.

Sawyer, R. K. (Ed.). (1997a). *Creativity in performance.* Greenwich, CT: Ablex.

Sawyer, R. K. (1997b). *Pretend play as improvisation: Conversation in the preschool classroom.* Mahwah, NJ: Erlbaum.

Sawyer, R. K. (1998). The interdisciplinary study of creativity in performance. *Creativity Research Journal,* 11(1), 11–19.

Sawyer, R. K., John-Steiner, V., Moran, S., Sternberg, R., Feldman, D. H., & Csikszentmihalyi, M. (2003). *Creativity and development.* New York: Oxford University Press.

Sawyer, R. K. (2006). *Explaining creativity: The science of human innovation.* New York: Oxford University Press.

Sawyer, R. K. (2011). *Explaining creativity: The science of human innovation* (2nd ed.). New York: Oxford University Press.

LETTER TWENTY-THREE

Who Knew? Being Part of a Thought Community on Creativity
An Essay in Honor of Vera John-Steiner

David Henry Feldman

I met Vera in about 1975 in Aspen. We were there for different meetings. I knew Vera's work as a language development specialist, one of the best in the field, but was unaware of her other interests. The other time I met Vera was in Cambridge several years later when she was doing research for her stunning book *Creative Collaboration;* she interviewed and tested my wife Ann and me (we apparently didn't make the cut for the book, but Vera did ask me to write a foreword to it, an honor for which I am still very grateful). As far as I remember, these are the only two times that I met Vera in person. We have had mail and e-mail exchanges over the years on various topics and projects, but being part of Vera's thought community for me has been a mostly virtual experience.

I am pleased to have this opportunity to reflect on Vera's profound influence on the field of creativity studies, which for me came as a surprise and a delight when I read her article in 1992 in the *Creativity Research Journal* that introduced the terms "thought collective" and "thought community" to the field, along with introducing that field to the work of Lev Vygotsky (which, to be sure, I did know she had studied). In this essay I will discuss my understanding of the thought community that Vera situated me in and how I experienced it before and after reading her article "Creative Lives, Creative Tensions" in the early 1990s.

As some of you know, the field of creativity studies (which was not labeled as such then) was going through a major set of changes, with the critical period of change at almost exactly the same time as I met Vera in 1975. That year, the Social Science Research Council received funds from the estate of Esther Katz Rosen to help rejuvenate research in the field of giftedness. Howard Gardner was one of the people the Council asked to help with the project, including whom to appoint to a SSRC Committee to serve as a kind of Board of Directors to make decisions about how to spend the funds. This part of the story was not in Vera's article, but it is hard for me to discuss how our thought community formed without this context, which is, when you think about it, perfectly consistent with the overall point of Vera's article, i.e., that creativity cannot be understood out of context and without careful consideration of the social/cultural/historical influences on it.

My colleagues and I have written about this part of the story elsewhere (Feldman, Csikszentmihalyi, & Gardner, 1994), so I will not go into detail here, but the role of the SSRC, of a deceased donor, and the early days of the committee are critical to the story. Essentially, what happened was that the SSRC created a committee with several leading scholars with long histories of contribution to the traditional fields of giftedness and the study of creativity as psychometrically assessed individual traits, and Howard Gardner, who insisted that a small number of nontraditional scholars be included in the group. In fact, Howard put his reputation on the line by making his own participation contingent upon the addition of scholars who would, three years later, become the core members of what Vera later described as a thought community (following Ludwik Fleck, of course, whose work I had not heard of until I read her article).[1]

---

[1] The original members of the SSRC Committee were Jeanne Bamberger, David Henry Feldman, Howard Gardner, and Howard Gruber on the revisionist side; on the traditionalist side were James Gallagher, Halbert Robinson, Julian Stanley, and Michael Wallach.

We became a thought community largely, as they say about grandchildren and grandparents, because we had a common enemy. The SSRC scheduled meetings of the committee that were abject failures in every way except that they drove the four of us together, closer, and helped us find common ground. We never agreed completely, but we were so much more in agreement with each other than with our counterparts across the table that the common ground needed to create our thought community was firmly established. Even after one of the most distinguished senior psychologists alive (Bob Sears) was called in to help find a way to move the committee forward, we failed. The SSRC disbanded the committee in 1978.

Seeing the committee's failure as an opportunity, Howard Gardner told me to organize a *new* committee to replace the failed one, with only members who shared our views about where the field (fields, really, since giftedness and creativity studies were only the same field in the traditional perspective). Again, the key catalyst for the success of the new committee was funding; fortunately, we were able to secure a generous grant from the Andrew W. Mellon Foundation that supported our activities for nearly ten years.

It was the sponsorship of the SSRC and the Mellon Foundation, along with several other grants secured as part of the committee's work that gave us the opportunity to spend significant amounts of time together and develop our joint and individual perspectives. Certainly one of the emphases of Vera's article was to show the importance of culture and context on creative expression (e.g., the importance of commissions and a collective desire to create a "new Athens" in Florence early in the 15th century). An accurate description of the thought community I helped create requires that the point be made explicit that it could not have been successful without the contributions of prestigious organizations and foundations. Vera is very aware of this; I am simply adding it to the account because it was so important to how I experienced the effort to move a field in a different direction in those early years.

And there is no doubt that we fully intended to change the direction of the field of creativity studies. Paradigm shift might be too strong, but a major change of direction was at the top of our agenda. The emphasis in Vera's chapter on the nature of the change was on the shift from individual-centered toward social/cultural/historical aspects of creativity, particularly the collaborative nature of creative work. However, this only became a theme of our thought community several years after its beginnings when we recruited Mihalyi Csikszentmihalyi to join the team. It was certainly not part of my vision for the field when I entered it nor was it a major interest for several years after even the new SSRC group was started. The major initial features of the new view of creativity were, following Howie Gruber's work on Darwin, that it should focus on *great* creativity; also, following Michael Wallalch, the field needed to recognize that few if any traits apply across all *domains*. In fact, it became clear to us that creativity was best studied within domains. Finally, we shared the commitment to a *developmental* approach to creativity, seeing it more as processes of change and transformation than as traits.

It was in many ways the synthesizing and conceptualizing work of Csikszentmihalyi (1988) and his systems framework that gave coherence and clarity to the shared vision we had for the field. A major feature of Csikszentmihalyi's framework is the interplay of individuals, domains, and fields, and the cultural/historical context within which they carry out their various efforts and activities. But this feature of the thought community was among the last to be integrated into its vision; we had in fact been reluctant to give up our individual-oriented approach to the study of creativity. In our first joint publication (Feldman, 1982), Csikszentmihaly's work was not included; indeed, he was not yet a member of the group. Even as we did begin to embrace Mike's integrating vision, Howie Gruber expressed a shared concern that the unique qualities that make great creators so extraordinary would be lost in the complexity of the new system and its emphasis on the larger social, cultural, and historical forces that affect their work (Gruber & Davis, 1988).

My aim here is not to diminish Vera's insights about the nature of the thought community, nor question that the thought community she described was described accurately (if this were not a celebratory occasion I would say the same thing). My point is that Vera was struck with an important feature of our point of view, but that it is a feature that was not part of the original vision. I wonder if Vera would have even identified our group as a thought community if Csikszentmihalyi's contributions had not been added. I am guessing not, and probably rightly so. What Csikszentmihalyi was able to do was integrate all of our efforts to date into a framework that at the same time showed how incomplete the work was. I actually remember the meeting in 1983 of the group in Cambridge when Csikszentmihaly presented his systems framework for the first time. I knew instantly that he had made a major contribution to the group's efforts. I remember thinking, "Why didn't I think of that?"

What is interesting to me as I reflect on the development of our thought community is that it was itself an evolving process. Although I was the head of the committee I was not the "leader" of the group in the way that Vygotsky became the leader of the Moscow group, nor the way Freud took control of the Vienna group, nor the way that Piaget built his large-scale "factory" in Geneva. All of these were top-down enterprises with a clear leader. For our group I was more of an organizer and convener than a leader in the way that most thought communities have a leader. Recall that it was Howard Gardner who simply told me I had to find a way to sustain the work we had begun with SSRC. I accepted the responsibility, but not because it was clear that I would be its intellectual leader.

And so as I reflect on Vera's remarkable effort to capture and describe a major shift in the field of creativity studies as involving the formation of a thought community, I see that she actually contributed to the effort to give it clarity and became a member of that very thought community itself. It seems clear that the thought community of which we are now both members is an unusual and interesting one, with a developmental history that is in some ways different from other known examples, yet without doubt is well captured in her account.

Our thought community on creativity studies is in some ways an example of the kind of contemporary collaboration and joint effort that Vera wrote about in her path-breaking millennial book on that topic (John-Steiner, 2000): less hierarchical than in past examples, often virtual, with lively disagreements between and among members, and with shifting roles and responsibilities as the group goes about its individual and shared activities. I was not aware that I was helping to construct a thought community when I began to work with the talented colleagues who would join the effort until Vera came along and showed me what I had been doing. I am grateful to Vera for her extraordinary insights and scholarly contributions to our emerging field and to my own understanding of its development.

DAVID HENRY FELDMAN, Ph.D., is Professor in the Eliot-Pearson Department of Child Development at Tufts University. His areas of interest encompass cognitive development, extreme giftedness and creativity, and developmental theory including the study of cultural knowledge domains as developmental entities, Piaget's genetic epistemology, and non-universal theory's continuum of developmental domains.

REFERENCES

Burman, J. (2011). Jean Piaget: Images of a life and his factory. *History of Psychology*.

Csikszemtmihalyi, M. (1988). Society, culture, and person: A systems view of creativity. In R. Sternberg (Ed.), *The nature of creativity* (pp. 325–339). New York: Cambridge University Press.

Feldman, D. H. (Ed.) (1992). *Developmental approaches to giftedness and creativity*. San Francisco: Jossey-Bass (a volume in the New Directions in Child Development series).

Feldman, D. H. (2000). Preface. In V. John-Steiner, *Thought communities: The dynamics of collaboration*. New York: Oxford University Press.

Feldman, D. H., Csikszentmihalyi, M., & Gardner, H. (1994). *Changing the world: A framework for the study of creativity*. Greenwich, CT: Greenwood/Praeger.

Gruber, H., & Davis, S. (1988). Inching our way up Mount Olympus: The evolving-systems approach to creative thinking. In R. Sternberg (Ed.), *The nature of creativity* (pp. 243–270). New York: Cambridge University Press.

John-Steiner, V. (1992). Creative lives, creative tensions. *Creativity Research Journal*, 5(1), 99–108.

John-Steiner, V. (2000). *Creative collaboration*. New York: Oxford University Press.

LETTER TWENTY-FOUR

Dignified Interdependence

Patricia A. St. John

"One of my central claims is that *the construction of a new mode of thought relies on and thrives with collaboration.*"

Dear Vera,

While I have had many opportunities to express my gratitude to you for your faithful friendship, my admiration for your inspiring work, and my appreciation for your sustaining mentorship, I am delighted to write this letter to you. Far from that first seminar on Vygotsky when you were a visiting professor at Teachers College and I was a second-year doctoral student, I am reminded of our conversations at my kitchen table and our AERA lunches together, our collaboration for CHAT sessions and *Vygotsky and Creativity* (2010). As I reflect on these many connections, the main theme from your work that has influenced my own research is collaboration and complementarity.

Creative Collaboration (2000) played a central role in my dissertation as I explored the notion of the community of learners and how children, in particular, scaffold learning for each other and sustain *flow experience*. What wonderful complementarity for me in the Fall of 2001 as I took both of your courses: *Vygotsky Seminar* and *Creativity*.

Vygotsky's (1978) theoretical model suggests that meaning is socially constructed—that Sociocultural approaches to learning and development emphasize the interdependence of social and individual processes in the co-construction of knowledge (John-Steiner & Mahn, 1996). Reflecting on community through a Vygotskian lens, I sought to understand how young children find and make meaning for self and others while collectively making music.

Building community is at the heart of creative collaboration (John-Steiner, 2000): It is relationship that leads to the development of thoughts, ideas, and projects. A safe place, which enables growth in confidence and trust, is the genesis of creating a classroom community. I believe that finding a place to be, the child is free to discover competence through exploration and negotiation built on mutual trust. Participating in this kind of collaborative environment allows the community of learners to collectively experience the exhilaration of enabling each other to belong, to grow, and to learn. You have referred to this complementary experience as "dignified interdependence," where each of us realizes and contributes our subset of human possibilities (personal communication, December 2001).

In my own work in early childhood music education, I seek to honor and incorporate the contributions of all participants in the music learning community, to invite children as creative collaborators to shape the curriculum. As we observe children's interpretation of teacher-presented material, we are afforded a window into their perception and cognition. These observations show us what they know, tell us what they next need to know, and direct us where the curriculum must go to facilitate their learning.

Your own collaboration with sociocultural theorists (e.g., John-Steiner, Panofsky, & Smith, 1994) has added breadth and depth to the concept of the *zone of proximal development* to conceptualize learning. Consideration of the dynamic interplay of exchanges in the *zpd* has resulted in such terms as *distributed, interactive, contextual,* and the result of the *learners' participation in a community of practice*. These imply rich and divergent environments. Holzman (2010) has offered a dynamic interpretation of the *zpd* and the role of the community in creating that learning space. The community of learners scaffolds the emergent understanding of all the participants. The convergence of the many and varied socio-cultural contexts of each member of the learning community results in a complex counterpoint of experience. Through exploration and discovery, the classroom community draws upon this wealth of multi-layered resources. In what you have called *mutual appropriation*, children manipulate ideas as they offer and receive contributions, moving from imitation to mastery. Through their collaboration, in the give-and-take of collective gifts found in the environment, they creatively collaborate to construct meaning, to elaborate on it, and to transform it.

It has been hypothesized that children are in a constant state of flow; "they enjoy 'unfolding their being' as they learn to touch, throw, walk, talk, read, and grow up" (Csikszentmihalyi et al., 1993, p. 191). Csikszentmihalyi purports that, once children go to school, their efforts at "unfolding" are thwarted; their growth is forced into patterns "over which they have no control" (p. 191). Reflected in young children's spontaneous music making is their ability to create challenge for themselves through manipulation of the music material. Opportunities for meaningful challenge and the sense of control, communicated through perceived choice, have been linked to optimal experience and intrinsic motivation (Rathunde, 1988).

I was curious to understand how children maintain this *flow* state as the implications for an early childhood music setting seemed exhilarating. What would teaching and learning look like if both experiences were *flow* producing? Through our collaborative thinking in your *Vygotsky Seminar*, in particular those *peer exams*, and with the mentoring of my doctoral advisor, Lori Custodero, I imagined a model for teaching and learning that combined *flow* experience with Vygotsky's *zone of proximal development*. The complementarity of Custodero's (e.g., 1998, 2002, 2005) *flow* work with young children and Vygotskian theory led me to discover learning strategies which I believe children use to sustain *flow* and to scaffold learning for self and others (St. John, 2004, 2006).

The flow paradigm linked with Vygotsky's socio-cultural prototype provides a vibrant framework to consider young children's music making experiences in the rich social context of the community of learners. This dynamic interplay results in a thrilling learning space; it creates an intense texture of experience, celebrating the multiple layers of contributions from all participants.

Your questions, Vera, as the second reader for my dissertation, helped me to define what scaffolding looks like in a music setting and prompted me to consider how aural and visual musical cues facilitate learning. In discussing cognitive pluralism (1995), you suggest that, while language may be a critical tool for semiotic mediation, there are multiplicities of semiotic means available which are represented in various modalities and based on cultural practices. It appears that the music environment provides a wide variety of multi-sensory experiences that assist the learner in discovering music content and in developing musical skill.

Collaborative efforts are often observed with rapid exchanges occurring among the community of learners that scaffold the experience into an expanded event. You speak to the power of the community and the development of relationship that lead to creative collaboration: "…the construction of a new mode of thought relies on and thrives with collaboration" (2000, p. 7). The expanded and transforming effects of mediating signs in these interactions follows in this excerpt from one of my videotaped observations.

The music content had been focused around a weather theme. The children learned the "Dr. Foster" chant and sang a series of rain songs. After discussing how composers sometimes use music to create a story, depict a scene, or communicate an emotion, the children listened to a short excerpt of "Cloudburst" from the *Grand Canyon Suite* by Grofé. A brief exchange ensued about what was heard and a movement activity followed. The children were given scarves and were asked to "move as the music tells you." The recording was a gentle song about the wind. As a boy twirled his scarf in a circular fashion, another child suggested that a tornado was approaching; he began twirling the scarf vigorously as he turned in circles, forming the funnel shape of a cyclone. Returning to the singing circle, one child relayed to another, "Not all storms have tornados, you know." This activity led to the creation of a weather story in which props as well as instruments were employed.

Finally, the use of verbal and non-verbal exchanges, reflective of the salience of language in Vygotskian theory, particularly in effective scaffolding, has led me to consider the function of narrative in the music learning community. In particular, I have been interested in what Nelson (1983) calls *social scripts* and how these *event representations* provide an entry point for future realization of musical concepts. This *scripting* and *cross-scripting* can be heard during young children's free-play with instruments. At first glance, the *scripting* appears un-related to music learning. However, by using a culturally familiar *script*, the child explores the instrument's qualities in non-traditional ways, switching from cultural tool to music artifact. Through this self-initiated exploration, s/he finds musical concepts (St. John, 2010). In *Notebooks of the Mind* (1997), you write:

> In more complex construction of concepts, the individual is engaged in streamlining, accentuating, and categorizing impressions that are then crystallized into larger entities. These acts of knowing are both individual and social in nature because categorizing is rooted in and influenced by the cultural framework of experience. (p. 108)

Thank you, Vera. Your *Gift of Confidence* not only offers insight for my work, but provides inspiration for my life. Thank you for bringing Vygotsky alive for me through your scholarship, your mentoring, and your friendship. My life and my life's work are richly blessed because of our creative collaboration.

With much love and deep admiration,
Patricia

DR. PATRICIA ST. JOHN is Founder/Executive Director of Carondelet Music Center, and Adjunct Assistant Professor of Music at Teachers College, Columbia University. A music practitioner and performer, her research employs cultural-historical and activity theories to explore early childhood music making and the social dimensions of musical experience.

REFERENCES

Connery, C., John-Steiner, V., & Marjanovic-Shane, A. (Eds.). (2010). *Vygotsky and creativity: A cultural-historical approach to play, meaning making, and the arts*. New York: Peter Lang.

Csikszentmihalyi, M., Rathunde, K., & Whalen, S. (1993/1997). *Talented teenagers: The roots of success & failure*. New York: Cambridge University Press.

Custodero, L. A. (1998). Observing flow in young children's music learning. *General Music Today* 12(1), 21–27.

Custodero, L. A. (2002). Seeking challenge, finding skill: Flow experience and music education. *Arts Education Policy Review*, 103(3), 3–9.

Custodero, L. A. (2005). Observable indicators of flow experience: A developmental perspective on musical engagement in young children from infancy to school age', *Music Education Research*, 7(2), 185–209.

Holzman, L. (2010). Without creating ZPDs there is no creativity. In C. Connery, V. John-Steiner, & A. Marjanovic-Shane (Eds.), *Vygotsky and creativity: A cultural-historical approach to play, meaning making, and the arts* (pp. 27–29). New York: Peter Lang Publishing, pp. 27–39.

John-Steiner, V. (1995). Cognitive pluralism: A sociocultural approach. *Mind, Culture, and Activity*, 2(1), 2–11.

John-Steiner, V. (1997). *Notebooks of the mind*. New York: Oxford University Press.

John-Steiner, V. (2000). *Creative collaboration*. New York: Oxford University Press.

John-Steiner, V., & Mahn, H. (1996). Sociocultural approaches to learning and development: A Vygotskian framework. *Educational Psychologist* 31(4), 191–206.

John-Steiner, V., Panofsky, C. P., & Smith, L. W. (1994). *Sociocultural approaches to language and literacy: An interactionist perspective*. New York: Cambridge University Press.

Nelson, K. (1983). The derivation of concepts and categories from event representations. In E. Scholnick (Ed.), *New trends in conceptual representation: Challenges to Piaget's theory?* Hillsdale, NJ: Erlbaum.

Rathunde, K. (1988). Optimal experience in the family context. In M. Csikszentmihalyi & I. S. Csikszentmihalyi (Eds.), *Optimal experience: Psychological studies of flow in consciousness* (pp. 342–363). New York: Cambridge University Press.

St. John, P.A. (2004). 'A community of learners: An investigation of the relationship between flow experience and the role of scaffolding in a kindermusik classroom', unpublished doctoral dissertation, Teachers College/Columbia University, New York.

St. John, P. A. (2006). Finding and making meaning: Young children as musical collaborators. *Psychology of Music*, 34(2), 238–261.

St. John, P. A. (2010). Crossing scripts and swapping riffs: Preschoolers make musical meaning. In C. Connery, V. John-Steiner, & A. Marjanovic-Shane (Eds.), *Vygotsky and creativity: A cultural-historical approach to play, meaning making, and the arts* (pp. 63–81). New York: Peter Lang.

Vygotsky, L. (1978). *Mind in society: The development of higher psychological processes* (M. Cole, V. John-Steiner, S. Scribner, & E. Souberman, Eds.). Cambridge, MA: Harvard University Press.

LETTER TWENTY-FIVE

Cognitive Pluralism and Creative Collaboration

Kimberly Cotter-Lemus

"The main challenge is to capture creativity in the making...and to focus on the social transformation of emotional and cognitive experience." (John-Steiner, 2000, p. 84)

Dear Vera,

It is with honor and gratitude that I write this letter. As a "distant teacher" (Carolyn Panofsky was my teacher as you were hers), you have shaped my thinking and influenced my practice of teaching music in profound ways. Your scholarship in cognitive pluralism and collaborative creativity speaks to me on a professional and personal level; I hope that in sharing with you ways I've woven your work into my own teaching and life experience, you will understand how critically important your concepts are to education outside academia.

Your concept of cognitive pluralism opens a window to student learning whilst providing language to talk about educational inequities in schooling. Schools narrowly (and often exclusively) emphasize verbal and mathematical thinking, creating a twofold problem. First, in emphasizing only two languages of the mind, schools marginalize those students whose preferred mode of thinking is otherwise. I am reminded of a particularly musical student I once taught. She moved with her whole body whether playing an instrument or simply clapping a rhythm. The inflection of Lizzette's speech was slightly drawn-out and modulating in pitch; the rise and fall of pitches in a smooth, legato voice gave a melodic quality to her speech. My perception of Lizzette was that she embodied music–she seemed to feel music on an intuitive and visceral level, expressing it through her physical gestures and speech. As musical as she was, Lizzette was not held in high esteem by many of her classroom teachers—her grades were not the best and teachers complained she spent too much time socializing and not enough studying. As you have noted, "most public schools fail to encourage or extend their pupils' artistic growth. On the whole, teachers often prefer highly intelligent and studious pupils to those with creative abilities" (John-Steiner,

1997, p. 93). Lizzette's musical intelligence was neither appreciated nor encouraged by most of her teachers.

Second, emphasis on two modes of thinking also limits the thought processes of all students. "One of the important bases for the development of a preferred mode of thought is to be found in the prevalence of certain activities in childhood" (John-Steiner, 1997, p. 35). By not providing opportunities for children to think in a variety of modalities (e.g., music, dance, art), we severely limit how they think and approach problems in life. As an example, Kayla was a fifth-grader in the "gifted" program, an academically strong student across the curriculum. In music classes, she was much stronger in the music content standards that emphasize literacy skills rather than those of music performance. Kayla was highly regarded by classroom teachers and classmates for her academic accomplishments throughout the years. However, outside the realm of verbal expression, she was painfully ineffectual. Once, when presented with teaching a group of students a piece she had composed, Kayla was unable to explain what she wanted the others to do. In communicating her ideas, she relied solely on her verbal ability. In the arts, words are not always the most effective way to convey meaning—in fact, words sometimes get in the way. With no other way to express herself, Kayla grew increasingly frustrated and unsuccessful in her efforts to convey meaning to the other children. In this instance, she was severely limited in her thinking and in her approach to the problem presented. I think her exclusive reliance on verbal concepts led to a certain "rigidity of thought" (John-Steiner, 1997, p. 86).

In schooling, we compartmentalize ways of thinking based on the subject/content area of the curriculum. Even music is traditionally taught in isolation from the other arts. And yet, as you point out, it is erroneous to assume that, for instance, writers are limited to verbal thinking or that painters are limited to visual thinking. Additionally, you illustrate in *Notebooks of the Mind* and *Creative Collaboration* how composers work closely with artists from other fields such as choreographers in order to expand their own musical thinking. This validates my own teaching in which I combine language, sound, and movement to teach musical concepts. For instance, after reading a short picture book and discussing the illustrations, students may explore movements to interpret parts of the story. I may offer a variety of percussion instruments for students to create a "sound carpet" (underlying sounds or melodies used to enhance the text) to accompany the story. There are multiple "solutions," and students must critique their instrument choices. In this way, they develop aesthetic awareness as they learn to think in multi-modal ways. We also use poetry for exploring language, sound, and movement through elements of mood, tempo, rhythm, imagery, and tone color. It is an integrated learning experience incorporating and combining the various languages of the mind, not only enhancing the poetry but also creating a deeper, more embodied understanding of language.

Schooling has traditionally emphasized individualism; likewise, creativity has widely been thought of in terms of the individual. However, your scholarship introduced an important shift in creativity studies from an individual approach to a sociocultural one. As you have found, creativity comes about from ideas developed not just within the individual but also through collaboration with others—a dynamic interdependence of social and individual processes. However, there is very little creative collaboration fostered in schools—and, as you clearly state, "brainstorming and other similar group processes do not represent the characteristics of collaboration, which are long-term engagement, voluntary connection, trust, negotiation, and jointly chosen projects" (John-Steiner, 2000, p. 82). In the current educational climate of prescriptive curricula and high stakes testing, creativity has been squelched, eliminated from schooling (especially in urban districts like mine) for teachers and students. Classroom teachers used to be professionals who had opportunity to craft lessons based on student needs and interests, and could bring their own interests and imagination into the classroom as well. Now, teachers are treated as technicians with precise scripts to follow—any opportunity for imagination and creativity no longer exists. At the elementary level, students' days are carefully regimented with emphasis on time-management in an effort to improve test scores. Particularly in urban districts, the school experience has been severely limited; there is no time in the schedule for field trips, recess, or even bathroom breaks due to failed AYP (Adequate Yearly Progress) growth targets. As has been predicted, "the children of the poor will receive even more limited instruction, curriculum and school experiences because their schools will be the first to be reported in need of improvement" (Meier & Wood, 2004, p. xii) under the federal No Child Left Behind (NCLB) legislation.

Fortunately this madness has not yet been imposed on me due to supportive building administrators, so I am able to provide opportunities for students to engage in creative collaboration with each other. I have witnessed the transformation of which you speak in students engaged in arts projects, for creativity transforms materials and the creator (John-Steiner, 2000, p. 78). Of course, such transformation does not happen in thirty-minute music lessons that meet once per week. Rather it is during the in-depth, intense hours spent in community working together to create an original opera, compose music for their poetry, or write a play for the wayang kulit (Indonesian shadow puppets) and Javanese gamelan during ensemble times and after school. In forming these 'communitas' students "become more aware of themselves, they profit from the criticism of their peers, and they learn new ways to claim their experience" (John-Steiner, 1997, p. 208). I have also witnessed positive risk-taking behaviors resulting from these creative collaborations. Taking risks and overcoming fear is a recurring theme for students involved in my ensembles as shown in the following journal entries after a public performance at school: "I was really scared but

I managed it and stayed strong." "I never thought I would make it. I was scared but I felt great." "I was scared at first but once I noticed the group with me I was fine." I think this is evidence of strong interdependence and "risk sharing" in which risk is spread between partners, thereby supporting and encouraging each partner to take more risks (John-Steiner, 2000, p. 79).

I am also fortunate to have found a colleague with whom I have successfully collaborated on creative endeavors with students. As with the partnerships you describe in *Creative Collaboration*, we are two individuals with complementary skills who interact to create shared understanding that neither of us could know on our own (Moran & John-Steiner, 2003, p. 82). Equally important is the emotional nourishment our collaboration provides which sustains us through the current dark times of education.

As you can see, your scholarship has been more than an interesting theoretical framework for me. Through "capturing creativity in the making," I hope to advance your ideas and concepts beyond the walls of higher education and into classrooms where they are most needed.

Kimberly Cotter-Lemus

KIMBERLY COTTER-LEMUS is a teacher-researcher currently teaching music and performance at an urban elementary school in Providence, RI. An avid blogger about the arts and urban education, her specialty lies in organizing multicultural arts ensembles in which students are given responsibility for creating and producing their own original works.

REFERENCES

John-Steiner, V. (1997). *Notebooks of the mind: Explorations of thinking*. Oxford, UK: Oxford University Press.

John-Steiner, V. (2000). *Creative collaboration*. Oxford, UK: Oxford University Press.

Meier, D., & Wood, G. (Eds.). (2004). *Many children left behind: How the No Child Left Behind Act is damaging our children and our schools*. Boston: Beacon Press.

Moran, S., & John-Steiner, V. (2003). Creativity in the making: Vygotsky's contemporary contribution of the dialectic of development and creativity. In M. Marschark (Ed.), *Creativity and development* (pp. 61–90). Oxford, UK: Oxford University Press.

LETTER TWENTY-SIX

Reverberations

Shirley Brice-Heath

"Generative ideas emerge from joint thinking, from significant conversations, and from sustained, shared struggles to achieve new insights by partners in thought." (John-Steiner, 2000, p. 3)

Dear Vera,

In recent years, I've returned often to your writings, reading them alongside the ideas of some of my new-found intellectual companions from the worlds of science, art, and the cognitive neurosciences. I smile frequently in my zig-zag reading and thinking, for I cannot help wondering what you would have thought back in the 1980s had you been able to see how key themes of your thinking would play out and who the primary actors would be in future years. This letter conveys some of my thinking on that question and also my abiding appreciation for all that you have inspired me to look for in every learning environment I have sought to understand over the years. I write the body of this letter as my side of an imagined response to a graduate student who might ask: "So where has the idea of creative collaboration come from, and how far is it likely to take us in understanding human learning?"

To me, it is no surprise that Vera John-Steiner (hereafter J-S) wrote the seminal work on collaborative creativity. Always a collaborative spirit and generator of innovative ideas, she has led several generations of scholars to question graduate-school cautions surrounding the need to "protect" one's ideas until publication legitimates them and acknowledges the author as individual. Never inclined to push or preach her convictions about the mutual benefits of working and thinking together, J-S instead modeled, narrated telling instances, and offered provocative questions to those in need of being reminded that "going it alone" is a myth about how the life of the mind really works.

In my career of studying young people learning in environments they select for themselves in their play, work, and friendships, the ideas of J-S have taken me to a micro-view of human interactions around symbol systems ranging from language to musical notation to the codes within graffiti arts. Head nods, eye gazes, overlaps and interruptions in conversation, and simultaneous talking and sketching stand out as some of the most obvious ways in which individuals communicate and create as they talk about ideas not immediately present in objects, models, actions, or representations. In these instances, the joint work of imagining what is not seen relies on mutual tuning of attention to mental sketching and collectively imagining.

Grassroots community organizations in which young people work through art and science to create products and services for which clients pay and in which young people find expression offer ideal settings for studying how collaborative creativity happens. Stimuli may be external (a client needs prototypes of a new product design) or internal (a single individual has an idea to put before the group). In either case, what follows incorporates what I view as the foundational elements of collaborative creativity among young people: complementarity of talents and channels of access to information, shared motivation to achieve, recognition of the need for productive failures, and mutual acceptance of both vertical and horizontal guidance. Generally unacknowledged until years later is the "sticky wisdom" that remains long after the often painful repeated processes of working together to bring about a product or process that wins praise from curators and critics (Allan, Kingdon, Murrin & Rudkin, 2002).

In 2011, twenty years after a group of middle-school boys and their art teacher started a blended value (for-profit/non-profit) community organization in Boston, MA, three of the original young men remained as executives within the highly successful enterprise, Artists for Humanity (hereafter AFH, www.afhboston.com). The organization's mission had remained as it began: "to bridge economic, racial, and social divisions by providing under-served youth with the keys to self-sufficiency through paid employment in the arts."

From the beginning years of the organization, young men and women (ages 14–18) have come to AFH in their after-school hours and worked systematically through several studios, learning the basics of arts forms, such as painting, photography, sculpture, and graphic design. They work collaboratively on commissions made to the organization as a whole, and they also work in different studios on their individual pieces, the profits of which are divided evenly between the organization and the individual artist. All members of the organization take part in deliberations around issues related to operational procedures, fund-raising, curation, and expansion and development of facilities and programming. Alumni of AFH overwhelmingly undertake both further education and small-business development within their first decade after leaving the organization. Periodic reviews of reflections on AFH by its alumni reveal three lingering sets of habits from time spent there during their adolescence. First among these reflections have been affirmations of the vital need to communicate "what's on my mind to others with a sense of what my thoughts might mean for the group's benefit and not just my own." Just behind this remembered value has been the need to "work in a group to make new stuff happen that will turn around people's thinking." Finally, alumni inevitably remember "how hard it was to learn that art never stands alone." They recall their annoyance during those times at AFH when they had to reckon with the fact that painting a picture for a specific outdoor site meant knowing the weather conditions the paint could withstand.

Others noted further irritations over logistics: hanging a picture in a public space meant dealing with health and safety regulations, building codes, and the need to protect the work from damage by viewers. Many alumni admit that they came to AFH "because I just wanted to do my own thing [e.g., graffiti art, photography, website development, social media]." Years later, they report that what they learned during their years at AFH was not just that they had to listen to and learn with others, but that they also had to take responsibility for the quality of work and services provided by the organization. Alumni working in or managing successful small businesses today see the necessity of this idea in their workplace. Alumni laugh and shake their heads as they remember how hard it was as a teenager to see the importance of learning that any art form will always be interdependent with much more than the individual's talent or the product or performance created (Heath, 2012; Heath & Smyth, 1999).

In her writings, lectures, and conversations, J-S has prepared us to hear what these alumni think about their experiences with creative collaboration. J-S has reminded us often that any creative work, most especially that done in science and art, will always be more integrative and far-reaching than initial innovators can envision. The relational nature of both science and art lies not only in the human dimensions of creative interactions but also within the "connexity" of the phenomena and processes involved (Mulgan, 1997). The Western world's celebration of individualism and separate disciplines since the Renaissance has led to the mistaken idea that the end point of identity is autarkeia, independence from external factors as the optimal goal of each subject. Human history points decidedly toward oppositional narratives.

No individual can live, think, know, or create except in interdependence with others. We understand this to be the case for us as socio-cognitive beings, because we hear at every turn the public media report scientific studies that reveal how the brain's interlocking computational neural systems enable simultaneities of processing. The senses we experience are not discrete or independent, for they continuously work in collaboration with each other: vision links to language, smell to long-term memory of spaces and sounds, touch calls up emotion and image. Almost daily, researchers in the neurosciences discover ways in which divergent populations of neurons collaborate to generate reciprocities.

Vera made us see the integration of patterning in relations—among humans, in works of art, and behind science experiments and ventures of discovery. She must certainly have done so knowing that others would someday find this kind of integration in new kinds of evidence from developing fields and disciplines. And indeed that is the case. Today ideas from both *Notebooks of the Mind* and *Creative Collaboration*, my favorites of her books, echo for me as I read new studies from sub-disciplines named only in the 21st century: cognitive neuroscience, neuroaesthetics, and neuromarketing (Stafford, 2007).

The irony that makes me smile whenever I return to Vera's works is this: Identifying as a psychologist, she came from a field that centered on the individual as learner. The era in which she received her training was full of "individual" pioneers, inventors, artists, corporate leaders, adventurers, and statesmen (with few women acclaimed as individuals in any of these areas of achievement). Yet she looked around her and pushed back against what others all around her proclaimed as individual genius. She drew quietly and persistently from the worlds of art to show us how artistic performance and production, in particular, rely on a combination of symbol systems, conversations, and connections of ideas, imagination, and critique.

The challenge in going forward is to take inspiration from Vera John-Steiner's pioneering spirit, encompassing energy, and counsel to seek a "durable 'we'-ness, built on a shared vision, patience and time, careful planning, and a chance to be playful as well as critical with each other" (2000, p. 9).

Thank you Vera,
Shirley

DR. SHIRLEY BRICE-HEATH is Professor Emerita at Stanford University. A prolific teacher, writer, and researcher in language, literacy, and sociocultural studies, her key research interests include later language development and adolescents in the contemporary world, along with the collaborative efforts of studios and laboratories.

REFERENCES

Allan, D., Kingdon, M., Murrin, K., & Rudkin, D. (2002). *Sticky wisdom: How to start a creative revolution at work*. Oxford, UK: Oxford University Press.

Heath, S. B. (2012). *Words at work and play: Three decades in family and community life*. Cambridge: Cambridge University Press.

Heath, S. B., & Smyth, L. (1999). *Artshow: Youth and community development*. Washington, DC: Partners for Livable Communities.

John-Steiner, V. (1985). *Notebooks of the mind: Explorations of thinking*. New York: Harper and Row.

John-Steiner, V. (2000). *Creative collaboration*. New York: Oxford University Press.

Mulgan, G. (1997). *Connecity: How to live in a connected world*. Boston: Harvard Business School Press.

Stafford, B. M. (2007). *Echo objects: The cognitive work of images*. Chicago: University of Chicago Press.

LETTER TWENTY-SEVEN

The Influence of Vera John-Steiner's Work on Sabra Sowell-Lovejoy
Artist and Educator

Sabra Sowell-Lovejoy

"Through the development of creativity, a person comes to be a flexible, intentional inventor of his or her personal future and a potential contributor to his or her cultural endowment" (Moran & John-Steiner, 2003, p. 5).

Dear Vera John-Steiner,

As a graduate student at the University of New Mexico studying art I struggled with my own creativity and its place within a rapidly changing field. The art of the past was no longer acceptable. Art had to change to meet the ambiguous, fluctuating, globalized, twenty-first century. I wanted my artwork to communicate that sense of change and transformation while engaging in both new and old artistic techniques. The desire for my work to show that "Human beings are flooded with information; the challenge to notice, to remember, to construct coherence out of this complexity is awesome" (John-Steiner, 1995), was strong, but not well conceptualized. My work was not effective. One day while looking for an answer to solve the problem, I wandered into the bookstore on campus. I thought that anything that was related to art, but not strictly about art, art history or art theory might possibly help. That is when I discovered *Notebooks of the Mind*. That book changed my life. Not only did it offer directions for my artwork, but it also influenced my teaching style. After reading the book, I could not wait to take a class with Vera John-Steiner. The following semester I took the class on creativity. I remember one specific class discussion; we were asked to recall a phone number without writing it down. The diverse manner in which my fellow classmates recalled the phone number was so varied that the notions presented in *Notebooks of the Mind* immediately became solidified. I had always known that I was a visual and kinesthetic thinker, but to hear my fellow classmates explain their modes of thinking was interesting. I immediately began to fill my sketchbook with new possibilities of art making. I theorized that if I could make art that specifically communicated through various processing modalities then I could expand my own intellectual understandings of society, language and thought. Throughout the course of the semester, I learned how various people think, construct knowledge and how they creatively process that information into cultural artifacts. Not only did I learn about famous individuals, but also about my fellow classmates. The pedagogical structure of the class provided a collaborative experience, perception and support for myself, a young artist who fit the description: "young artists are frequently beset with anxiety. They are confronted by self-doubt.

In addition to encouragement derived from studying the lives of their artistic models, these individuals also need support from those around them, from their parents, teachers and friends" (John-Steiner, 1997, p. 61). Your class, knowledge, books and insights provided that support. The peer exams and the case study assignments required for class were eye-opening. I realized that the problems I experienced with my studio work were a result of failed communication. I knew the domain of art. What I didn't know was that others did not think nor communicate like myself; therefore, the work was inaccessible. I was not creating powerful art as it was so eloquently described in *Notebooks of the Mind*: "the power of a work of art is that it draws the audience into the artist's own interpretation of these physical forces thus producing a 'mass dream'" (John-Steiner, 1997, p. 62). Listening to the final case studies presented in class, I noticed that the other students chose an artist whom they could identify with in some manner. They had a personal attraction to the art or the artist. That was a very different approach than I had taken. I knew that I had to determine whether or not I wanted to communicate to the general public or to the art-world. The latter would more likely lead to possible advancements within the domain and up to that point in my development it had been my audience. However, with the art-world in such Postcolonial unrest, I determined the best approach was to communicate to both, by recognizing the social, historical constructs of the visual, verbal and emotional languages.

The introduction to Lev Vygotsky's theories in both the book as well as the class led to a methodological approach to my queries about thinking and communication patterns within society. I needed a framework for my art practices that would allow the observation of the viewer's interpretations. The work had to function in a continuous cycle of idea, language and the production of art that recognized the various constructs of thought. On the wall of my studio I wrote, "The relation of thought to word is not a thing but a process, a continual movement backward and forth from thought to word and from word to thought. In that process, the relation of thought to word undergoes changes that themselves may be regarded as developmental in the functional sense. Thought is not merely expressed in words; it comes into existence through them. Every thought tends to connect something with something else to establish a relation between things. Every thought moves, grows and develops, fulfills a function, solves a problem" (Vygotsky, 1962, p. 125; 1986, p. 218). My subsequent artwork followed the above-mentioned cycle. Decisions were made in correlation to process, observational-feedback and reflection in continuous relational progression until the problem was solved. I took Vygotsky's theories on social language and applied them to visual symbol systems. I found that visual imagery was more flexible and more cohesive to my expertise than the verbal language: "The power of visual thinking is that it illuminates and makes manifest this ability to conceptualize our experiences as structures in motion, as relationships" (John-Steiner, 1997, p. 106). Because of this, artwork could be flexible and fluid to a point that its purpose became one of dialogue and inquiry, not one of absolutes.

"While language is a socially constructed and conventionalized mode of expression, no corresponding single visual language exists"(John-Steiner, 1997, p. 86). In order to grasp that notion I experimented and explored the visual artifacts of various cultures, in hopes that I would eventually be able to spontaneously express my ideas to a global audience.

For the last sixteen years I have taught art in several different colleges in New Mexico. That has given me the opportunity to study the thinking/communicating processes of rural Anglo, Native American and Spanish cultures. I've noticed that the Native American and Spanish students were more visually oriented, while the Anglo students were more verbal. All groups have had a localized, culturally specific view of the world. Those facts were intriguing to the art side of me while difficult for the educator. As a teacher at a time when "societies have become more global and people must learn to interact with a diversity of others" (Moran & John-Steiner, 2003, p. 3), I've not been able to instruct in the same manner that I was trained.

Once again I looked to you, Vera John-Steiner, for assistance. I was pleased to find that your observations of Native American children in the Southwest were in keeping with my findings (John-Steiner, 1997, p. xix). As an instructional framework, I choose to use the quote:

> A person comes to know about the world not through absorbing but through transforming the information received from other's speech and actions; s/he must reconstruct knowledge based on these experiences. Through the transformation of this social interaction and use of cultural tools and signs, a person can free himself or herself from the constraints of the present environment and take control of his or her own future." (Moran & John-Steiner, 2003, p. 4)

To implement that, students were exposed to socio-historical creative art processes through a series of group and individual projects that engaged visual and verbal thinking modalities. Influenced by the collaborative group structure of the creativity class, I encouraged a communicative, creative dialogue between the students so that they could navigate their own output with the idea that that you share further in the same article.

Creativity actualizes the inherent, latent possibilities of people and environments; it not only broadens what we singly and collectively have done, but also what we can and may do. It allows people to step out of the present moment, reflect on the past and plan future behavior; it connects us to what could be. Through the development of creativity, a person comes to be a flexible, intentional inventor of his or her personal future and a potential contributor to his or her cultural endowment. (Moran & John-Steiner, 2003, p. 5)

Vera John-Steiner, thank you for your insights. As you can see your work has greatly influenced both my art and my educational endeavors. I look forward to your next contribution.

Sabra Sowell-Lovejoy

SABRA SOWELL-LOVEJOY, M.F.A., is a nationally known, professional artist with an interest in the ecological implications of sociohistorical interactions who has exhibited nationally. Chair of the Art Department at the University of New Mexico's Taos branch, her work weds the disciplines of art, science, linguistics and land management into land work, sculpture, video, installation, painting and performance.

REFERENCES

John-Steiner, V. (1995), *Cognitive Pluralism, Mind, Culture, and Activity*, Vol. 2, No. 1). Albuquerque: University of New Mexico.

John-Steiner, V. (1997). *Notebooks of the mind.* New York: Oxford University Press.

John-Steiner, V. (2000). *Creative collaboration.* New York: Oxford University Press.

Moran, S., & John-Steiner, V. (2003). Creativity in the making: Vygotsky's contribution to the dialectic of creativity and development. In K. Sawyer et al., *Creativity and development.* New York: Oxford University Press. http://www.lchc.ucsd.edu/mca/Paper/CreativityintheMaking.pdf

Vygotsky, L. S. (1962). *Thought and language.* G. Vakar (Ed.). Translated by E. Hanfmann. Cambridge, MA: MIT Press.

Vygotsky, L. S. (1978). *Mind in society.* M. Cole, V. John-Steiner, S. Scribner, & E. Souberman (Eds.). Cambridge, MA: Harvard University Press.

LETTER TWENTY-EIGHT

Bridges Are Made for Movement
Robert Lake

"Language is communication; as such it serves as a bridge between individuals who wish to overcome divisions born of the diversity of human experience. It is also a bridge between inner thought and shared understanding: the past and the present, the world of the senses and the realm of thought." (John-Steiner, 1985, p. 111)

Dear Vera,

I am writing you this letter while traveling on the Amtrak train from Georgia to North Carolina. I will visit my mother and some friends and return tomorrow to get ready for class on Monday. I am one of those people who find creative release while literally moving. Some of my best ideas come to me while driving or riding a bike or mowing the lawn and today I am able to write while in motion. Your work and scholarship are very much concerned with *movement* and *motion* in a wide range of applications. In fact, you mention these two words a total of 32 times in *Notebooks of the Mind* as a means of releasing the dynamic and creative processes that exist in the fusion of self speech, inner speech and outward expression in communication, as you so wonderfully state in the above citation.

I have been traveling for less than two hours and have already crossed quite a few rivers, tidal streams and ravines on bridges of various designs and heights and ages. They all have one aspect in common and that is a set of rails that allows this train to make progress. The bridge metaphor is used several times in this volume in describing your life and scholarship, but like your life's work confirms, bridges are only as valuable as the movement that takes place on them in bringing about connections. A bridge that is not traversed while connecting at least two specific points eventually gives way to the forces of entropy. But bridges that are traveled on become the means of reaching and embodying all that your scholarship embodies as well as that of your "distant mentor" Vygotsky. In this letter, I want to highlight some of ways that you have helped me across some ravines and rivers of my own.

I first met you in 2006 when I was working on my dissertation. The annual AERA meeting was in San Francisco that year. I wrote to you and asked you if you would be willing and available to join me for breakfast. For me, this was a long shot, so you can imagine my surprise when you agreed to meet with me. We met in the restaurant inside the Warwick Hotel.

You enjoyed herbal tea and toast while I had coffee and oatmeal. I was amazed at your focused gift of empathic listening in the crowded and bustling atmosphere during the peak of the breakfast period in a hotel filled with educational researchers.

You helped me cross the wide expanse of my dissertation topic which was titled "A Curriculum of Imagination beyond Walls of Standardization." I was in need of a way to connect the inner processes of incubated thinking and meditation with curriculum and pedagogy. Your notion of "cognitive pluralism" (1995) and the entire text of *Notebooks of the Mind* was the bridge I needed to help me move forward (and backwards) without being waylaid in Gardner's (1985) biologically based *Frames of Mind*.

Reading your work instilled me with a greater sense of personal agency by providing me with a language that allowed me to make sense of my own experiences. in Allow me to share an example from my own life history that is affirmed by what you so clearly write in *Notebooks of the Mind*. In this work I am able to map my journey across the bridge of music as a language of the emotions to a verdant, safe and creative setting in the land of verbal thinking and expression far beyond my "biological" homeland (John-Steiner, 1985, pp. 111–158). The following is a slightly revised excerpt from a book I recently finished called *Vygotsky on Education Primer*.

> I grew up in a working class home of very humble means in a large family that loved to sing and play the kind of music that could best be described as Americana and classic rock. Music certainly was a prominent facet of my zone of early experiences of proximal development. When I was around 9 years old, I remember bringing two spoons to a room in our basement where all of the empty canning jars were kept. I would tap each jar with a spoon to hear the tone each one created and add or remove water to tune each one and then line them up to play simple songs. The experience with the canning jars helped me to teach myself how to play the blues harmonica. There is so much about this genre of music that is intuitive. I remember reading a few sentences of "method" on the paper insert enclosed in my newly purchased instrument, but learning to play fits Vygotsky's idea of imitation, internalization and externalized expression. These formative experiences led me directly to the internal dimension of learning. I had already taught myself the basics of the guitar, so when I was asked to join a band and play the harmonica, I became a guitar intern as well. I learned quite a bit by observation, as well as direct instruction from the lead guitar player. Playing in a garage band was truly one of the most productive experiences of the value in the zone of proximal development that I could have ever imagined. Out of that experience, I came to understand more fully, Vygotsky's emphasis on the role of tool and sign in the release of higher levels of consciousness and agency in personal development. In

my case, "tool and sign" are in the form of music that is internalized as a symbol system and externalized in holistic expression that incorporates imagination, cognition and emotion.

At the same time that I was having such a struggle as a high school student outside of school, I began to flourish as a musician. One strongly defining moment took place in my second year of high school. I remember hearing a song by the Lovin' Spoonful (1965) featuring a harmonica solo by John Sebastian called *Night Owl Blues*. I was so drawn in by the emotional tone and skill expressed in that song that I said to myself, "I will learn to play just like that!" A few months later, I could play most of it! Not long after that, I was asked to play in a band. My level of self-confidence was altered considerably.

Fast forward through performing in several garage bands and later accompanying myself on the guitar, to the time I met my wife Elizabeth. She once confessed that she married me "because I was nice and played the guitar." On several occasions, we lived with her parents. Her father was a lawyer and her mother was an art teacher and their home was rich with academic language and books. By daily interaction in this zone of proximal development, I found myself thinking, speaking, reading and writing much more expansively in ways that brought positive changes in my view of myself as a person and life partner as well as a father and teacher (Lake, 2012, pp. 147–149).

Vera, your work helped me revisit, name and cross these bridges of musical and verbal thinking not only for myself, but for also my own students. Today, I continue to write and teach on expressing imagination through multiple dimensions of literacy.

Three years after our first meeting, your work drew me more deeply into a greater dialogue. Oakeshott once noted, "As civilized human beings, we are the inheritors, neither of an inquiry about ourselves and the world, nor of an accumulating body of information, but of a conversation" (1962, p. 490). I was interested in expanding "the conversation" that took place between you and Nan Elsasser (1977) as you collectively searched for convergence in the work of Lev Vygotsky and Paulo Freire on language and literacy. I remember contacting you to see if you would be willing to participate in a panel discussion on Freire and Vygotsky at AERA for the 2010 conference. You immediately agreed to do so and we were joined by LeAnn Putney, Susan Jean Mayer and Miguel Eduardo Cortes. In the unpublished paper for this event you wrote:

> These two theories place culture into the center of human learning and thus meet the needs of contemporary, increasingly complex multicultural societies. In this new context theories which are universalistic and ignore historical changes are limiting (i.e. Piaget). In addition, cultural historical theories emphasize the availability of new artifacts which transform cognition. The most significant concept that these two authors share is their view of the learner as active and engaged, rather than as recipients of what Freire famously called "banking education." While they lived in different historical times, these authors saw education as essential and liberating. They viewed true learning as the fulfillment of human potential rather than the transmission of knowledge and the training of skills. Both empha-

sized that by "breaking the silence" of the oppressed and impoverished learners embark on a trajectory of participation in their societies. These authors saw the full development and use of language and communication as part of empowerment. (John-Steiner, 2010, n.p.)

I had already deeply researched Freire's work for my dissertation and I have to admit that I did not yet know the real Vygotsky's work. Once again, your work provided and continues to be a much traveled bridge to a deeper, true reading of Vygotsky, especially regarding his work on thinking and speaking. Indeed, in your 2007 piece for the *Cambridge Companion to Vygotsky* you provide the clearest reading of Vygotsky's notions of "thinking and speaking" I have ever read! I use this chapter as a bridge to Vygotsky's work with my own students. (See my student Laura Richly's letter.)

As my train races across the tracks, I am gently rocked into a half sleep like a child in his mother's arms. Houses, buildings and trees flash past. I am reminded of the swift passage of time. Today the bridge of your life's work enables us to draw a new generation of students, colleagues, friends and family into Oakeshott's conversation that began "in the primeval forests and extended and made more articulate in the course of centuries. It is a conversation which goes on both in public and within each of ourselves" (1962, p. 490). This book is rich with the content of the extended conversation that has been expressed through those of us who cherish what your mentoring and scholarship have inspired us become. At the same time I am deeply aware that there is so much more to add to the conversation, so many more inward and outward expanses to traverse. I cannot thank you enough for connecting all of us into to a larger unfinished collective conversation and to this traveling musician, harmonica in pocket, to his own internal speech.

With immense gratitude,
Robert Lake

ROBERT LAKE is an Associate Professor in Social Foundations of Education at Georgia Southern University where he teaches courses in multicultural education and curriculum theory and design. His most recent book is *Vygotsky on Education Primer*.

REFERENCES

John-Steiner, V. (1985). *Notebooks of the mind*. Albuquerque: University of New Mexico Press.
John-Steiner, V. (2007). Vygotsky on thinking and speaking. In H. Daniels, M. Cole, J. V. Wertsch, (Eds.). *The Cambridge companion to Vygotsky*. New York: Cambridge University Press.
Oakeshott, M. (1962). The voice of poetry in the conversation of mankind. *Rationalism in politics and other essays* (197–247). London: Methuen.

LETTER TWENTY-NINE

Tapestry
Interwoven Minds, Emerging Meanings
Seana Moran

"Each individual realizes only a subset of the human potential that can be achieved at a particular historical period. In partnerships, starting from the youngest age, we broaden, refine, change, and rediscover our individual possibilities." (John-Steiner, 2000, p. 189)

Dear Vera,

You have been the warp for the weft of my intellectual journey as a scholar. From the entwining of your ideas and encouragement with the opportunities I have taken in the last 15 years, a tapestry—a "bigger picture" interlacing creativity, collaboration, motivation, meaning-making, and ethical contributions to the greater good—has emerged. I am so grateful for the caring, innovative example you have set. Like all weavings of minds, I could not have done it alone. From this tapestry, I draw out a few yarns, or stories, to show the beauty of your contributions.

In 1995, you launched my academic career. I was a "practicing creative" in advertising when I took your course on creativity at the University of New Mexico. At first, I thought it would enrich my job performance. Little did I realize that the thread of my intellectual life had found a new loom. You suggested I "pursue the life of the mind." Since that time, I have been a weaver of your scholarship and teaching methods in different venues.

Some of the benefits of your teaching I recognized during that first semester. I particularly loved your metaphor of the onion: learning, research, and creativity were like an onion because they were stories, and our job was "peeling away levels of meaning." I had taken psychology courses before yours. But the creativity class made focal that not only variables or knowledge were relevant, but also subjective experience and self-awareness of what one could and does contribute.

Other benefits of that first course I did not recognize until later. Your teaching methods were unlike any I'd encountered before. The emphasis you placed on interlacing personal experience with conceptual knowledge (both your own and students'), the focus on meanings not just findings, and the fluidity of conversations became standards against which I judged later courses I took or taught. While teaching a course on leadership to undergraduates in a liberal arts college, I employed your Peer Exam format. A Peer Exam is a dialogical context in which partners engage each other in topics each brings to the conversation such that both minds are enriched by the inquiry (Wix & John-Steiner, 2008). The Peer Exam provided a perfect "holding venue" for the students to stretch as leaders by practicing guiding a conversation without fully controlling it, incorporating multiple perspectives in real time, and maintaining momentum despite not knowing where the inquiry might lead. In anticipation of the Peer Exam, the students were quite nervous; afterward, they felt empowered by how moved they and their partner were—not only intellectually but motivationally as well!

You changed my mind about creativity. Prior to your influence, I had subscribed to the standard conception of creativity as a static, trait-based, norm-deviant, male-dominated competition of ideas. Afterward, creativity became a contribution to the flow of cultural development over historical time through the caring interaction among ideas and persons (Moran & John-Steiner, 2003). You transformed the view of creativity from a "lone genius" to a collaborative endeavor (John-Steiner, 2000). You interwove emotions and motivations into the previously cognition-dominated thinking about creativity (Moran & John-Steiner, 2004), and made timescales an important analytical aspect of creativity.

Your work emphasized how creativity is a search for meaning (John-Steiner, 1997). In Vygotskian terms, "meaning" is a socially agreed-upon understanding of a concept, whereas "sense" is a penumbra around meaning that encompasses the idiosyncratic connotations or understandings that each individual may also hold about the concept. This variation in sense is significant not only to creativity but also to both individual development, as we learn from each other's perspectives, and to societal functioning, as "more heads are better than one" in approaching issues. Creative work builds on the vibration caused by this sense-variation in relation to cultural meanings as filtered through the self-awareness of personal experience (Moran & John-Steiner, 2003).

Not only in your publications, but also in your personal demeanor and actions, your contributions embody and extend Vygotsky's ideas of interpersonal meaning and sense-making. Co-construction comes not from simply throwing people together. For example, a group of people in conformity is "groupthink" and potentially dangerous, despite how it may feel easier to those who conform. Instead, it is good to have multiple semiotic means, different personal and cultural lenses, or our experiences would be a blur because we could not parse them into meaningful units. Each of us appropriates—selects and makes our own—from what others have contributed to culture and society. In turn, we contribute in ways others can appropriate from us. Although different perspectives knit together—what you termed "cognitive pluralism" (John-Steiner, 1995)—is a necessary prerequisite, you took the concept further. Co-construction in "thought communities" requires a mindset to influence and be influenced by the other, to accept a process of emotional as well as cognitive engagement, and to commit to our interdependence as constructors of knowledge and possibility (John-Steiner, 2000).

Your work on productive thinking and collaboration was groundbreaking in its emphasis on dynamic systems (John-Steiner, Meehan, & Mahn, 1998). People and tools, which bring importantly different resources and perspectives to society, change each other through interactions with both other minds and with symbolic tools of a domain. These changes ripple across conversations, short-term interactions, lifetimes of creative pursuits, fields of creative practitioners, and historical timelines of domain-altering contributions. Through this process, both the creators and their worlds can be enriched and enlivened (John-Steiner, 1992).

Much of my current thinking about creativity stems from the chapters we wrote together. I often describe the progress and momentum of how individuals contribute to cultural development in terms of a tapestry. The individual threads—each a different color and texture—weave together to create a bigger picture of community understanding. When one thread connects to other threads, the thread's color and texture interact with those of other threads. Connected, they create something bigger than each thread individually. They build the greater good.

Thus, my recent work on the intersection of creativity and ethics also stems from your teachings and writings. You have talked about a "communitas" that unites individuals in a common pursuit, and how individuals hold—and perhaps share—continua of concerns. Individuals can develop "an intense awareness of their own inner lives" that also is sensitive to the outside world (John-Steiner, 1997). We can create moral meaning as we allow others' insights and meanings to "disrupt us" based on the tensions that different perspectives cause. I am encouraged to see other scholars furthering these lines of thinking (e.g., Wall, 2003).

Yet, you also have heightened awareness of the limits or obstacles we face in striving for a better world. You recently said to me, "The 20th century shows that we cannot rely solely on thought as a way to create a good society." New ideas may be useful (to at least someone), but not necessarily good. Your ideas on multiple timescales suggest that foresight about the longer term implications of our contributions are needed. Even more important, we need to keep cognizant about how we are connected in intricate ways. What each of us contributes matters immensely to the way the world will be. Both individualism and collectivism can go too far: individualism into solipsism and greed; collectivism into totalitarianism. We not only create artifacts and tools for each other to use, we create each other. As you said, "Humans come into being in relation to others." Perhaps our greatest creative achievements are the kinds of people we develop through interaction and role-modeling.

You have been the avant garde in the notion of collaboration, especially applied to creativity. You broached this "crazy idea" that countered the "lone genius myth" in the 1980s and 1990s. *Creative Collaborations* helped open the field (John-Steiner, 2000). Only now, in the late 2000s and early 2010s, has it become center stage in scholarly, business, and education publications. My most recent research position is part of an effort to launch a whole new university based on the foundations of creativity and collaboration. Slowly, the world is catching up with you! There is hope that, as scholars and as members of society, we are following your lead in "constructing 'we-ness' in a world where separateness of individuals is still highly prized" (John-Steiner, 1997, p. 204). After all, as you so eloquently stated, "Together we create our futures" (John-Steiner, 1997, p. 204).

Over the years, your continuing passion to create knowledge, such as your most recent book on the emotional lives of mathematicians (Hersh & John-Steiner, 2010), inspires me to keep going, despite discouragements and setbacks. As you quoted, in *Creative Collaborations*, Simone de Beauvoir's salute to her longtime collaborator, Sartre: "You did me a great service. You gave me a confidence in myself that I should not have had alone" (Beauvoir, 1984; see also Mahn & John-Steiner, 2002).

Thank you,
Seana.

SEANA MORAN, Ph.D., studies motivational and ethical dimensions of creativity, particularly the social and cultural impact of creators' contributions to others and to entities larger than themselves. She was the research director for the Stanford Youth Purpose Project and most recently a fellow at the Edmond J. Safra Center for Ethics at Harvard.

REFERENCES

Beauvoir, S. (1984). *Adieux: A farewell to Sartre* (p. 168). New York: Pantheon Books.
Hersh, R., & John-Steiner, V. (2010). *Loving and hating mathematics*. Princeton, NJ: Princeton University Press.
John-Steiner, V. (1992). Creative lives, creative tension. *Creativity Research Journal*, 5(1), 99–108.
John-Steiner, V. (1995). Cognitive pluralism: A sociocultural approach. *Mind, Culture, and Activity*, 2(1), 2–11.
John-Steiner, V. (1997). *Notebooks of the mind*, (2nd ed.) New York: Oxford University Press.

John-Steiner, V. (2000). *Creative collaborations.* New York: Oxford University Press.

John-Steiner, V., Meehan, T., & Mahn, H. (1998). A functional systems approach to concept development. *Mind, Culture, and Activity,* 5(2), 127–134.

Mahn, H., & John-Steiner, V. (2002). The gift of confidence: A Vygotskian view of emotions. In G. Wells & G. Claxton (Eds.), *Learning for life in the 21st century: Sociocultural perspectives on the future of education* (pp. 46–58). Malden, UK: Blackwell.

Moran, S., & John-Steiner, V. (2003). Creativity in the making: Vygotsky's contribution to the dialectic of creativity and development. In K. Sawyer et al., *Creativity and development* (pp. 61–90). New York: Oxford University Press.

Moran, S., & John-Steiner, V. (2004). How collaboration in creative work impacts identity and motivation. In D. Miell & K. Littleton (Eds.), *Collaborative creativity: Contemporary perspectives* (pp. 11–25). London: Free Association Books.

Wall, J. (2003). Phronesis, poetics, and moral creativity. *Ethical Theory and Moral Practice,* 6(3), 317–341.

Wix, L., & John-Steiner, V. (2008). Peer inquiry: Discovering what you know through dialogue. *Thinking Skills and Creativity,* 3, 217–225.

LETTER THIRTY
Vera John-Steiner on Creativity and Collaboration
A Scholar Ahead of Her Time

Nancy J. Uscher

"Creativity lies in the capacity to see more sharply and with greater insight that which one already knows or that which is buried at the margin of one's awareness." (John-Steiner, 1985, pp. 51–52)

"Creativity requires a *continuity of concern,* an intense awareness of one's active inner life combined with sensitivity to the external world." (John-Steiner, 2000, p. 220)

Dear Vera:

In the dozen years that we were faculty colleagues at the University of New Mexico (1992–2004) you greatly inspired me (and so many others) with the imaginative and thorough quality of your scholarship and teaching. As chairperson of the faculty committee (a subcommittee of the university's Research Policy Committee) that chooses the recipient of the Annual Research Lecturer award—the highest such faculty tribute at UNM—I had the privilege of reading the accolades provided by your distinguished colleagues in 1998, the year that you were chosen for this honor. Your thought-provoking lecture that year was entitled "Creativity and Collaboration: A Sociocultural Approach." After interviewing me for your book *Creative Collaboration*, you wrote about my own creative process and collaborations in this volume (pp. 162–63). Being included in such an important body of work was very meaningful to me. Over our years together at UNM, I observed with admiration your profound dedication to your students and the ways in which you mentored them as emerging scholars and encouraged their early professional opportunities and growth. More than anything else, I recall your passion and love of the work that you undertake. You carry a sense of excitement and deep satisfaction and exude a feeling of well-being through this wonderful search for knowledge.

Beyond UNM, of course, your work has been an inspiration to the scholarly community, creative thinkers and thought leaders throughout the globe. Your work has had profound impact. Like John Cage, whose hundredth birth anniversary was celebrated in 2012, and other influential and original thinkers, you are a scholar who thinks ahead of your time. I believe that your work will have increasing resonance with the passage of time. In your elegant writing, you delve into the rich and textured stories of creativity and collaboration and help us all think through how the mind works, and examine the genesis of how people grow into their passions. You distill the key elements of significance in those you study.

Powerful aspects of your work include the respect with which you write about artists and their creative minds, and the rich examples you share enhanced by your own meaningful reflections. Indeed, writing included in *Notebooks of the Mind* provides nurturing ideas to which one can return over and over again. I find that the stories about the creative lives of scientists and artists actually become catalysts for the reader's own creative thinking. Put another way, reading about what has fueled the creativity in seminal figures in world history can easily serve as a vehicle for being creative. The many and varied examples are motivating and somehow fertilize the mind and can produce a tremendous desire to make something original. "Creative individuals' openness to all their feelings and reactions distinguish them—according to psychologists who have studied them—from others less able to confront their emotion" (John-Steiner, 1985, pp. 67–68). In your writing, you reference not only the lives of creative individuals, but also concepts that are original and have considerable resonance for all disciplines. One of these is "distant teachers." The idea that one's mentors can be chosen at will by an individual—customized to the person's interests and aspirations—is a very hopeful and exciting way of viewing lifelong learning and can be a helpful step toward the quest of achieving "a distinctive voice, a creative identity" (John-Steiner, 1985, p. 37).

Another concept of note is the role of personal loss and illness in the lives of creative thinkers. Pointing out that a creative life is bound to include setbacks and struggles in addition to the joy of discovery underscores the rich complexity of being human and can be well used by young scholars in the contemporary era. A third concept is this: "The influences affecting the growth of creative thinkers are not arranged in a neat chronological order: It is the totality of their experiences that musicians, actors, painters, and scientists bring to bear on their work." (p. 57, *Notebooks of the Mind*) This is a very reassuring perspective, and encourages a long view of the artist's life. It reminds me of wisdom from the celebrated violinist Isaac Stern that I once heard imparted to a group of young musicians who were worried that one performance or one event could define them. Stern said something to the effect that "It is the whole life that one should look at—not just a small example of it." A fourth concept is that of structure and discipline as a critical "invisible tool" inherent to the creative process. I particularly liked your choice of the quote by Tchaikovsky: "A self-respecting artist must not fold his hands on the pretext that he is not in the mood." You go on to conclude that "one of the most neglected areas of the study of creativity is that of discipline, the structure that the individual who works outside of institutions imposes upon him or herself. Discipline has many functions among these creative individuals, For Tchaikovsky it contributes to his sense of self-esteem." Here you have hit upon a fundamental issue: confidence for many artists is very much linked to intense practice and preparation. Decades after you shared these ideas with your readers and scholarly community, opinion leaders such as Malcolm Gladwell in his work built upon this general theme with regard to the kinds of preparation one needs to earn the designation of "expert" in contributing to society from a specific disciplinary perspective.

Your discussion about patterns of collaborations among artists, complementarity in partnerships and supportive alliances that lead to shared vision and growth in *Creative Collaboration* are very germane to the lives of young artists in colleges like Cornish College of the Arts, where I currently serve as president. A major learning goal for students across the performing and visual arts disciplines in such arts schools is to learn to work with others in just the ways you describe in this wonderful book.

Both in your discussion of individual creators and of more universal concepts about the creative mind, you have shown your ability to be a global thought leader who is reaching for the future. Indeed, many of your theses have surfaced in the contemporary discourse about creativity. This large topic seems to be of increasing significance to society, perhaps because of the fear that the education offered today to many students in American society is missing this precious element: creativity, about which you write with such passion and authority. Your work has been central to the construction of knowledge regarding the essence of creativity and others have built upon it. I believe that as a scholar ahead of your time, your voice will continue to have powerful reverberation in the years ahead.

With affection and admiration,
Nancy J. Uscher

DR. NANCY USCHER is a concert violist and President of Cornish College of the Arts in Seattle. In addition to a distinguished career as an administrator at several arts-based institutions of higher education, she has served as a professor of music and women's studies.

REFERENCES

John-Steiner, V. (1985). *Notebooks of the mind: Explorations of thinking*. Albuquerque: University of New Mexico Press.

John-Steiner, V. (2000). *Creative collaborations*. New York: Oxford University Press.

LETTER THIRTY-ONE

And Perhaps Our Research Leads Us Back to a World We Lost

Eleni Bastéa

"Creativity lies in the capacity to see more sharply and with greater insight that which one already knows or that which is buried at the margin of one's awareness" (John-Steiner, 1997, pp. 51–52)

Dear Vera,

Recently, I watched the documentary *Race to Nowhere* (2009) about the excessive homework meted out to our young students (K–12) and its destructive emotional and physical effects. The film captured stories of struggle with pressure-cooker school systems. There were small victories, to be sure, of students and parents who just about survived in one piece. Yet nowhere did we see children immersed in learning, discovery, and experimentation for the pure joy of it. In fact, joy was present only when students *escaped* into their worlds of creativity, be it music or art, sports and family activities, seeking to counterbalance school pressure. But creativity's primary mission is not therapy. Creativity, as your work reminds us all, is a way of life.

"In the life of the adolescent," you note, "the need to reach somebody by words, written words, is important, as the young person frequently feels too tentative for self-expression in the presence of those he or she respects and loves" (John-Steiner, 1997, p. 50). Instead of anticipating these words that come from our young people, we are silencing them under the weight of repetitive and prescriptive homework. In fact, I see disturbing similarities between the way information is rammed down our students' throats and medical drugs are overprescribed. Just as we are robbing our bodies of their natural ability to heal, we are drowning our young minds in a deluge of information and requirements, suppressing their ability to make their own discoveries.

Today, most formal educational environments avoid engaging with deep inspiration and creativity, as if teachers are afraid to address the spirit of learning and making. I fear that if we, teachers and academics, forget to celebrate the love of learning and creating, then we are willing them into obscurity. Eventually, we might all forget that learning, like playing, is innate and self-generative. And that creativity needs to be continuously nurtured in order to thrive.

But it doesn't have to be this way. I am encouraged by the explosion of opportunities for learning and sharing knowledge that surround us now through various internet groups. Consider the powerful energy that brings together knitters and dressmakers, potters and craft artists, poets and fiction writers on the web. As a "guerrilla" creative person myself, doing sewing or pottery or creative writing in between my academic work—which I also consider a creative affair—I seek out these communities and draw daily inspiration from them. Participants in sewing forums ask each other questions, post photos of their work-in-progress, comment on patterns, share tips and praise, and continue looking for new challenges. Similarly, there are circles of potters who share short videos on process and techniques, insights and breakthroughs, advice on the art and the business of ceramics. Is that so different from the way a master builder used to train his crew? Our students might not be finding creative outlets in the academy right now, but they can seek them in the borderless world of the internet.

Last month, I signed up for two on-line sewing classes in part because of the young instructor's infectious enthusiasm for traditional couture techniques. What drives people with full and busy lives, people like myself, to enroll in virtual courses, when there is no "material" reward, like a grade or professional advancement? We join these communities for the love of learning, of a good challenge, or of fulfilling a secret desire. We wish to connect again with a relative or friend, here or gone, who once inspired us to sew or weld or write poetry. We strive to create a whole that is larger than the sum of parts, to be part of a community again, to contribute and receive, to learn and to pass down information. There is comfort in watching a master craftsman turning a wood bowl or a grandmother explaining the bramble stitch in a short video. Traditionally, we would have learned these crafts from our own families. And some we did. Now, we can learn them also from someone else's family, be it in Brazil or Michigan. This is an exciting explosion of community learning that cuts across all fields, from crafts to TED talks, from writing circles to MIT Open Course Ware. This energy about learning, teaching, and creativity that we share on the web right now is bound to transform formal education in the near future as well. I believe that we are already in the process of "constructing 'we-ness'" in our world (John-Steiner, 2000, p. 204).

I came to your work on creativity and collaboration over ten years ago, when I joined the University of New Mexico as an architectural historian, because of my own interest in memory and the creative process. Many creative people, you write, "echoed Albert Einstein's belief that people come to art and science to create 'a simplified and lucid image of the world,' hoping in this way to attain some peace and serenity amid the cruelties of daily life" (John-Steiner, 1997, p. xiv).

In architecture, we often work with similar concepts that explore the power of words and of imagined, remembered, and imaginary places. For example, I have asked my students to consider the following: "Cut out doors and windows in order to make a room. Adapt the nothing therein to the purpose in hand, and you will have the use of the room" (Lao-Tzu, 1963, p. 67).

We seek words for spaces never seen before. We study the "empty spaces" between words and images. We work with ambiguity, as that, too, triggers our imagination to complete the picture. We create spaces that have never existed before, yet somewhere deep inside us, they were always there. In a roundabout way, I realize that we, in architecture, come back to your own findings: "Creativity lies in the capacity to see more sharply and with greater insight that which one already knows or that which is buried at the margin of one's awareness" (John-Steiner, 1997, pp. 51–52).

For the last couple of years, with my colleagues Ted Jojola (Community and Regional Planning, UNM) and Lynn Paxson (Architecture, Iowa State University), we have been studying contemporary Native American architecture. We are focusing on new buildings constructed for Indigenous communities by Indigenous architects. Although most of the buildings look similar to many others across North America, what sets some of them apart is the fact that they grew out of a collaborative process between the community and the architects. In those cases, there is a strong sense of ownership and pride for the new buildings and a connection between makers and inhabitants. You write that *"humans come into being and mature in relations to others"* (emphasis in the original) (John-Steiner, 2000, p. 187). In our research we are finding that buildings, too, develop and mature best when they are conceived in relationship both to the people inhabiting them and to the larger physical world.

In closing, Vera, I would like to confess that I have also been reading your books as a biographer, searching for clues of your own childhood, your own experiences of the life of the mind. I would venture that some of your descriptions are partly autobiographical: "The intensity with which most creative individuals approach their work is frequently nourished by a highly supportive and stimulative environment in one's home, although at times, loneliness or conflict may contribute to the lure of the world of one's own making" (John-Steiner, 1997, p. 35). Is it possible to describe the dance with knowledge, the restless search for the life of the mind without first having experienced it personally? I see your work on creativity and collaboration in part as a tribute to your family and the culture that nurtured you, a world full of books, passion for learning, and for charting new paths in the company of other seekers. Even if parts of that culture have perished tragically, we are able to capture glimpses of it, vibrant and alive, as expressed through your own work. And that alone is a most worthy legacy.

Eleni

ELENI BASTÉA, Ph.D., is a teacher, writer, and historian of the history of architecture. The recipient of several honors including the Graham Foundation Grant and the Association of Collegiate Schools of Architecture New Faculty Teaching Award, she additionally serves as an editor, writer, and lecturer on creativity, the arts, and urbanism.

REFERENCES

Abeles, V., & Congdon, J. (2009). *Race to Nowhere*. [Documentary].

John-Steiner, V. (1997). *Notebooks of the mind: Explorations of thinking* (rev. ed.). New York: Oxford University Press.

John-Steiner, V. (2000). *Creative collaboration*. New York: Oxford University Press.

Zhu, L. (1963). *Tao te ching*. (D. C. Lau, Trans.). Baltimore: Penguin Books.

LETTER THIRTY-TWO

Creative Collaboration as Revolutionary and Transformative

Robin Oppenheimer

"Through collaboration we can transcend the constraints of biology, of time, of habit, and achieve a fuller self, beyond the limitations and the talents of the isolated individual." (John-Steiner, 2000, p. 188)

Dear Vera,

I don't remember how I first discovered your book, *Creative Collaboration*, in 2007. I probably googled the phrase and your name popped up. But as soon as I started reading your book, I realized you were different from the other collaboration researchers. You drew on multiple fields of knowledge to eloquently describe the oft-elusive, deeper complexities of collaboration from inside the process. You found a common ground of collaboration that connected the distinctly different worlds of the arts and sciences. And you brought a feminist perspective to your research that uniquely emphasized the emotional, intuitive aspects of collaboration. Since I was researching how Greenwich Village avant-garde artists Robert Rauschenberg, John Cage and many others collaborated with Bell Telephone Labs engineers in 1966 to create huge multi-media performances using new technologies, your work was both a revelation and a new path to follow.

Now it's 2011 and I've just received my PhD in interactive arts and technology from Simon Fraser University while teaching at the University of Washington's Bothell campus for three years. You served as External Examiner for my dissertation defense, and you are now a colleague, mentor, and dear friend. During these past four years, you and your work have been an inspiration and integral part of my new life in academia, where I recently transitioned from a long career working with experimental media artists and running media arts centers in Atlanta and then Seattle. Now I'm teaching the hidden histories, ideas and techniques of artists who have experimented with media technologies for the last hundred years and how the fruits of their creative collaborations can be applied to today's electronically networked Web 2.0 world of social media and games.

I can still remember the visceral rush of reading your words in great long gulps of astonishment and inspiration. Here was someone who could eloquently explain what I had thought to be artists' individual achievements as, instead, the complex social interactions of creative collaboration. You invoked ideas from outside the arts (Vygotsky's especially) about human cognitive development and learning, and wove them into compelling stories about how major artists like Pablo Picasso or Martha Graham collaborated and created art. You connected the historically separate worlds of art and science by uncovering their similar creative, experimental practices involving working with people with different "ways of knowing" that have changed our world. And you emphasized the nurturing, empathic qualities of women as essential aspects of successful collaborations that are seldom mentioned in other research. Your work transformed how I saw the worlds of art and science, and how I understood and explained creativity (artistic and scientific) and collaboration as I researched and wrote my dissertation.

When I had the good fortune to become a lecturer at UWB in Fall 2008, with the opportunity to develop and teach a new course focused on creative collaboration, I invited you to Seattle as a guest presenter, and you graciously accepted. I hadn't realized how rare my department's interdisciplinary culture was until your visit, and I'm grateful that you trusted me, someone you had only met by e-mail, to take care of you. Getting to know you and your amazing personal story, and having you validate and support my research was a crucial part of my graduate school experience. You embodied your concepts of intergenerational creative collaboration, giving me encouragement to keep working on my research and complete my dissertation.

I entered graduate school at age fifty-three to get a PhD after working in the fringe non-profit art world of experimental media for over twenty years. I wanted to teach current and future generations what artists have learned about the language and power of media through their experimentations with film and video technologies. When I started graduate school in 2005, I had already been researching a historical group of artists and engineers who founded an organization called Experiments in Art and Technology (E.A.T.) in 1966 right after creating a series of huge multi-media performances in New York called 9 *Evenings: Theatre and Engineering*. E.A.T. was a forward-thinking global networking organization created decades before personal computers, connecting artists with engineers in order to create technology-based artworks that emerged out of their collaborations. There were chapters of E.A.T. organized in cities around the world, including a group formed in Seattle and Portland. I knew some of the artists who were in that group and started talking to them about E.A.T. in 2000. I began meeting others and collecting their stories that included unlikely collaborations of Boeing engineers, painters, and early computer artists; psychedelic light shows staged by artists for the Seattle Opera; and multi-media art exhibitions by then-unknown artists Claus Oldenberg and Hans Haacke shown at UW's Henry Art Gallery in the late 1960s. This is where I began what would then become my PhD dissertation research.

What I didn't recognize at the beginning of this journey was the importance and centrality of the collaborative process to these histories. It took finding a graduate program at SFU in Vancouver, Canada, by way of presenting my early E.A.T. research at a 2005 Creativity and Cognition conference in London to lead me to yours and others' creative collaboration research. I've been intrigued by how and why artists have experimented with new communications technologies since discovering the world of the media arts in the early 1980s. The art world's focus was mostly on the technologies and the resulting artworks, not on the invisible process-based interplay of artists, technologies, and many others (often engineers and technical types) who invented and modified those technologies. From your book I realized that media artists have always collaborated with people with complementary skills and ideas both inside and outside the art world. And it is those collaborative processes, not just the technologies, that enable artists to create visionary works (experimental films, video art) that have influenced our current media environment.

Your writings also enabled me to see how the collaborative practices of artists and scientists help bridge the centuries-old dichotomy of the arts and sciences as two separate worlds. One of my key dissertation findings is how this dichotomy was intentionally transcended by the 9 *Evenings* artists and engineers through their collaborations. The artists learned to think differently about technology from the engineers, and the engineers learned from the artists how to push their traditional working methods, along with their inventions' limitations in playful, creative ways. Your elegant, insightful theories about creative collaboration as personally and collectively revolutionary and transformative enabled me to define my research as "collaboration aesthetics" and develop a framework of successful collaboration elements instead of focusing on the technologies and the resulting performances.

In addition to your important research, your long, distinguished career as a woman scholar and educator is a great inspiration to me. I hope I can maintain your high level of enthusiasm and passion for learning and mentoring younger scholars as I continue in my new career. I will carry forward the transformative spirit of creative collaboration you have gifted to me and many others for the rest of my life. It is now my students who will benefit from your life's work and the revolutionary ideas you have generated throughout your incredible lifetime of teaching, learning, and collaboration.

Thank you,
Robin Oppenheimer

DR. ROBIN OPPENHEIMER is an internationally recognized media arts historian, curator, and scholar. A former director of two media arts centers, she currently lectures at the University of Washington while contributing to the emerging literature on creative collaboration and digital culture studies.

REFERENCE

John-Steiner, V. (2000). *Creative collaboration.* New York: Oxford University Press.

LETTER THIRTY-THREE

Creativity in All of Us
A Dialogue with Vera John-Steiner
Anna Stetsenko

"The intense focus upon the work of an accomplished person or persons yields insights that are not easily acquired in the more traditional settings of learning.... The tools and skills used for solving daily problems may not be so different from the tools and skills used by individuals engaged in creative endeavors. (John-Steiner, 1985, p. 208)

Creativity is a topic of unwaning interest and everlasting importance to scholars of human development. It appears to tap into the qualities of infinite appeal and desirability—including novelty and singularity, uniqueness and generativity, discovery and innovation, all marking movement beyond "the given" in a search for new, uncommon and unconventional ways of being, acting and knowing. Perhaps in a fitting vindication of these core qualities of creativity, it is only fair that psychologists do not seem to be ever satisfied with what we know about creativity, continuing on a never-ending quest to rediscover and rethink it in novel and creative ways. Vera John-Steiner's works are among these important quests, representing the best example of a novel and imaginative—indeed creative—achievement of the human mind. In her approach, Vygotsky's insights are creatively put in the service of uncovering the workings of human imagination. The genetic and historical methodology, the emphasis on continuous interactions of persons with their world including collaboration with others, the richness of varied forms of thought, the enduring importance of cultural tools for thinking and doing and hence of apprenticeship in using them, and finally the ineluctable role of commitment and passion in creative endeavors—all of these ideas unite Vera's work with the direction charted by Vygotsky. Because of these parallels, the two scholars appear as immersed in a dialogue and collaboration, as partners in search for answers to common questions, who enrich and complement each other's quests and insights. Perhaps their kindred spirits have roots in strikingly similar childhood experiences. After all, what Vera describes her childhood to be, most likely applies to young Vygotsky too. As Vera writes, growing up in precarious years before World War II, when nothing was certain and adults were filled with fear for their future, the most valued human activity was developing and working with ideas, engaging in impassioned conversations about the great achievements and traditions of human knowledge. From what we know about Vygotsky, the same atmosphere most likely permeated his childhood in the world on the verge of World War I and the turmoil of events that followed.

This analogy is not mentioned just for the sake of drawing interesting parallels. The point that I want to make is actually theoretical and goes to what I see to be at the heart of the study of creativity. In comparing Vera's and Vygotsky's works, is there a danger of pushing the limits too far? Can we ever compare ourselves, the "mere mortals," or our colleagues and contemporaries, to the giants such as Vygotsky who is widely acknowledged to be a genius among truly outstanding pioneering figures in psychology? The answer to me is that such comparisons are absolutely legitimate, and fair especially in cases such as Vera's works that are amazing in their breadth and ingenuity. Moreover, such comparisons are quite useful and even necessary in a broader sense, as they highlight something about creativity that might otherwise be overlooked. Creativity, as I want to argue in dialogue with Vera's approach, is an ineluctable feature of all and every person in their even utmost mundane activities and pursuits of everyday life. That is, creativity and its attendant features of novelty and uniqueness, generativity and innovation are the defining qualities of how we all act and know the defining qualities of being human. No human action is possible without a degree of creativity and ingenuity even when solving everyday, mundane problems and common tasks of life because no task of life is ever completely common and no life is ever completely mundane.

What we are used to admire in creative giants like Einstein and Newton, Darwin and Vygotsky, whom we are taught to picture as standing apart from the rest of us, dwelling at unattainable Olympian heights or in the Pantheon for the chosen few, is actually something we all share as human beings. Descriptions provided by studies of creativity and prolific contributions, in this sense, rather than affording a glimpse into the unusual and the exceptional, might be actually supplying us with insights about the workings of the mind that all humans can be credited with, revealing with unusual clarity its important dimensions. It is as if the scholars of creativity, by looking deeply into the workings of exceptional persons, have de facto focused the lens of our more generic understandings and uncovered aspects that are mired, yet nonetheless necessarily present, in all forms of human acting and knowing—such as intuitive and imagistic side of any thought and the role of dialogue and self-reflection in all development—thus reflecting on perhaps no less than the true meaning of humanness.

Vygotsky's theory has actually prepared grounds for just such an understanding. His broad perspective can be interpreted as positing that human development has to do with active and purposeful, as well as always collaborative, activities and practices of transforming the world, rather than with mere adaptation to its status quo. This idea (often overlooked or only formally acknowledged) in fact signifies a radical departure away from traditional portrayals of human beings and their development. Whereas these portrayals dissociate cognition from feeling and imagination on the one hand, and from action and collaboration on the other, presenting humans as passive recipients of stimuli or computer-like processors of information, an alternative approach grounded in Vygotsky's theory, views humans as co-creators of their world. In this model (which I have discussed in detail elsewhere), human existence can be understood to be grounded in answerable and responsible (rather than responsive) deeds of individuals as agents in the social drama of life (rather than simply "undergoers" of solitary experiences), suggesting that individuals come into being while creating their world in a relational, synergistic process of reciprocal recognition and mutual becoming. This model is based in understanding that humans live within dense and constantly changing social webs and hierarchies of interactions and collaborations with other people, infused with tacit and not so tacit social contracts, rules, responsibilities, expectations, and obligations and fraught with complex meanings, conflicting interests and high degrees of uncertainty. This model highlights that people have to take stands and make decisions, on a daily basis, as to what is right or wrong and what to do next under the pressures of uncertainty, unpredictability and urgent demands to innovate, facing problems and dilemmas that had never existed before—all in the context where the only permanent "given" is that the world is in constant change that can and does spin off in unexpected directions all the time.

The gist of this radical shift is that it integrates agentive capacities for transformative change and activism as central, indeed formative constituents of human nature, into accounts of human development and models of personhood. Accordingly, it is not the originality and novelty of human conduct such as ingenuity in acting and thinking that require explanation—because these come "with the territory" of being human—but instead, abilities to rigidly stick to the rules and act as automatons and mechanical information processors. It is these latter abilities that unfortunately are often drilled into children thus circumventing their agency and activism and stalling their development as agents of history and society. Having now re-read Vera's works, I think it is important to explicitly include creativity among these formative constituents of human nature, asserting that it is human nature to be creative and innovative, rather than seeing these as exclusive properties of unique individuals.

Vera has given us plenty of insights that this is indeed the case, as reflected in the quote at the start of this piece. Moreover, by zooming in on this perspective, many of her observations on creative individuals can be applied to elucidate the most generic ways of how humans develop and learn. The role of continuous seeking for varied directions and meanings, sustained commitment to queries and creative life, immersion and exploration, continuity of concern, perseverance, independence and flexibility, nonconformity—all of these qualities that Vera has discovered in creative individuals point to key dimensions of what it is we need to nurture and help our children to develop, including in educational settings. It is quite telling that what matters about these qualities, in Vera's exposition, is how pronounced they are, the degree of their intensity, rather than merely whether they are present or not in people—thus supporting the view that they are always present to some degree in all of us. The realization of how rarely these qualities are indeed made the focus in education should be a concern and Vera's works open up ways to mitigate this concern and act on it, in creative and innovative ways. Putting emphasis on the notion that there is a creative genius in all of us might be the best way to fashion development and learning that indeed can set us on a path of true creativity, as equals with even the greatest giants whose shoulders we stand upon yet also walk hand in hand and participate in dialogues with, as partners in search for answers to common questions, just as Vera has done.

ANNA STETSENKO, Ph.D., is a Professor at the Graduate Center, City University of New York, with joint appointments in Developmental Psychology and Urban Education. An international researcher, Dr. Stetsenko's expertise revolves around the issues of self, agency, identity, gender, and social transformation, as they relate to development and learning in educational contexts and social institutions.

REFERENCE

John-Steiner, V. (1985). *Notebooks of the mind: Explorations of thinking.* Albuquerque: University of New Mexico Press.

LETTER THIRTY-FOUR

Collaboration Is at the Heart of the Human Condition

Andy Blunden

Dear Vera,

I write to encourage you to continue your study of collaboration, and hopefully encourage students to take up collaboration as an area of specialist research. You are really the only person who has made a genuinely deep study of collaboration, while in my opinion, collaboration is the archetypal human relationship and ought to be at the centre of *all* social and psychological research.

It is hardly possible to exaggerate the importance of collaboration as a concept which provides a lens through which the whole universe of human life can be viewed. Your typology of collaboration has been of great assistance to me. In your book *Creative Collaboration* (John-Steiner, 2000, 196–204) you suggest a 4-way typology of collaboration:

1. *Distributed collaboration*, which "takes place in casual settings and also in more organized contexts. These include conversations at conferences, in electronic discourse communities, and among artists who share a studio space. In these groups, participants exchange information and explore thoughts and opinions. Their roles are informal and voluntary."
2. *Complementarity collaboration*: which is "characterized by a division of labor based on complementary expertise, disciplinary knowledge, roles, and temperament. Participants negotiate their goals and strive for a common vision."
3. *Family collaboration*: "a mode of interaction in which roles are flexible or may change over time." The long period of time over which these collaborations extend often brings about transformative changes in the participants and their roles.
4. *Integrative collaboration*: which "require a prolonged period of committed activity. They thrive on dialogue, risk taking, and a shared vision. In some cases, the participants construct a common set of beliefs, or ideology, which sustains them in periods of opposition or insecurity. Integrative partnerships are moti-

vated by the desire to transform existing knowledge, thought styles, or artistic approaches into new visions."

In my view, collaboration is always mediated by a project, and indeed, the concept of collaboration is incoherent in any other way; collaboration which is not furthering some project is not collaboration at all. Conversely, I believe that projects are always essentially collaborative, whether knowingly or not. So as I see it, the *collaborative project* is the essential unit of human, social life (rather than the individual, social group, family, state or whatever). If this is true, then in the above typology of collaboration, you have given us the first anatomy of human life adequate to understanding the modern world.

Your work has focused on *creative* collaboration. In general, 'collaboration' is recognised as a distinct mode of activity in creative work, computing and software design and in collaboration between *institutions* in science and technology, research and services. Collaboration is adopted when projects are particularly challenging, requiring creativity, problem-solving and resources across a wider domain than any one person or institution can provide. But in my view, 'collaboration' is a *universal* mode of human activity.

This does not mean simply that 'everything is collaboration'. Such a view would reduce the concept of collaboration to a cipher. The point is that collaboration is *normative*: that is, engaging in collaboration with another subject entails agreement to certain norms of action in relation to the other parties which have normative force. Any breach in these norms has psychological consequences and threatens to undermine the project. The powerful emotions and personal transformations which you describe in your book are testament to this fact. Collaboration creates expectations which have to be fulfilled.

This idea is supported by Lev Vygotsky's psychology, which conceives of learning as arising from collaboration in a problem-solving task, in which the neophyte learns from the aficionado how to use a cultural artefact to solve some problem they are facing. In this way, the neophyte learns to include the artefact in their autonomous sphere of activity, and thereby appropriates a cultural means of solving problems. In Vygotsky's view then, collaboration is the very essence of becoming human. As one of the four co-authors of *Mind in Society*, the 1978 book which introduced the ideas of Lev Vygotsky to a mass audience in the West for the first time, you have also a long association with Vygotsky's work, so it is no surprise that your work on collaboration has a depth which other approaches do not have. For most modern social theory, collaboration is something organisations and individuals can choose to do if it suits their purposes. Few see that our very purposes themselves arise from collaboration, particularly the desire for recognition and inclusion.

It is only through working together that we can live. Even purchase and sale of products is a limiting case of collaboration: in order to live one person works to produce something which someone else needs, and by exchange of commodities, our ends are met. But this is a distorted and non-normative type of collaboration—one labours and the other decides whether or not to accept the product. Nonetheless, this limiting mode of collaboration is one which is normalised in this capitalist society in which we live. Another limiting kind of collaboration is command-and-obey, collaboration achieved by command. This also is a ubiquitous type of collaboration which remains the dominant mode of government and *modus operandi* inside capitalist and public service enterprises where top-down line management is applied. Here one thinks while the other acts, and any effort to learn from mistakes is often taken as a challenge to the hierarchical relationship of command.

What is lacking from both these distorted modes of collaboration is the *combination of cooperation and criticism*. It is the presence of mutual criticism *within* the process of design and production of a product or activity which makes collaboration such a powerful form of activity. What modern society has done is to separate out these two functions so that the essential collaborative nature of the overall project becomes invisible, and people suffer from the illusion of having free choice as a customer and the right to do as we please as a manager. In reality, both customer-service provider and master-servant relations turn out to be collaborative relations, but relations which have been distorted so as to lose the creative potential of the great collaborations which you have studied.

Overcoming these distortions of the collaborative relationships brought about by modern society, whilst retaining the great power which has been unleashed by the highly developed division of labour in modern society, is the challenge before us. As I said above, your study of collaboration offers an important milestone in understanding the human condition and how we can live humanly, that is, collaboratively.

From,
Andy Blunden

ANDY BLUNDEN, Ph.D., is editor of the flagship journal *Mind, Culture and Activity*. An expert in activity theory, he currently resides in Melbourne and is a member of the Independent Social Research Network.

REFERENCE

John-Steiner, V. (2000). *Creative collaboration*. New York: Oxford University Press.

LETTER THIRTY-FIVE

My Awakening

Patricia A. Richard-Amato

"Partners need to learn to listen carefully to each other, to hear their words echoed through those of the collaborator, and to hear the words of the other with a special attentiveness born of joint purpose" (John-Steiner, 2000, p. 190; also in Marjanovic-Shane, Connery, & John-Steiner, 2010, p. 225).

Dear Vera,

The only regret I have concerning my graduate studies at the University of New Mexico in the early 1980s is that I did not get to know you better. However, I am immensely grateful that I was able to sit in on some of your sessions. You were the first person to make me aware of Vygotskian theory. And what an awakening that was! It was not only Vygotsky's ideas that fascinated me, but the skillful way you expressed your own insights as they related to his work. I remember many years later telling our mutual friend, Cathrene Connery, that you spoke in cogent paragraphs, complete with parallel structures and transitions—almost as though you were writing a book in the air with your every word.

After being allowed to sit in on the first lecture (you had kindly given me your permission), I immediately got my hands on the book *Mind in Society*. This excited me and motivated me to read his earlier work *Thought and Language*. I was convinced at the time that Vygotsky's theories would have a huge impact on how we approach second language teaching and on education itself. Your research and the works you developed over the years were some of the more potent and important sources to which I later referred in my own writing.

When I first came to UNM, I had brought with me not only a strong desire to learn, but 19 years of experience in the public schools of Arizona and Colorado, where I worked extensively with second language students from Mexico and a variety of Asian cultures. Vygotskian theory allowed me to meld this experience with the knowledge to which I was exposed in my graduate program. You might say that his theory formed the hook I was seeking on which to hang what I had learned from my own experience. Out of this synthesis came the first edition of *Making It Happen* back in 1988.

When I had earlier begun to teach large groups of English as a Second Language students in an ESL center at Alameda High School in Lakewood, Colorado, I came to the realization that I would not be able to meet their needs without additional help, even though I was fortunate enough to have two adult assistants hired by the school district. Eventually I found a resource within the school itself: English-proficient peers who could act as peer facilitators. I soon learned that these peers (with a little guidance from me) were able to effectively negotiate meaning, give encouragement, work with the language learners to solve problems, and complete joint projects in which both the student and facilitator had an interest. In addition, they often served as social links to the rest of the students in the school and to the community surrounding it.

The peer facilitators had in effect helped to create Zones of Proximal Development, but only to the extent that mediation was involved in the academic discourse that took place. In fact, the students and the peer facilitators with whom each worked appeared to form *mutual zones of proximal development* (John-Steiner, 2000) as they became collaborative in a variety of subject areas. As you and your colleagues note in *Vygotsky and Creativity*,

> In this broader view of the ZPD, scholars have come to identify that the co-construction of new ideas include the sharing of risks, constructive criticism and the creation of a safety zone. Partners can live, however, temporarily, in each other's heads. (John-Steiner, Connery, & Marjanovic-Shane, 2010, p. 9)

You note too that Wells (1999) had earlier called similar dynamics within even larger groups and whole classrooms the "communal zone of proximal development," an idea he had originally credited to Hedegaard (1990). This extension of the ZPD concept made a lot of sense to me through my own experience earlier with cooperative group work as well as with whole class interaction and full participation, meaning that students were more likely to have a personal investment in what they were learning.

I would also like to tell you that ever since reading *Mind in Society*, I have counted myself among the many educators who greatly value the work you did with Cole, Scribner, and Souberman to bring this book to us. You were able to make more clear the cryptic style you had encountered in some of Vygotsky's papers. You had mentioned this problem in *Notebooks of the Mind* and had indicated that the problem may have been due to his deteriorating physical condition. Had it not been for your efforts and the earlier efforts of Hanfmann and Vakar, Vygotsky and his work may have indeed remained in the shadows of history.

Your afterword in *Mind and Society* with Ellen Souberman helped me sharpen my understanding of dialectical thinking and what it meant in more concrete terms. I was able to better comprehend its relationship to dichotomous thinking, which seemed to have permeated the literature at the time. Your emphasis on the term "interlacement" provided the clarity I needed to more fully realize what the dialectical process was all about and to discuss it with my graduate students. Seeing what may have originally appeared to be opposing ideas "interlace" with one another, e.g., biological forces and cultural forces, the interpersonal plane and the intrapersonal plane, psychological dimensions and sociological dimensions, and the like, facilitated my being able to talk about such relationships in a more nuanced way.

Your work with Holbrook Mahn, published in *The Educational Psychologist* in 1996, also emphasized the dialectical process. You and Holbrook talked about dialectical thinking as it related to the research of the socioculturalists in their efforts to study cognitive and social change. The two of you put it this way:

> Sociocultural researchers emphasize methods that document cognitive and social changes. Rather then seeing a dichotomy between quantitative and qualitative research, approaches are chosen that emphasize development, and multiple ways in which both can be revealed. (John-Steiner & Mahn 1996, p. 198; also in Richard-Amato, 2010, p. 12)

Even as late as 2000, verbal battles were still taking place between the cognitive and sociocultural camps. In fact, these battles didn't come to a head until 2006 when almost the entire volume of the *TESOL Quarterly* ("TESOL at Forty: What Are the Issues?") was devoted to the differences. The search for definitive answers had caused many a cognitivist to favor quantitative research over qualitative research. As I'm sure you are aware, many researchers in the field of applied linguistics to this day consider the sociocultural and affective aspects to be too messy and difficult to measure to be of real value.

Over the years, I have admired your work and the scholarly approach you and your collaborators have brought to your many publications. I would like to return to the quote that begins this letter and continue where it leaves off: "...living in the other's mind requires trust and confidence" (John-Steiner, 2000, p. 190). You have indeed built that trust and confidence with the others with whom you have worked. I only wish that I had had the opportunity to be one of them.

Respectfully yours,
Patricia Richard-Amato

DR. PATRICIA RICHARD-AMATO is Professor Emerita at California State University, Los Angeles, where she coordinated graduate programs in TESOL. An internationally known textbook writer, lecturer, and school teacher, Dr. Richard-Amato was awarded the prestigious Mildenberger Medal by the Modern Language Association for her work in the field of teaching foreign languages and literatures.

REFERENCES

Connery, M. C., John-Steiner, V., & Marjanovic-Shane, A. (2010). *Vygotsky and creativity: A cultural-historical approach to play, meaning making and the arts.* New York: Peter Lang.

Hedegaard, M. (1990). How instruction influences children's concepts of evolution. *Mind, Culture, and Activity, 3,* 11–24.

John-Steiner, V. (2000). *Creative collaboration.* New York: Oxford University Press.

John-Steiner, V., Connery, M. C., & Marjanovic-Shane, A. (2010). Dancing with the muses: A cultural-historical approach to play, meaning making and creativity. In M.C. Connery, V. John-Steiner, & A. Marjanovic-Shane (Eds.), *Vygotsky and creativity: A cultural-historical approach to play, meaning making and the arts* (pp. 3–16). New York: Peter Lang.

John-Steiner, V., & Mahn, H. (1996). Sociocultural approaches to learning and development: A Vygotskian framework. *Educational Psychologist, 31*(3/4), 191–206.

John-Steiner, V., & Souberman, E. (1978). Afterword. In L. Vygotsky, *Mind in society* (pp. 121–140). Cambridge, MA: Harvard University.

Marjanovic-Shane, A., Connery, M. C., & John-Steiner, V., (2010). A cultural-historical approach to creative education. In M.C. Connery, V. John-Steiner, & A. Marjanovic-Shane (Eds.), *Vygotsky and creativity: A cultural-historical approach to play, meaning making and the arts* (pp. 215–232). New York: Peter Lang.

Richard-Amato, P. (2010). *Making it happen: From interactive to participatory language teaching: Evolving theory and Practice.* White Plains, NY: Pearson Education.

Vygotsky, L. (1962). *Thought and language.* Cambridge, MA: MIT Press.

Vygotsky, L. (1978). *Mind in society.* Cambridge, MA: Harvard University Press.

Wells, G. (1999). *Dialogic inquiry: Toward a sociocultural practice and theory of education.* Cambridge: Cambridge University Press.

LETTER THIRTY-SIX

From Vygotsky to Vera to All of Us
The Mentoring Magnifies

LeAnn Putney and Joan Wink

When asked to think about what we have gleaned and gained from the work of Vera John-Steiner, our thoughts turned to the notion of *mentoring*. John-Steiner and Meehan (2000, p. 37) describe Vygotsky as a "distant teacher" whose work continues to inspire us to think and rethink his constructs as well as our own educational processes. In our own studies of Vygotsky's work (Wink & Putney, 2002), we refer to Vygotsky as a distant mentor or a mentor from the past who contributes to our present and future as educators. We can say the same for Vera, a more proximal mentor, whose work has translated and extended the work of Vygotsky, thus helping us better understand the complexity of Vygotsky's theories.

For example, Vera (1997) has published on the importance of creativity in the development process and her work on complementarity has shown that the relationship of mentor to novice is not a one-way relationship. In our own educational

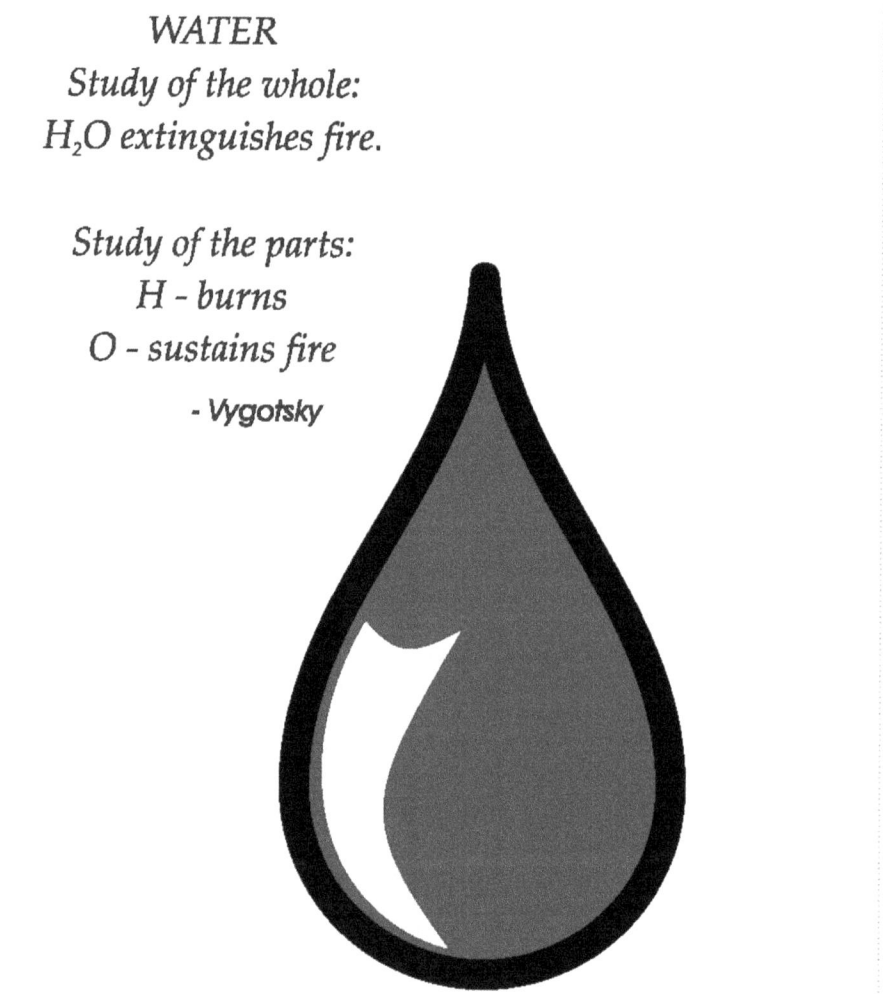

FIGURE 1. THE VYGOTSKIAN METAPHOR OF WATER

spaces we have noted the complex relationships offered between mentor and novice and how that relationship becomes reciprocal as well.

The reciprocal relationship of mentor and novice is but one example of Vygotsky's use of dialectics. In our own work we have used the metaphor of the water drop (Wink & Putney, 2002), as did Vygotsky (1986) to explain the complexities of teaching, learning, and development. When separated into its parts, water is qualitatively changed. It is the union of the atoms of hydrogen and oxygen that creates the properties of water as we know it. The uniqueness of the property of water that extinguishes fire is made more interesting when we consider that separately, hydrogen (H_2) burns, and oxygen (O) sustains combustion (Figure 1: The Vygotskian Metaphor of Water). The illustration of the water drop is significant in our attempts to understand individuals, especially students in diverse classrooms, in relation to their social, cultural, historical, and political contexts. In addition, we value pedagogy as a dialectic as well, considering the reciprocal relationship between teaching and learning as creating more than the sum of its parts (Wink & Putney, 2002). In understanding Vygotsky's zone of proximal development, Vera taught us that learning and development are thoroughly situated in culture, and development of the individual is "a process in which children grow into the intellectual life of those around them" (Vygotsky, 1978, p. 88).

REFORMULATION OF THOUGHT THROUGH IMAGES

In all of our work related to Vygotsky we found the act of creatively reworking his words into illustrations helped us to better understand and reformulate (Putney & Floriani, 1999; Vygotsky, 1978) the complexity of his theories. In addition, this reformulation of Vygotsky's theories helped us in discussing his work with classroom teachers, graduate students, and colleagues. What has been clear to us is that what Vera helped us understand about Vygotsky's work in relation to child development is also central to our understanding of developing novice scholars.

REFORMULATION OF THOUGHT THROUGH LANGUAGE: HEAPS TO COMPLEXES TO CONCEPTUAL THINKING

Just as Vygotsky's image of the water drop assists in the reformulation of thought, so too does Vera's language lead to reformation and deeper thought. In her work (2007), she captures Vygotsky's (1986) point that concept development is a complex process that moves from *heaps* of things that the child thinks belongs together, proceeds into *complexes* in which the connections between the items are functional, and then evolves into *conceptual thinking* that requires and demonstrates a generalized understanding (John-Steiner, 2007, p. 138). Furthermore, this progression of conceptualizing happens in relation to problem solving actions on the part of more experienced others who scaffold the process. Thus, "the meaning of a fully developed concept involves cultural and intergenerational transmission, verbal thinking, and practical application" (John-Steiner, 2007, p. 138).

It is not lost on us that Vygotsky was studying development of the child. However, in our own educational contexts, we have marveled that the process is strikingly similar when we scaffold the learning *of* and *with* novice scholars. We also note that their awakening and their view of the concepts often sparks in us a different way of rethinking and reformulating what we already know. This reciprocal relationship leads to problem solving and research of new ideas that keeps us moving through our own personal zones of proximal development.

Le has captured an example of such conversation with a doctoral student, Cynthia Kimball, which illustrates the process of developing conceptual thinking. Le illustrates through this dialogue what Vera described for us as Vygotsky's theory of conceptual thinking as a way of moving from *heaps*, to *complexes*, to *conceptual thinking*.

> Le: "So, Cynthia, tell me what is happening with you and your work on hope-base leadership."
>
> Cynthia: "I've got all of this stuff in my paper about the idea of hope-based learning, but I just can't seem to figure out exactly what it is and how to explain it to anyone else. It's like I know, but I don't know."

At this point, Cynthia has information in **heaps**.

> Le: "But, you do have this. I have heard you tell me on other occasions. So just tell me now what you have learned from all that you have been reading and doing. You collected data from people you consider to be hope-based teachers, so now tell me what you learned from studying them."
>
> Cynthia: "Oh, well, hope-based leadership is about the way the teachers react and relate to the learner. You don't hold learning over their heads as a prize. You unfold it for us in a way that makes us want to know more. You get us excited about learning, and you also instill in us the confidence to know that we will get this. We may not understand it right now but if we just keep talking it through, if we keep sharing the ideas with each other, if we keep reading and thinking and working through it, we will come to understand it. Not out of fear of getting the right grade, but learning for the sake of learning. We're learning because we are excited to know more."

Gotta love this Cynthia, who is moving toward **complexes** related to hope-based teaching/learning.

Le: "Ok, that's a great start to show your understanding. You are really beginning to solidify your response, and now I want you to go to the data and show me what you have identified in the data as hope-based teaching. Show me the categories you constructed so that we can zoom in and label what it is."

Cynthia: "Well, hope-based teachers give *second chances* because they believe in the potential of their students. But they also give their students *tough love* meaning that they acknowledge that the work is hard to do, but they don't let up on their students and lower their expectations of them; they give their students the resources they need to keep going. Hope-based teachers *create a culture* in their classroom that supports students and convinces students *yes, I can*. They are *flexible, positive, and they never give up* on students."

Cynthia is moving toward **conceptual thinking** at this point as she is generalizing what she learned from her data.

So you see, in her own way, Cynthia was showing us what it takes for adults to conceptualize and generalize as they reformulate their thinking. It is not exactly the same process as for children, yet we see similarities in the process. Joan has talked about this as taking a tiny idea and adding more words to it and watching it grow. Then experiencing the idea, which adds more thoughts and more words to it until we have a full understanding. And just about the time we think we really get it, another novice comes along, full of great ideas and new twists, and we think it through again with renewed energy.

This takes us back to Vera's work on mentorship. She notes that the novice/mentor relationship is mutually beneficial when they are working together creatively and collaboratively in problem solving situations. Vera stated that such collaborations, when successful result in novices developing fluency, while also offering renewal for the experienced individual. From a Vygotskian point of view, these interactions are central to the transformation of the novice into an experienced thinker (John-Steiner, 1997, p. xxiii).

THE MENTORING ENDURES

What we have learned from Vera is that the Vygotskian legacy is not only a theory. As we have seen in her life, that legacy is exactly what we have lived as well. The mentor, Joan, of twenty years ago has consistently been led to reexamine, rethink, and regenerate her principles and practices as the assumed novice, LeAnn, invigorated, expanded, and transformed pedagogical insights. Vygotsky's concept of mentoring is reciprocal; so was ours.

So here we are writing together, years after learning from and about Vygotsky, often times from Vera. Our roles are changing, our experiences have varied, and our sociocultural historical context has evolved; the world has changed. We have changed. By reflecting on our journaling with each other over the past twenty years, it is clear to us that our roles have often been fluid and flexible, depending on the context in which we were working. As there were no set boundaries constraining the roles within our mentoring relationship, we were both able to grow in our collaborative efforts, resulting in richer understandings of mentoring. Because our assumptions allowed our roles to change and grow, the zones of possibilities and potentialities for each of us were and continue to be unlimited as we reformulate our understandings to think more deeply (Wink & Putney, 2002).

From Vygotsky we have come to know that our experience has primacy in our learning, and that experience is reflected in our language and our thoughts. The sociocultural, historical context of the teacher and the learner becomes a zone of proximal development that informs both active participants through this dialectical experience. We suggest that the dialectic of the mentor–apprentice relationship is the same as that of teacher–learner. It is through the original metaphor of the waterdrop that these seeming opposites are unified. As the relationships between teaching–learning develop, inquiry is the unifying principle (Wink & Putney, p. 166).

We have developed in new and surprising ways through our mentoring relationship. Our continual reformulations bring us to a place where we are partners in our learning and teaching. Sometimes we are teachers, learners, professors, practitioners, inquirers, but we are always teaching, learning, and developing. For some our work may be about new thoughts and new language. However, the ideas we work from today are grounded in the antiquities of dialectical learning. "The ideas of Vygotsky have a long tradition that we are simply revisiting as we listen to the voices of the past and present who lead us to our future" (Wink & Putney, 2002, p. 167).

LEANN PUTNEY, Ph.D., is professor and department chair at University of Nevada, Las Vegas. She has focused a Vygotskian lens on studies of individual and collective development and collective classroom efficacy in K–12 settings.

JOAN WINK, Ph.D., is professor emerita of California State University, Stanislaus and has focused on languages, literacy, and learning in pluralistic contexts. Now, partially retired, she divides her time writing on the family ranch in South Dakota when she is not teaching and consulting nationally.

REFERENCES

John-Steiner, V. (1997). *Notebooks of the mind* (2nd ed.). New York: Oxford University Press.

John-Steiner, V. (2007). Vygotsky and linguistics: On speaking and thinking. *The Cambridge companion to Vygotsky* (pp. 136–152). H. Daniels, M. Cole, & J. Wertsch (Eds.). New York: Cambridge University Press.

Putney, L. G., & Floriani, A. (1999). Examining transformative classroom processes and practices: A cross-case analysis of life in two bilingual classrooms. *Journal of Classroom Interaction, 34*(2), 17–29.

Vygotsky, L. S. (1978). *Mind in society: The development of higher psychological processes.* Cambridge, MA: Harvard University Press.

Vygotsky, L. S. (1986). *Thought and language.* Cambridge, MA: MIT Press.

Wink, J., & Putney, L. (2002). *A vision of Vygotsky.* New York: Pearson.

The authors wish to thank Cynthia Kimball, of UNLV, who is now in the process of analyzing her data, as she creates a model for hope-based leadership, teaching and learning.

LETTER THIRTY-SEVEN

A Researcher's Grail
A Search for an Alternative to Conventional Teacher–Student Discourse

Ronald Gallimore

"[We may discover our own mentors] through...recognition of the importance of an intense and personal kinship [that arises from the work of another, even from the distant past]. Once such a bond is established, the learner explores those valued works with an absorption which is the hallmark of creative individuals. In this way, they stretch, deepen, and refresh their craft and nourish their intelligence, not only during their early years of apprenticeship, but repeatedly, throughout the many cycles of their work-lives. (John-Steiner, 1985, p. 54)

Dear Vera:

Around the time you, Roland, and I finished our orphan chapter on mentoring, my colleagues and I were wrestling with a paradox—elementary teachers seldom used at school an attractive form of teaching that many probably employed at home with their own children.

The paradox was suggested by emerging studies of early language and literacy development. Conducted mainly by developmental and sociolinguistic investigators, evidence was mounting that literate parents engaged in a powerful form of "conversational teaching." This teaching included extended dialogues, leading questions, connections to a child's existing knowledge, more equitable turn distribution, collaborative inquiry over an extended period, and co-instructed text and event interpretations. Even toddlers were treated as legitimate conversational partners rather than game-show contestants expected to quickly answer a series of unrelated questions. Interspersed with this more conversational form of "natural teaching" were instances of parents engaged in direct instruction—how to sound out a word, noting similarities between words, and other decoding issues. This mix of teaching forms we began to call *instructional conversation*.

Instructional conversation (hereafer IC) is something of a contradiction in terms. Instruction implies one participant has an agenda—some kind of learning objective. A conversation implies a balanced exchange of thoughts and sentiments, usually unhinged if one or more interloctuer suspects a conversational partner has an ulterior motive. Contradictory or not, the instructional benefits of "teaching through conversation" seemed evident in compelling video tape examples of parents engaging in intellectually demanding exchanges with their young children. Such interactions that nurture thinking and speaking might be described as scaffolding, assistance in the zone of proximal development, or intellectual midwifery.

Despite many being parents, few teachers we observed in schools used a conversational approach to scaffold students' thinking and speaking. When discussion was called for, some relied mainly on the hoary practice of asking one known-answer question after another—a practice described as recitation as far back as the 1860s. Students were expected to deliver up short-answers to questions about the literal details of narrative texts. Questions did not build on previous student contributions, so extended discourse was seldom used to probe deeply into a topic or issue.

Many teachers used direct instruction strategies, such as step-by-step instruction, augmented by teacher models, opportunities for guided practice, and checking for understanding. Although disparaged by some, there is ample evidence of direct instruction's benefits for some educational goals. For example, direct instruction has been shown to be effective teaching literal comprehension. However, direct instruction is not always as effective in developing higher-order comprehension functions such as text application, analysis, synthesis, and evaluation. Direct instruction might help teach well the facts of *Hamlet*, but not so much the play's meaning.

If teachers who are also parents can combine instruction and conversation at home, why don't they carry over this form of teaching when they are at work in classrooms? Can they, for example, use a conversational approach to teach reading comprehension in combination with direct instruction?

Our initial quest included researchers and teachers collaborating to develop a form of IC that promoted higher-order reading comprehension. A series of studies indicated that teachers could, with ample and extended professional development, learn to conduct ICs, and that ICs produced greater gains in higher order comprehension than direct instruction.

However, a problem was apparent. Conventional forms of professional development (PD) did not work for IC. Even those who might be doing ICs with their own children struggled to employ it at school because of the number of students and a faster, more deliberate instructional pace ("got to cover the material"). Even if they mastered IC, usage typically faded once scaffolding PD support was taken down. Teachers, working as individuals on instructional improvement, seemed unable to sustain the practice. This quest was ended because of cost: to provide rich enough PD long enough cost more than most schools could afford.

At this point we began a new quest. We posed the following question to ourselves that connected to your work on mentoring; can teachers learn and implement ICs through some form of peer mentoring and apprenticeship? After all, those who use conversation at home with their own children could surely help each other deploy some of those practices at school.

Beginning in the late 1980s, a team at UCLA worked on what is now referred to in our lab as "teacher learning teams." The basic idea is simple enough. Most schools have ubiquitous and durable settings—faculty meetings, elementary grade-level meetings, and secondary department meetings—where day-to-day work gets done. Yet, almost never do these settings focus on instruction as a subject of extended inquiry about and discussion of instruction. We've very rarely observed in typical school meetings anything like your description of the kinship that can arise between mentors and apprentices (John-Steiner, 1985, p. 54).

To convert grade-level and department meetings into settings that supported instructional improvement turned out to be more difficult than we imagined. After years of tinkering and experimentation, some features of learning teams were identified that make these settings better work as laboratories for instructional improvement. Here are the key features: teams should be 6 or 7 teachers all teaching the same subject to approximately the same age group; teams need stable and protected meeting times; a trained peer-facilitator is needed to keep the team focused; teams need an inquiry protocol that guides but does not prescribe their efforts to study improve teaching and learning; and teams must persist working on learning challenges their students share until there is tangible evidence of achievement gains.

With these factors in place, public school teachers approach that special kinship of which you have so compellingly written. It is not the classic dyad of master teacher serving as mentor to an apprentice. It is a sociocultural phenomenon that arises when a small band of individuals set and share a common quest, commit to searching until they find a solution, develop and try out solutions, collect, share and reflect on results, and return to the old problem or turn to a new one. Their grail is better teaching and more learning, a search that makes meaningful progress but is never ending—in the best circumstances it beomes a career-long pursuit of continuous improvement.

As the continuous improvement process plays out, the mentoring/teaching role rotates from one individual to another within the team; sometimes it's hard to distinguish among the peers who at any moment is acting as mentor and apprentices. Like families under duress, infantry squads, and disaster responders, teacher teams can forge a bond and a unity that is hard to describe but is instantly understood as that preculiar kinship forged by working together to solve a common problem. Team members might not be attracted to each other; they may not like one or more colleagues very well. Their joint efforts are fueled by teamwork they cherish, comradeship they value, and satisfaction derived from persisting to a solution that benefits their students.

At their best, teacher learning teams "stretch, deepen, and refresh their craft and nourish their intelligence, not only during their early years of apprenticeship, but repeatedly, throughout the many cycles of their work-lives (John-Steiner, 1985, p. 54). However, there is a sobering reality about teacher teams. The teaching improvements we observe are, for the most part, incremental, small steps. Only very, very rarely do teacher teams, however effectively they operate, move toward teaching practices as challenging to learn and sustain as instructional conversation. On the surface this seems disappointing. But perhaps not.

In the 1999 TIMSS Video Study of Teaching in Seven Countries, my colleagues and I compared 8th grade U.S. teaching practices with those in some extraordinarily high achieving countries. When the project began I expected to see at least in some countries relatively common use of instructional conversation or some like form of challenging, extended classroom discourse. We did not. The high achieving countries were more different in teaching practices than similar, but they did share a few commonalties. In high achieving countries, for example, each week a handful of problems were worked on at length until students more fully understood the mathematical reasoning beneath the solution methods they were learning to apply. The instruction was typically more similar to direct instruction than anything like instructional conversation.

Perhaps seeking instruction that has conversational elements has been this researcher's grail. Forever hoping to find it, pressed to continue by teasing evidence that seems to disappear on approach, and wondering from time to time if it is just a romantic illusion.

Ronald Gallimore

RONALD GALLIMORE, Ph.D., is Distinguished Professor Emeritus at the University of California at Los Angeles. The author of over 5 books and 130 scientific papers, Dr. Gallimore's research and courses focus on the improvement of teaching.

REFERENCE

John-Steiner, V. (1985). *Notebooks of the mind: Explorations of thinking.* Albuquerque: University of New Mexico Press.

LETTER THIRTY-EIGHT

Dr. Vera John-Steiner as a Key
Unlocking a Theory of Receptive Discourse

Laura Rychly

"Such a process of dissolving, of placing a thought into its verbal and social context, is required in turning thoughts outward. It is through making explicit not only what is new inside one's mind, but also what is the implicit background of ideas, knowledge, and beliefs that novelty and insight arises." (John-Steiner, 1997, p. 139)

Dear Dr. John-Steiner,

My copy of *The Cambridge Companion to Vygotsky* falls open to page 143, the eighth page of your chapter, "Vygotsky on Thinking and Speaking." This reading was recommended to me by my professor Dr. Robert Lake, who was helping me access Vygotsky's (1986) ideas in *Thought and Language*. I needed Vygotsky because I was trying to build an idea that has become central to my dissertation research, an idea that is a way for teachers to use language to access students' thinking and convince them of their own agency as meaning makers. Vygotsky's conceptualization of the relationships between our thinking, the words we use to share that thinking, and meanings we attribute to the words we use are fundamental to the case I am building. Unfortunately, my first attempt to read *Thought and Language* felt like trying to pry open a locked box; I knew what I needed was in there, but I didn't have the key.

Dr. John-Steiner, your work has proven to be my missing key. Your clear and insightful explications of some of Vygotsky's seminal ideas, such as the development of and differences between inner speech and outer language, and the difference between our private thoughts and the language we use to share those thoughts, clarified for me the ways that my research relies upon Vygotskian theory. Also, it was in your work that I discovered the label *linguistic relativity* for a phenomenon I had encountered in bits and pieces, mostly in coursework related to teaching English to speakers of other languages. Your reasoning about this gave me the confidence to extend the theory that the availability of particular conceptual understandings is based on available ways to speak about them into classrooms where, technically, teachers and students speak the same language but nonetheless share misunderstandings that are the result of linguistic relativity.

Receptive discourse is the name I have given to my idea under construction, about the special way for teachers to hear their students. It is a pedagogical possibility for a way that teachers can listen to their students. Instead of listening to students from their own thinking, teachers can learn to listen for their students' thinking behind the words that they use. Receiving and responding in this way maximizes the potential of classroom discourse to help students know themselves as agents of meaning construction, which will help them develop persistence in the face of confusion or frustration. The theory that it is even possible to listen to students in this way exists at an intersection of many ideas about ways that language works with dual directionality to reveal our inner selves outward at the same time that we internalize our unique understanding of the world, including our sense of self. Two of these ideas are linguistic relativity and Vygotsky's explanation of the relationship between thought and language.

Linguistic relativity, as you have helped me understand, is a phenomenon whereby speakers of two different languages will not share the same realities because "a particular language channels the speaker's attention according to the categories provided by the native language...part of acquiring a native language is learning particular ways of thinking for speaking (John-Steiner, 2007, p. 150). Actually, I have an uncanny experience to share about my study of this theory. One afternoon, while reading your chapter "Vygotsky on Thinking and Speaking," I suddenly and involuntarily looked up from the page. You had quoted from Sapir his idea that "Language is not merely a more or less systematic inventory of the various items of experience which seem relevant to the individual, as is so often naively assumed, but is also a self-contained, creative symbolic organization..." I looked up because I knew I had read those words before. I knew right away that this same quote appears in Harry Hoijer's 1954 essay "The Sapir-Whorf Hypothesis," which is printed in the proceedings of the American Anthropological Association's 1954 conference, Language in Culture, a volume of which I own a treasured copy. You and Dr. Hoijer quoted from the same essay by Edward Sapir's 1931 essay, "Conceptual Categories in Primitive Languages." It cannot be a coincidence that these writings have come together in my world.

I think that in classrooms there exists a potential for linguistic relativity whether students and teachers speak the same, or a similar language, or two altogether different languages. This is because teachers and students will have different lexicons and levels of syntactic and semantic fluency with which to access and share their thinking, due to their different levels of proficiency with the subject under study. There exists then the potential for a mismatch, or a disconnection, between the meaning that one speaker is trying to convey, and the meaning that the other is presuming. Given this, the task facing teachers of nurturing conceptual understanding is more complex than perhaps is acknowledged, and requires a special way for teachers to hear their students.

Vygotsky's important work on the relationship between spoken words, their meanings, and the thoughts they represent added to linguistic relativity make a strong case for there being a need for teachers to learn to practice a sort of reverse interpretation. He showed that spoken words represent a convergence of private thinking and public speech into presumably what a child *means* to share with another person. The response a teacher immediately begins preparing is a response to the meaning she perceives based on the words she hears, and is weighed against the meaning she expected to hear. But it is possible that neither her perception nor her expectation of meaning was what her student was *thinking*. Vygotsky explained that this is because the words we use are not direct copies of our inner thoughts (John-Steiner, 2007). Instead, verbal language is a means through which we condense our inner thinking so we can share it with others. You led me to the idea of a reverse interpretive moment, a moment in which teachers can separate a students' words from the teacher's perception of their meaning, and imagine other possible thoughts as the origin of the produced meaning-in-word.

Receptive discourse is possible if teachers are careful to access that which lies below, or behind, the first level of the words that they hear students say. In *Notebooks of the Mind* you explained that "verbal thinking" is how students give teachers access to "not only what is new inside one's mind, but also what is the implicit background of ideas, knowledge, and beliefs [in which] novelty and insight arises" (p. 139). It is in this 'background of ideas, knowledge, and beliefs' that all new experiences are interpreted and made meaningful by students, and to which teachers might be said to have a responsibility to honor. Listening for and responding to students' thinking, which may be different than it seems given the words students share their thinking through, is a way to honor this responsibility.

Your book *Notebooks of the Mind: Explorations of Thinking* has been an especially important resource for me for understanding how humans can come to be powerful and creative thinkers. You present myriad examples of individuals who developed thusly, and your language and descriptions supported my emerging thinking about learners being 'received' by the world in order that they should persist in their learning. What many of your subjects seemed to experience was permission, granted either by themselves, or families, or teachers, to continue their thinking or practice such that a line between the self and this thinking or practice was no longer discernable. To explain this idea from the other direction, what I mean is that the people you studied seemed to be free from a sort of blocking that would have prevented them from persisting and then from becoming the powerful and creative thinkers that the world came to know them to be.

Now, in the dissertation stage of my doctoral degree in Curriculum Studies, I will have the wonderful opportunity of getting to know you as you serve on my dissertation committee. I am, as I should be, a bit nervous, and very grateful. I appreciate the influence your work has had on my ability to generate and articulate my own research ideas and I humbly recognize the privilege it is to work with such an esteemed scholar as yourself.

Laura

LAURA RYCHLY, Ph.D., is a recent graduate of the Curriculum Studies program at Georgia Southern University. She is interested in how school-aged children develop a sense of self resulting from language interactions with their teachers including the cognitive-affective and sociocultural dimension of identity.

REFERENCES

Hoijer, J. (1954). The Sapir-Whorf hypothesis. *The American Anthropologist: Language in Culture,* 56(6), 92–105.

John-Steiner, V. (1997). *Notebooks of the mind: Explorations of thinking* (2nd ed.). New York: Oxford University Press.

John-Steiner, V. (2007). Vygotsky on thinking and speaking. In H. Daniels, M. Cole, & J. V. Wertsch (Eds.), *The Cambridge Companion to Vygotsky* (pp. 136–152). Cambridge, MA: Cambridge University Press.

Vygotsky, L. (1986). *Thought and language.* Cambridge, MA: MIT Press.

LETTER THIRTY-NINE

The Constellation, Maker

Robert Danberg

"During these diverse apprenticeships, creative adolescents immerse themselves in the work of their elders. This is also a time in their lives when they first explore their inner resources, these varied invisible tools that help transform a gifted young person into a productive artist or scientist." (John-Steiner, 1985, p. 59)

"The ability to apply and extend productive ideas only succeeds when an individual can join these with a profound knowledge of his or her craft or the tools of a discipline. But tools are both external and internal: an individual's self knowledge, an awareness of the specificity of one's talents, the rhythms of one's cycles of work, and the need for sustenance and support, all contribute to the realization of a thought. As I wrote at the beginning of this work, 'A new work of an artist may start with a phrase or a scientist may start with an image, which often represents that nucleus of understanding which unfolds through labor, craft, inspiration and careful mustering of time that separates the beginner from those with experience.'" (John-Steiner, 1985, p. 222)

I've begun with two quotes, although I was asked for one, for reasons I hope the letter that follows will make clear, but before I do, I want to say I include them because the book they are from, *Notebooks of the Mind*, passes what a teacher of mine once called the "Heschel Test." His "Heschel Test" referred to his experience, one I shared, of reading anything Rabbi Abraham Joshua Heschel wrote. Open to any page at random and you will find some beautiful, memorable prose that expresses something you otherwise knew but could not say. For example, this phrase from *Notebooks*:

INVISIBLE TOOLS THAT HELP TRANSFORM

Or these careful clauses—
Tools are both external and internal:
An individual's self knowledge,

> An awareness of the specificity of one's talents,
> The rhythms of one's cycles of work
> And the need for sustenance and support
> All contribute to the realization of a thought

Or

> That nucleus of understanding
> Which unfolds through
> The Labor
> Craft
> Inspiration
> And careful mustering of time
> That separates the beginner from those with experience

Looking back over the twenty years since I first encountered *Notebooks of the Mind* I see its ideas and observations formed an "image which represented the nucleus" of an understanding which unfolded and was transformed through a life of teaching and thinking about teaching, against a life of writing and solving a writer's problems.

I teach college composition. The students who enter my writing classrooms do not come as artists-to-be, but all have been *makers* in some way, and *Notebooks* describes what I believe we intuit, but often ignore: creators share elemental qualities of work, intention, and intuition. In our everyday lives, we tend to assume that the chef, scientist, and writer differ and that their work and learning are incommensurable with one another. Although some of my students may become artists, almost all will become something other than writers. Some may want to make something beautiful from words, but most simply wish to make something true out of them, and by true, I mean in the way a carpenter might make true a door so that it hangs right in the space it was meant for.

I know that my students have been enriched by the practice of creation, often privately, away from school, from home, on the field, in the studio, in the kitchen, among friends, and yet, they come to the college writing classroom like the nonbeliever in the Jewish legend who dares two sages to teach him the entire Torah while he stands on one foot: a provocation. In the tale, the nonbeliever approaches Shammai first, a sage known for his strict reading of Law. Shammai chases him off, with a carpenter's rod, a sturdy stick used, fittingly, for measurement. The nonbeliever goes to Hillel, Shammai's opposite number, who is known for kindness and interpretations tempered by the circumstances of Exile. Hillel utters the line that's made the legend central, "That which is hateful to you do not do to others. The rest is commentary; go and learn it." The nonbeliever is converted.

In a letter to Martin Buber in the 1920s, the philosopher and educator Franz Rosenzweig observed that although the legend was known for its ethical aphorism, "That which is hateful to you," the last part of Hillel's admonition, which readers typically passed over and forgot, was powerfully suggestive to him as an educator. "The rest is commentary. Go and learn it."

Over time, I've reached the conclusion that learning commentary is the goal of the writing classroom and in my work with writers, *Notebooks* helped me understand what it means to learn the commentary and teach it. The writing class itself is the commentary, each member, the time we take, the work we do, our perceptions, efforts, and the rhythms of return that comprise our movement from beginning to end, all are the commentary we learn.

For Rosenzweig, to learn the commentary meant that the learner becomes a "chooser," one who makes herself a link in a chain of tradition. To be one who chooses, Rosenzweig asserts, one must face ambiguity and, over and over again, choose. And so the writing student does the same, forging herself as a link in a chain of tradition. Rosenzweig also observes that while a teaching is a useful guide, it becomes a platitude when it does not become an "invisible tool" subject to lived experience, as when the student resists the ambiguity of commentary in favor of the certainty of rule. A teaching can be transmitted, honed as it is by tradition, tradition an expression of communal experience. A "teaching" becomes a "true teaching," as Rosenzweig calls it, when it lives within the individual and thus enables her to face those situations which require the courage of everyday life, situations which transform and unfold in time.

My work takes places when the nonbeliever leaves the scene of a teaching, the scene of "that whiches" for the "go and learn its." First year writing classrooms—writing instruction up and down the school system—tend to focus on the "that whiches," which is why they cause so much consternation to those who teach in them, to those who administer the programs these classes comprise, to those who observe and reflect upon those classes, and those who often from a distance ask, since we know what good writing looks like, and who good writers are, why is it so hard to teach? New teachers often want what the nonbeliever wants, a "That which…" Writing students want the same; however, the ambiguity of creation, and of ethical decision, requires things other than what we can tell, but are certainly knowledge.

Vera John-Steiner reminds me today, as she showed me many years ago, and as Rosenzweig reminds us, the learning is in the commentary. What I understand as the commentary in a writing classroom is the lived experience of making work together, the way students and I face one another, sustaining and provoking each other, the way we labor together, in time, that I, as a teacher, have shaped so that they can take up those invisible tools to see if they can make the materials of tradition yield to inspiration. I help them become aware of their gifts not through my observations necessarily, but through what the work throws back upon them when it does not yield.

I close with a-not-so-found-poem, made in collaboration with her text, just as my teaching life in some way collaborates with her text, or conspires with it. I've drawn a line to link some words, the way the night sky and the stargazer collaborate on a constellation.

> Invisible tools that help transform
> Tools are both external and internal:
> An individual's self knowledge,
> An awareness of the specificity of one's talents,
> The rhythms of one's cycles of work
> And the need for sustenance and support
> All contribute to the realization of a thought
>
> That nucleus of understanding
> Which unfolds through
> The labor
> Craft
> Inspiration
> And careful mustering of time
> That separates the beginner from those with experience
> Call the constellation, *maker*.

ROBERT DANBERG, Ph.D., is a visiting Assistant Professor in the Writing Initiative at Binghamton University. With an M.F.A. in Poetry and Ph.D. in Composition and Cultural Rhetoric, Dr. Danberg's scholarship focuses on ways to create learning experiences that facilitate the acquisition of mindfulness, intuition, and experiential knowledge exhibited by creative and academic writers.

PART FOUR

Letters on Teaching and Mentoring

A Circle of Learning and Transformation

LETTER FORTY

You Will Meet Vera

Courtney Angermeier

You will meet Vera. She will look at you as you enter the room. Prepare to be SEEN.

Like an infant in a sling, she WATCHES, NOTICES, ABSORBS. All the while you will be aware she is holding something bigger than you or herself or the room or the day. You sense that she senses THE WHOLE.

She will ask you questions about yourself and want to KNOW the answers. She will make you wonder WHAT KNOWING IS.

She will encourage you (almost invisibly) to reclaim the infant's SUPPLENESS GRIP and INNATE HUNGER.

It is fine if you are a MESS (she seems to say). MESSES (sketches, processes, jottings, scratches, notes, scattered equations, and badly drawn diagrams) are all grist for the mill, works in the making... and can become, you see, the MAKINGS for the WORKS of others.

Each word and gesture of Vera's will have weight and wisdom and sanity. Each is ripe and full of MEANING. You will scribble in a notebook, trying to get it down... right. But it won't seem right. (Maybe you will try some diagrams) WORDS? you can't get it onto the paper. Nothing quite captures IT!

She will make you think about why. She will help you understand why.

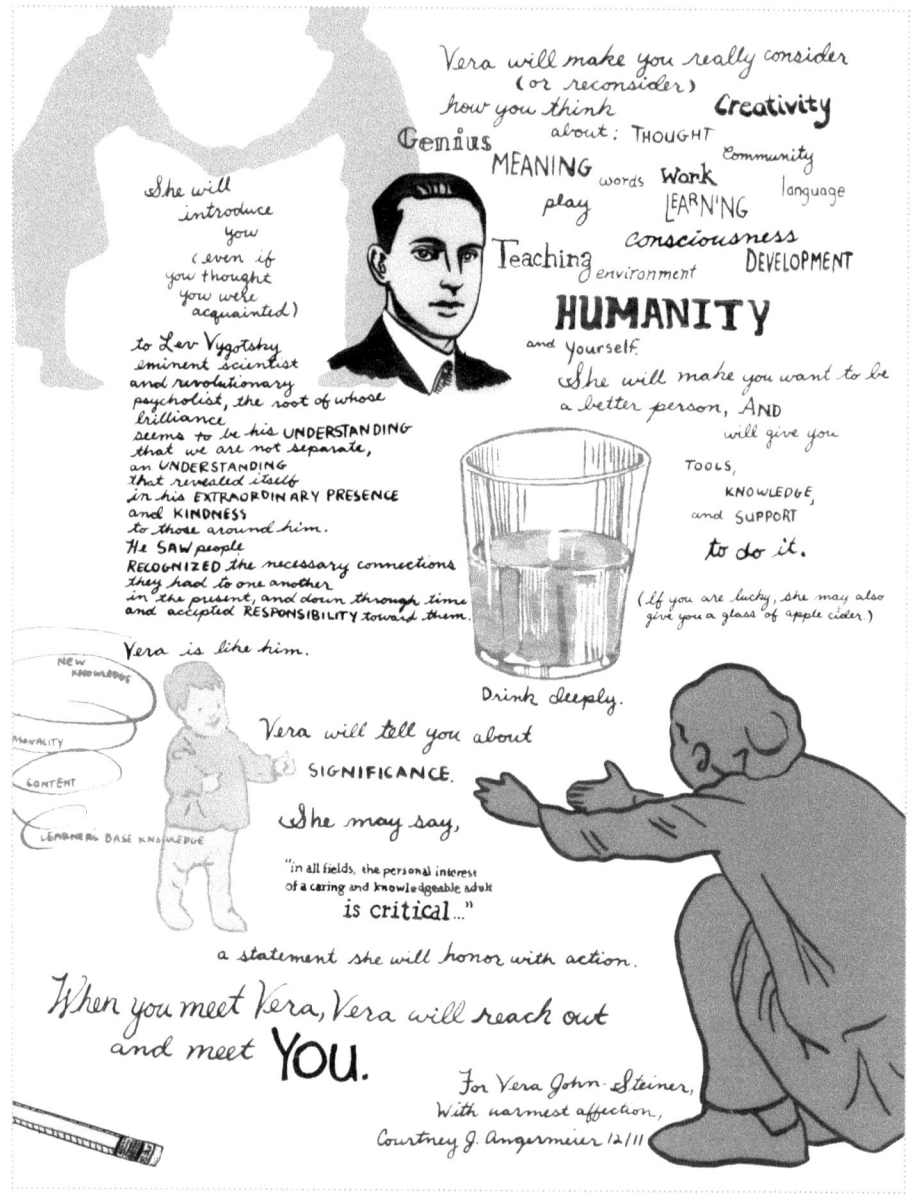

MS. COURTNEY ANGERMEIER teachers high school in Albuquerque, New Mexico. A fine artist and doctoral student at the University of New Mexico, her multi-modal work explores educational history and psychology, as well as human growth and development.

LETTER FORTY-ONE

Vera John-Steiner
Mentor and Collaborator

Christopher C. Shank

I was first introduced to Vera when I started as a doctoral student in the University of New Mexico's Educational Linguistics doctoral program in Fall 1999. Vera had agreed to be my first year advisor and while our first meetings were cordial I never imagined the relationship that would eventually develop as I moved forward in my studies from teacher to student, to advisor, to mentor, to collaborator, to colleague and, most importantly, to someone who I could (and still) call a friend. I also never imagined the degree that Vera would influence my understanding of and approaches to the domains of classroom instruction and discourse and the nature and rewards of engaging in collaborative activities and projects. It is within these two areas that I feel Vera has had the deepest and longest lasting impact upon me and my approaches to lecturing and researching and therefore these memories and experiences are what I would like to share in this letter.

Anyone who has attended Vera's classes, seminars or presentations is aware of her particular discourse and speaking style. A colleague once said she "speaks in such dense rich paragraphs" that it was hard to take accurate or complete notes. Indeed, in my experience Vera's lectures were typically thought-provoking, packed with information, terminology and ideas, plus she always seemed to elegantly integrate the themes and topics from the assigned reading into her prepared comments, observations and reflections. The combination of her distinctly methodical and illustrative lecture style, along with her experience and knowledge in the domains of language, cognition, psychology, bilingualism, and of course Vygotskyian theories and their application, usually created an environment of inquiry, robust dialogue, and discussion between Vera and her audience. It was within this resulting dynamic, as Vera worked to guide us through the complexity of the assigned literature and subject matter where I feel she made one of the most indelible impressions upon me as a student and teacher.

One of the first things I noticed about Vera's teaching style was regardless of either the nature, formulation, phrasing or even relevance of a student's question or comment Vera always, without fail or noticeable hesitation, seemed to effortlessly and adroitly find the relevant or germane element and relate it back to the topic under discussion. The net result was that Vera was almost always able to smoothly validate both the content of the question and the legitimacy of the questioner and thus maintain the speaker's sense of face and confidence and the larger atmosphere of risk-taking and inquiry in the classroom. It is a remarkably complex skill, one which I am certain that Vera has honed over her years in academia, but it really helped to create and sustain a very positive classroom and discourse environment for the students even when faced with the insecurity associated with dense or complicated reading assignments.

The best and most skilful example of this discourse and pedagogical tactic comes from a Vygotskyian seminar that Vera was teaching one semester with her collaborator Dr. Holbrook Mahn. It was early in the semester and all of the assigned readings up to that point dealt with the theoretical underpinning of Vygotsky's approach to learning, cognition and psychological development. During one discussion, an older student who had previously informed us of her occupation as a professional animal trainer and who rather forcefully projected a deliberate New Age/holistic persona and/or air about herself, calmly asked Vera with a degree of deliberation and seriousness "What implications do you think that Vygotskian theory has for my work with animals? How can I apply Vygotsky's ideas to my work rehabilitating animals?" I was a bit taken back by such a question, to me it seemed to originate in far, far left field and it was all I could do to disguise the look of sheer surprise and dismissiveness in my face and body language. Vera, of course, nonplussed, took a short breath and proceeded to give a lengthy answer that gently and skilfully redirected the focus back to the human dimensions, smoothly skipping by the hypothetical cross-species implications (or lack thereof), all while somehow validating both the premise of the question and individual who asked it. It was a remarkably deft performance and it made an indelible impression upon me in terms of demonstrating and reinforcing the importance of listening to one's students, striving to always try and validate students' questions even when only tangential in nature, and to do it in such a way that maintains a classroom atmosphere of congeniality, respect, risk-taking and inquiry. These were of course all qualities and ideals that I had always tried in integrate into my teaching practices but Vera's actions that particular day really reinforced the critical importance of this particular set of skills by providing a model that I strive to uphold and emulate to this day.

The second area where Vera has had a profound impact upon me as an academic and a researcher is in the domain of collaboration. At the start of my second year at UNM I worked for Vera as her graduate assistant. I was introduced to a number of important people in Vera's world, Dr. Teresa Meehan, Dr. Michele Minnis and Dr.

Holbrook Mahn, all individuals who Vera had collaborated with in the past. The notion of collaboration, versus teamwork or sub-division of labour, was new to me perhaps not so much in theory but definitely in practice, but this did not stop Vera from putting me on two projects that would result in public presentations, critical review, evaluation and feedback. The first project resulted in a poster, presented by Vera, at the 7th International Pragmatics Conference in Budapest, Hungary, and the second was in support of her newly released 2000 book entitled *Creative Collaboration*. This presentation was open to the public and given at the Santa Fe Institute in Santa Fe, New Mexico. Both projects involved a steep learning curve and a great deal of collaboration to be successful but it was the Santa Fe institute presentation that proved to be the most challenging and enduring learning experience because of the subject matter, the design and nature of the supporting PowerPoint presentation and the audience.

In the months prior to our SFI presentation Vera asked me to look at the raw transcripts from interviews that she conducted with a wide range of collaborative dyads as part of her research for Creative Collaboration. My task was to conduct an in-depth discourse-based analysis and identify the recurring metaphors, idealized cognitive models and image schematic structures (Lakoff & Johnson, 1981; Lakoff 1990) used by the participants to describe or frame their respective collaborative dynamics, practices and experiences. This was my first real application of Cognitive Metaphor Theory to actual discourse and given the range of participants and disciplines that Vera has looked at for her research it was a daunting task to work through this large body of work, to identify recurring themes and patterns, to extract what I thought were the underlying metaphors and schematic themes and to develop a current draft framework that we could then use to contextualize and gain further insight into the dynamics of creative collaborative endeavours. This research, as I would later find out, was an integral part of the public presentation and, furthermore, there was a good chance that some of the participants described in the book, and whose interviews were contained in the transcripts, could be in attendance. The stakes, I felt, were quite high and consequently the self-imposed pressure to develop the best framework possible for the others to expand upon and develop in new dimensions was quite great.

As Vera and I met regularly to discuss the project it also became clear that she also wanted me to explore the dynamic and imagistic dimensions present in the transcripts and to integrate a creative and artistic component into our slides. Unbeknownst to her, this was a domain that I felt completely lacking and inexperienced in, but I suppressed my fears and started exploring my creative side. While we worked on this project, discussing the results, identifying that we thought were substantial patterns and metaphor threads and collaboratively developing the narrative that would form a substantial part of our SFI presentation, Vera once again encouraged an atmosphere of risk taking, through discourse and feedback, that really encouraged me to explore my inchoate artistic and graphic design skills. Vera would work with me as I tried to graphically represent a process, a pattern or to schematize an underlying metaphorical transfer, and have me talk my way through the idea or image and so reshape it in a way we thought best. It was intimidating to be given free artistic and analytical rein with Vera's source material and to engage her on an equal level given her clear seniority and considerably more experience, but at no time did she ever deviate from the role of collaborator. I felt both valued and an important contributor though the entire process. This of course was particularly challenging because while I was working on this project with/for Vera I was also a graduate student in one of her classes and she was my PhD. supervisor; roles that inherently embody, at least theoretically, an asymmetrical power dynamic and relationship.

The project rolled forward and with Valerie's creativity and assistance the final presentation was assembled, edited and titled "Flights and Resting Places: Discovering Complementarity in Scientific Collaboration". The night of the event we all met up in Santa Fe. This presentation, once again, was in support of her book; therefore Vera presented it by herself on stage, in an auditorium in front of several hundred people sitting in the audience. I sat in the front row with several colleagues who had come up from Albuquerque and even though I was relegated to a more passive role for the actual presentation it still had a profound effect in further building up my confidence as a cognitive linguist, a colleague and a creative person.

That night, as the lights dimmed, and Vera was introduced, I was unbelievably nervous and my stomach was in knots. Once the basic introduction was over Vera did something entirely unexpected, she called attention to me sitting in the audience, referred to me as her collaborator, and very publicly acknowledged my role in the forthcoming presentation. I had never been in such a position before, I had always tried to shun the spotlight and my immediate reaction was a combination of shock and mortification. I wanted to crawl under my seat. In the past I was most comfortable remaining in the background but as I had learned from Vera through this process, and that night in Santa Fe that is not what a true collaborative endeavour is all about. Ideally, everyone contributes equally and therefore everyone should be recognized for his or her contribution. Once I had been exposed to the audience Vera began the presentation and perhaps 10 slides into it she transitioned into our metaphor research and the first of my many graphical representations of an underlying idealized cognitive model. As she moved into the heart of the presentation it was clear that the audience was responding quite positively to our findings, our discussion and our imagery. My initial feelings of unsettled nervousness and embarrassment turned to those of pride and accomplishment. It was an amazing emotional swing and by the time she had reached the final slide I was in an entirely new emotional state, one that projected a new degree of confidence and awareness of my understanding of the subject matter, my ability to successfully collaborate, create, and express myself creatively. It was a completely unexpected and inspirational learning experience that marked a turning point in terms of confidence and skills that I continue to draw from and build upon to this day. I would have never imagined such a long-lasting outcome when I first met with Vera to discuss this particular project but, as I learned, that is the nature of collaborative endeavours, they can take you in unexpected directions and have wonderfully long-lasting outcomes.

In the decade since those formative experiences with Vera I have continued to reflect upon and improve my classroom discourse practices and engage in a number of collaborative endeavours across a wide range of disciplines and domains. I don't know if Vera is aware of the effect that those experiences had upon me. I suspect my story and experiences may be shared by a whole slew of graduate students and colleagues who have worked with, worked for and studied under Vera given her long career in academia but these are experiences that I will always treasure and value greatly.

CHRISTOPHER SHANK, Ph.D., is an Assistant Professor in Cognitive Linguistics in the School of Linguistics & English Language at Bangor University in Wales. His primary research fields include cognitive semantics and syntax, figurative language, grammaticalization and language change / processes, corpus linguistics, and the exploration of cognitive aspects of bilingualism.

REFERENCES

John-Steiner, V. (2000). *Creative collaboration*. Oxford, UK: Oxford University Press.

John-Steiner, V., Meehan, T., & Shank, C. (2000, July). *Collaborative metaphors*. Poster presented at the 7th International Pragmatics Conference. University of Budapest, Budapest, Hungry.

Lakoff, G. (1990). *Women, fire and dangerous things: What categories reveal about the mind* (2nd ed.). Chicago: University of Chicago Press.

John-Steiner, V., & Shank, C. (2000, October). *Flights and resting places discovering complementarily in scientific collaboration*. Paper presented at the Santa Fe Institute, Santa Fe, NM.

Lakoff, G., & Johnson, M. (1981). *Metaphors we live by* (1st ed.). Chicago: University of Chicago Press.

LETTER FORTY-TWO

Creativity and Collaboration
A Student's Salvation?

Susan K. Metheny

"In today's information, technological and innovation driven society, creativity has become more of a necessity for psychological health and life success. It can no longer be viewed as a luxury or marginal to "the good life"; it is essential to society's ability to develop and work under conditions of fast-paced change." (Moran & John-Steiner, 2003, pp. 61–90)

Dear Vera,

I am writing this at the close of the holiday season, where wishes abound of peace and good will, and my thoughts, if focused, always rest upon the people who have been so interested in me and my life that they encouraged me to follow my own path and to pursue dreams of creativity combined with academia. In this group, you, most of all, rise above the others; you have been a role model, a coach, a mentor, an adviser, a friend, and, eventually, I hope, a colleague, to me.

These past years have been filled with trauma and hardship for many people, and I can't help but look at them through the lenses of your work—I've used your work with Vygotsky and creativity so many times to pull myself from the despair that threatened to engulf me and my research, my writing, and my life that I feel a very intimate cognitive connection with the "thought and language" so endemic to your work in sociocultural historical theory. I truly believe that nested within your work, within each sentence you write or each topic you talk about in your courses, are tiny pieces of the rich and challenging experiences that formed you from a small child to the premier scholar who always remains approachable and helpful, even as your own life presented and presents difficulties. These life experiences vibrate in tandem with the theoretical bases you explicate through the use of Vygotsky's writings; in a very real way, you yourself are the first and best evidence of the value of sociocultural historical theory, as your own life has been reflected, integrated, and pedagogically assimilated in your writings and your work with students. With every new insight and each amazing volume you produce, the progression of your life path is exposed, enabling you to inspire great work among all who incorporate your experience and oeuvre as part of their own everyday scholarly study.

As in the quote above, you emphasize the importance of including creativity for the healthy development of one's life, and indeed, 'fast-paced' might also refer to the difficulties encountered by students young and old whose lives include the trauma of deep and injuring events, which change their environments momentarily as the satisfaction of even their most basic human needs shifts precariously depending upon the emotional state of their family members. This quote also applies to the students in my own classes, students whose backgrounds often contain challenging situations, which make it difficult for them to attend classes and to succeed in a university setting. One of the most harrowing situations for a young person is the experience of entering an unknown culture; one of the most terrifying is entering the culture of higher education, and along with it, encountering the expectations of this system that s/he absorb and assimilate into that educational culture as quickly as possible. You realized this early on and acknowledged the difficulties of an individual student entering a classroom for the first time, and your course structures are flexible, allowing a student to adjust at his or her own pace. As the class progresses, you revel in watching the student community form, and you encourage these groupings through a unique method of assessment called "peer exams." This concept of "peer exams" is, I believe, the essence of your sociocultural historical pedagogy made manifest in an evaluative teaching tool, formulated from your work with Vygotsky's theoretical constructs, and linked with creativity and collaboration. As you describe it in the syllabus from your Vygotsky seminar:

> A peer examination is designed to give you the opportunity to seek out and reflect upon an issue of particular importance to you. It is an opportunity to explore and develop ideas that are meaningful to you and also of interest to your partner. The process requires that you combine individual research and discussion/negotiation with a partner (chosen in class) over a three-week period. During this time you will generate what you consider to be a major question regarding Vygotsky's cultural-historical framework. You and your partner will both be working on different issues; however, you will be formulating each of your questions collaboratively.

Your conceptual creation and implementation of the peer exam in your courses leads students who come from seemingly disparate disciplines into discussion, where they discover that there are common threads of inquiry underlying all disciplines. Used as a collaborative instrument to encourage interdisciplinary interpretation of a particular issue inherent in each participant's field of study, the peer exam takes place at midterm of the course, a time when the subject matter of the seminar and the experience and background of the students can be productively accessed and processed. It's very true that I fell in love with the idea of the peer exam. I had never experienced any sort of interdisciplinary collaborative work as a form of assessment before, and it struck a chord within me that hadn't been sounded since I worked in the theater, where without collaboration, none of the productions I was part of would ever have been mounted. The creativity required on the part of each partner in the peer exam is extensive; I recall searching and searching for ways to explain my topics of research to my partner who came from an entirely different discipline. The skills I developed during this process have served me well; I am now able to explain my work to almost anyone so that they can understand it, and this ability has also improved the written explication of my research.

I adopted the concept of peer midterm exams in my linguistics courses, and since I was working with undergraduates, I altered the procedure, hopefully maintaining the spirit of the collaborative effort. As a firm believer in the Vygotskian phenomenon of students learning to self-reflect and to self-instruct that I had studied in my courses with you, my adapted peer midterm exam in an introductory linguistics course adheres to the tenets of your insightful instrument. The students and I use the midterm as a time to exercise the skills acquired and/or to regain footing lost because of personal issues; the week before, preparations occur with optional group study sessions and Q&A sessions, often conducted by the students themselves. Students are made aware of the format of the exam, during which they are allowed to form groups or pairs, working together, exploring their notes or the textbook as needed in order to determine their responses. This approach alleviates much of the stress related to testing, instead turning the experience into something that the students almost look forward to and certainly, learn from. On the day of the exam, the small groups gather their resources, collaborating, discussing, making their choices on the test questions based upon the group's consensus. Because my courses are populated with students from many different disciplines, the peer exam experience transforms an ordinary classroom into a creative environment where there are multiple ways of explaining linguistic concepts, not by the instructor, but from student to student. Opinions are aired and solicited; laughter occurs intermittently, and the atmosphere becomes one of inquiry and of open and honest collegial aid and support.

As a result of this approach, the students in my course experience first hand the importance of creatively collaborating on a problem, and I believe they are much more likely to solicit the advice of their peers when they are faced with their own personal difficulties. My heartfelt thanks to you, Vera, for all of the insight, the advice, and the beautiful modeling of how teaching can be performed on behalf of the student; I'm a much better teacher for having had you as a resource and mentor, and teaching is a greater joy than I had ever imagined.

Yours in respect and friendship,
Susan K. Metheny

SUSAN METHENY, M.A., is a teacher, consultant, and doctoral candidate in Educational Linguistics at the University of New Mexico. Her many areas of interest and research include the development of a performance assessment tool for bilingual students, exploring the relationship between first and second language with broader implications for understanding language learning, as well as mathematics education for post-secondary second language learners of English.

REFERENCES

Moran, S., & John-Steiner, V. (2003). Creativity in the making: Vygotsky's contemporary contribution to the dialectic of development and creativity. In R. K. Sawyer, V. John-Steiner, S. Moran, R. J. Sternberg, D. H. Feldman, J. Nakamura, et al., (2003). *Creativity and development*. New York: Oxford University Press.

LETTER FORTY-THREE

Creative Collaboration in the Art Museum

Sara Otto-Diniz

Dear Vera,

"She will be retiring soon, so you must take Vera John-Steiner's 'Psychology of Creativity Class,'" urged Peter Smith, director of the University of New Mexico art education program in fall 1998. I had registered as a non-degree student for Peter's class, "Curriculum Development in Art Education," in order to confirm the theoretical validity of the curriculum I was writing for a non-profit art education organization (Art in the School, Inc.). So, in the spring of 1999, I followed Peter's advice and first met Vera John-Steiner and, through her, Teresa Amabile, Jerome Bruner, MihalyCzikszentmihalyi, L. S. Vygotsky, among others. Students in the class, including Cathrene Connery and Linney Wix whose letters are included in this volume, came from diverse fields such as art education, creative writing, dance, early childhood education, educational psychology, linguistics, and educational thought and sociocultural studies. You can imagine the rich discussions we had in this seminar-style class provoked by our weekly assigned readings! But, as "heady" as were the readings and class discussions, for me the novel experience of our mid-term Peer Examination made the deepest impression. Vera described the assignment in the syllabus:

> A peer examination is designed to give you the opportunity to seek out and reflect upon an issue of particular importance to you. It is an opportunity to explore and develop ideas that are meaningful to you and perhaps even intrigue you. The process requires that you combine individual research and discussion/negotiation with a partner over a three-week period. During this time you will (each) generate what you consider to be a major question relating to the issue at hand. This process will lead to an oral exam administered in class by your partner. He or she will ask you the question that the two of you have been negotiating over the past three weeks. (Retrieved from http://www.unm.edu/~vygotsky/create.pdf).

This seemingly simple assignment addressed a complex array of elements at the heart of Vygotskian theories of creativity and education while simultaneously and seamlessly interweaving Vera's own scholarship, teaching and mentorship. For me the assignment provided an academic opportunity to examine current theories of art education systematically through the lens of the social psychology of creativity. But, the lived-experience of that assignment of 13 years ago—particularly the experience of problem-finding as negotiated with a partner, the delay in closure on defining the problem, and the power of choice to foster intrinsic motivation—continues to reverberate through my current practice as an art museum educator. The next semester, I enrolled in Vera's course on "Creative Collaboration," and ultimately applied to the doctoral program in Educational Thought and Socio-cultural Studies, inspired by what I was learning in your courses.

Today, as I engage diverse visitors—elementary school children, international university students, and seniors—to the University of New Mexico Art Museum's exhibitions which range from "Man Ray, African Art and the Modernist Lens," to "Desire for Magic: Patrick Nagatani 1978–2008," "Through a Narrow Window: Friedl Dicker-Brandeis and Her Terezin Students," and "Re-Imagining American Identities," my practice reflects lessons learned from Vera's teaching. To clearly articulate the social nature of our relationship, I greet visitors on their arrival at the entrance to the museum and escort them to the door as they depart. I speak of them as "visitors," and our time together as a "visit," not a "tour." I position myself simultaneously as the facilitator and as a learner in our small group dialogue about the work of art by sitting in a circle on the floor with younger visitors or on museum stools with university students and in which the work of art is included.

We begin in silent, sustained seeing after which I gently invite them to share their observations and thoughts. University students have written about "how tranquil the room was" and how this centered or focused their attention on the art work. Collaboratively, we begin to construct an interpretation of the work of art as participants share prior knowledge and life experiences while building on each other's ideas. As Vygotsky (1971) wrote, "Art…brings the most intimate and personal aspects of our being into the circle of social life" (p. 249). A University student reflected that "the opinions and thoughts of others...made me think deeper about the piece and look at it in a whole different way." A sixth grader wrote, "I liked when we all sat down and discussed one painting. I heard a lot of other opinions and ideas that I never would have thought of." And, even a second grader told me that "you discover a lot from each other." Next, I send the students off with an art partner to choose a work of art with which to engage and have a conversation. Modeled after Vera's Peer Examination, students have the opportunity to choose a work that intrigues them and to explore it in depth with a peer. Elementary school children have confirmed that they "like that because we got to work together and it made it kind of easier." When I asked, "How does it make it easier?" one girl responded, "Cause we get to help one another understand it better." Artistic collaboration between like-minded participants, like that between theater director and playwright Bill Conte and choreographer Suki John, may lead to a state described by John as, "Ideas create ideas, it is like ping-ponging" (John-Steiner, 2000, p. 79–81).

Your work reminds us that, critical to such a relationship is the "need to learn to listen carefully to each other, to hear their words echoed through those of the collaborator, and to hear the words of the other with a special attentiveness born of joint purpose" (John-Steiner, 2000, p. 190). When we encourage young children to slow down and listen to each other and to what the works of art may ask of us, even second and fourth graders can enter into a similar synchronous state in which they finish each other's sentences as these art partners did in a kind of poetic duet while engaged with Pueblo pottery:

There's art in the sky, the constellations
    ...clouds...
...even the sun's rays.
    Everywhere you look, there's art, on the bottom of your shoes...
And there's color...
    ...when you step on the sand...
how the mountain's colors change from purple to green...
    the sky...when the sun sets.

Through the intense partnerships that you documented in *Creative Collaboration* (2000), partners "may develop previously unknown aspects of themselves through motivated joint participation. The collaboration context provides a mutual zone of proximal development where participants can increase their repertory of cognitive and emotional expression" (p. 187). My work with museum visitors who are engaged in focused dialogue toward a shared goal—the interpretation of a work of art—demonstrates the potential for even short-lived collaborations. When we as educators acknowledge this promise and provide our students with opportunities to co-construct knowledge with their peers, we all benefit. Students from middle school ("The tour made me be able to look into the **soul** of a painting and its meanings.") through university ("The most meaningful experience I had at the museum was when we discussed and focused on only one picture. It really opened everyone's eyes and got them thinking.") routinely write about such experiences as "life-changing."

More than any profession, teaching shapes the future. How fortunate for us all that you have been a teacher and generously shared with her students, her collaborators, and those she has never met but who have learned from her scholarship. Those of us in this volume are only a fraction of a much larger thought community that you have inspired. In concert with you and the ever-expanding community of like-minded individuals, your work has made we can continue to make tangibly real what you meant when you said that "together we create our futures."(John-Steiner, 2000, p. 204).

Fondly and with gratitude,
Sara

SARA OTTO-DINIZ, PhD., is an art historian and educator at the University of New Mexico's art museum. She specializes in providing meaningful engagements with works of visual for art museum visitors of all ages by tapping viewers' multiple modalities.

REFERENCES

John-Steiner, V. (2000). *Creative collaboration*. New York: Oxford University Press.
Vygotsky, L. S. (1971). *The psychology of art*. Cambridge, MA: MIT Press.

LETTER FORTY-FOUR
Collaborative Re-creation
Rod Parker-Rees

Dear Vera,

I heard you talk about your book *Creative Collaboration* (John-Steiner, 2000) in Bristol, shortly after it was published. I was deeply impressed by your accounts of conversations with artist, scientists and academics whose collaborative activity often extended well beyond the public surface of their work. I was reminded of your book recently when I joined a discussion on the *XMCA* (eXtended Mind, Culture and Activity) forum about *perezhivanie*. I had noted that much of the discussion about the importance of this concept seemed to focus on suffering, stressing the formative role of crises and traumas. The English verb 'to suffer' and its more Anglo-Saxon equivalent 'to undergo' are etymologically close to the root meaning of *perezhivanie* but they have both, to different degrees, shifted from the neutral sense still associated with 'to experience' towards a meaning which is more redolent of pain, hardship and grief. My own understanding of *perezhivanie*, based largely on Vygotsky's lecture on 'The Problem of the Environment' (Vygotsky, 1994), is more inclusive, incorporating the whole range of nuances, connotations and associations which are gathered up in the unique history which shapes an individual's emotional experience:

> The emotional experience [*perezhivanie*] arising from any situation or from any aspect of his environment, determines what kind of influence this situation or this environment will have on the child. Therefore, it is not any of the factors in themselves (if taken without reference to the child) which determines how they will influence the future course of his development, but the same factors refracted through the prism of the child's emotional experience [*perezhivanie*]. (Vygotsky, 1994, pp.339–40)

When we look back at our own childhood we tend to pay attention to 'stand-out' events and to credit these with a special role in the development of our adult identity, this is how attention works, but I wanted to suggest that our *perezhivanija* also include the routine, day-to-day events which inform our sense of what is ordinary or to-be-expected. It is only by comparing events against this 'baseline' of what happens 'as a rule' that we are even able to sift out and remember exceptional events and special occasions, so any discussion of *perezhivanie* should, I felt, acknowledge the formative influence of neutral and happy events as well as crises and hard times.

Andy Blunden, in a later post (2011), offered the following quotation from Vygotsky's *Educational Psychology*, which might seem to challenge this suggestion about the formative role of ordinary experience:

> People with great passions, people who accomplish great deeds, people who possess strong feeling, even people with great minds and a strong personality, rarely come out of good little boys and girls. (Vygotsky, 1997, pp. 232)

He added, 'I think the same goes for "happy little boys and girls"'. We have to acknowledge that 'good little boys and girls' may have had a particular significance for Vygotsky, writing in post-revolutionary, Stalinist Russia, but this quotation reminded me of your focus, in *Creative Collaboration*, on the ways in which 'people who accomplish great deeds' are supported by the dynamic flow of ideas, arguments and discussion which circulate in thought communities which may also include a proportion of 'good little boys and girls'.

In *Creative Collaboration* you focus on the outstanding achievements of extraordinary people but you show how these accomplishments are grounded in the day-to-day processes of living and working together; extraordinary deeds are rooted in ordinary experiences and outstanding people need friends and colleagues who can understand them. This argument is a particular focus for your chapter on 'A chorus of voices: women in collaboration', in which you contrast the individualist, 'isolated mind' model of traditional psychology with the more relational, collaborative, distributed model which you documented in the working practices of groups of feminist writers. Vygotsky's comment about 'good little boys and girls' reminded me of your argument that 'male-type autonomy is only possible when scaffolded by caregivers and partners—often women—who support the man's questing for fulfilment' (John-Steiner, 2000, p.106). Of course you point out that the gender distinction between autonomy and caregiving is socially constructed, not biologically inevitable, and you emphasise the functional advantage which comes from the flow of ideas between people who each have their own, complementary ways of thinking. As an example of this partnership you offer Cecile De-Witt-Morette's observation that her physicist husband described his mind as 'extremely focused, like a spotlight' while he saw hers as 'a more diffuse floodlight'. This distinction echoes the physiological differences between the left and right hemispheres of the cerebral cortex (McGilchrist, 2009) and in each of us, as in this intimate relationship between partners, the sum is greater than the parts. We are born already equipped with the potential for different kinds of thinking but close collaboration with familiar others also allows us to learn and to borrow a rich variety of different patterns of thought.

You describe Barbara Rogoff's way of working with her community of doctoral students and post-docs as 'a family approach to collaboration in which rules are flexible, newcomers are carefully socialised and values are negotiated and shared (John-Steiner 2000, p.172). The trading of cool, common meaning (*znachnie*) alone cannot engage the full benefits of distributed intelligence; to really understand another person we must reach a point where we also know them well enough to be able to read the sense (*smysl*) of what they have to say (Mahn & John-Steiner, 2002) and this seems to require an investment of time in relatively unstructured, social interaction.

Carey Kaplan writes about the process by which she and her collaborator, Ellen C. Rose, 'learned each other' by exchanging weekly letters which included 'gossip and daily-ness as well as intellectual exchange' (John-Steiner, 2000, p.97). This sharing of the whole self seems to be essential for the formation and maintenance of a thought community because it is by immersing ourselves in the ordinariness of daily interactions with another person that we are able to 'take them on board', to internalise their voice so that our *perezhivanie* can be modulated by our awareness of what they would have to say. Janet Surrey captures this when she writes that an effective mother-daughter relationship depends on a "capacity to learn to "see" the other and to "make oneself known" [which] highlights one's own self knowledge and fosters growth in the other and in the self. Thus "mutual care-taking" is a fundamental aspect of learning' (Surrey, 1991, p.58, as cited in John-Steiner, 2000, p. 128). The ordinary 'daily-ness' of this mutual care-taking enables us to incorporate and understand the different sense (*smysl*) which different others can be expected to attach to the common meanings (*znachenie*) which make up a particular culture. When we engage with others in relaxed, recreational activity we also contribute to the renegotiation and re-creation of these shared meanings, keeping culture flowing, alive and connected to the felt experience of participants.

When I worked as a nursery teacher, with three- and four-year-old children, I was constantly reminded of the value of time spent 'just chatting' with children and parents, particularly at meal times and on days out and now, working in a university, I can see how working relationships are supported by the 'daily-ness' of social chat over coffee. When we talk about a 'meeting of minds', I think it is important to recognise that minds extend well below the public surface of what people say or write. Another Russian word, *obuchenie*, alerts us to the relative narrowness of the common meaning of the English words 'teaching' and 'learning', both of which can sometimes be used to translate it but neither of which fully captures the sense of a meeting of whole selves, closer, I think, to Surrey's 'mutual care-taking'. At one of the wonderful summer schools jointly run by the Lev Vygotsky Institute of Psychology, the International Vygotsky Society and the Russian State University for the Humanities in Moscow, I was able to experience the rich mix of learning, talking, eating, drinking and dancing together with a group of academics from various countries, Russian students and lecturers from the Vygotsky Institute. The summer school allowed participants to hear about the application of Vygotsky's ideas about the place of play in learning but, by encouraging us to get to know each other around and outside the programme of lectures, it also allowed us to collaborate in the recreation of our understanding of how these ideas still live in the values, interests and concerns of today's Russians. You have shown how thought communities can help brilliant people to cope with the pressures and risks of exposing their ideas to public scrutiny but you have also identified how the seemingly unimportant, marginal processes which I am calling collaborative recreation weave the webs of shared sense out of which new, creative meanings can emerge.

ROD PARKER-REES worked as a nursery teacher before joining Plymouth University to co-ordinate Early Childhood Studies programmes. As co-editor of *Early*

Years: An International Journal of Research and Development since 1999, Rod's research interests include playfulness, cultural historical theory and pre-verbal communication.

REFERENCES

Blunden, A. (2011). Post to 'Notions of suffering, enduring, undergoing' thread. *xmca* November 05 2011 @ 06:11http://xmca.ucsd.edu/yarns/14180?keywords=#44726

John-Steiner, V. (2000) *Creativecollaboration*. Oxford, UK: Oxford University Press

Mahn, H., & John-Steiner, V. (2002). The gift of confidence: a Vygotkian view of emotions, In G. Wells and G. Claxton (Eds.), *Learning for life in the 21st century: Sociological perspectives of the future*, (pp.46–58). Oxford, UK: Blackwell.

McGilchrist, I. (2009). *The master and his Emissary: The divided brain and the making of the western world*. New Haven, CT: Yale University Press.

Vygotsky, L. S. (1994) 'The problem of the environment' in R. Van der Veer & J. Valsiner (Eds) *The Vygotsky Reader* (pp. 338–354). Oxford, UK: Blackwell.

Vygotsky, L. S. (1997). *Educational psychology*. Boca Raton, FL: CRC Press.

LETTER FORTY-FIVE

Coming into Being
Creative Collaboration as a Life-Long Gift
Judah Ronch

"Humans come into being and mature in relation to others." (John-Steiner, 2000, p. 187)

Dear Vera,

This celebration of your work as teacher, mentor and scholar is a most fitting and well-earned tribute to your intellectual and creative achievements. I am so honored to contribute, especially as the nature of your influence on me would have been totally impossible to predict when we first met in 1966.

In retrospect, the essence of your influence on me was evident very clearly on a personal level but not immediately evident in my work. I realize that despite your sincere efforts at the time, I just didn't get a lot of what you were teaching me. I listened, but didn't think I really "heard" it. Like the poet David Whyte, I have come to look at work as "a pilgrimage of identity" (Whyte, 2002), so I see that despite not having been your best student, your generous spirit and profound influence provided me with the basic tools to undertake the journey to "come into being" wherever it took me. Neither of us could have imagined that the start you gave me would be such a powerful influence that frames how I approach changing the culture of aging services through undergraduate and graduate teaching, research, leadership development, policy consultation, and how I have been able to address the philosophical basis of education is provided to the long-term care workforce.

As I re-read *Creative Collaboration*, the extent of your gifts as a teacher become more evident, especially since I am sure that most of the lessons I learned from you in the classroom were absorbed outside of my conscious awareness but have informed my work overall these years. You characterized the theoretical framework of your work on collaboration as "a life span approach. Social cultural, historical and biological conditions together contribute to the realization of human possibility" (John-Steiner, 2000). Let me share with you how in two eras of my life separated by thirty years your influence helped me "realize what was possible."

THE PERSONAL/STUDENT ERA

In May of 1966 you interviewed me when I applied to Yeshiva University's Master's program. Despite my less than stellar undergraduate grades you spoke positively about how I would like it at YU since it was a good fit for my values. I wondered how you knew my values, and you replied that you guessed them from my resume—by where I had worked and my activities in college. This being the turbulent sixties, and being just about to turn 21, it was so comforting for me to know that sympatico folks (at YU and at Einstein Medical School where I worked in research) could be role models and mentors in what was becoming an anxiety-filled world.

I was put at ease during the interview by your sweet voice, easy manner, genuine smile and warmth. The word "seductive" comes to mind to describe your effect and since many language scholars will read this, I want my meaning not to be misinterpreted. Your charisma defined the conversation and the relationship. Your poise, warmth, humanism and genuine interest in me felt like the welcoming embrace of family. In your calm, assertive way you became for many of your students the strongest creative and moral force in our education. When I was accepted into the ("your") new Language and Behavior Ph.D. program (once again thanks to you), I felt an even greater level of acceptance by you; I felt like I had arrived. I didn't realize how close I came to disappointing you and not fulfilling any possible promise you saw in me when I was admitted.

The late sixties were both politically and personally chaotic for many of us, so the goal was to make progress toward a degree. I continued to put one foot in front of the other as I trod down the path of "becoming" a Ph.D. and, due to what I now see as poor self-awareness, thought I was doing OK. One day my mentor and your colleague, Vivian Horner, told me and another likewise insouciant classmate the words that changed my life: "Dr. John thinks you two are a pair of screw ups (but she didn't use the word "screw"), but I don't think you are." I was horrified. (I later learned that this was called a "corrective emotional experience", and corrective it was!) I was so thankful that Vivian had taken that risk to try to set me straight. The idea that I had disappointed you made me get serious about school and pay attention to the reality that I had responsibilities to you, and all the others who believed in me. I had taken the first steps on my pilgrimage of identity to being an adult student.

A year or so later I joined the faculty at Vassar College in Poughkeepsie. I heard that you were pleased—I was very proud that I could honor your decision in this way. Our final meeting was at my oral defense in 1971, when you were, as always, supportive, kind, comforting and the leader. (Thanks for asking Marshall to go downstairs for the celebratory bottle of wine so you could open it when I passed the exam.) Just as at our first interview, your graciousness and charm infused this closing phase of our initial relationship as student and teacher. Our relationship went dormant, only to be revitalized again thirty years later.

THE PROFESSIONAL ERA

After four years at Vassar, my pilgrimage of identity took me to postdoctoral training in clinical psychology. In 1975 I relocated to Miami, Florida, and through a series of circumstances that made my magic circle even wider and richer, I became a specialist in aging. There were few of us then, and I certainly had not been educated about aging while in graduate school. Though I was a novice in gerontology, my background in language and cognition gave me particularly valuable insights into how persons with Alzheimer's disease and related dementias thought and communicated. Many of their behaviors were not merely dementia-based "noise," but instead evidence that they were trying to make meaning. I worked with caregivers to look for the meaning in the errors of speech and behavioral "misses" those with dementia demonstrated. The therapeutic model we developed relied on caregivers and those with dementia becoming co-creators of meaning as best they could. In looking back I now realize how your lessons had taken deep root and guided my work. I just didn't have the conscious awareness of how deep this influence was until in 2000 when I came upon *Creative Collaboration* and found you again.

Happily, I devoured the book and we reconnected by phone in early 2001 (thanks to the magic circle again) and we caught up on the thirty years that had passed.

> "The construction of a new mode of thought relies and thrives on collaboration." (p.7)

> In Vygotskian terms, partners create zones of proximal development for each other. (p.189)

Your influence on the architecture of my work jumped off the pages of *Creative Collaboration*. Reading it had a galvanizing impact on the work I was doing to change the organizational cultures of long-term care settings where elders live. It gave me a research based mental model and provided me with a vocabulary to make a more powerful argument about why the long-term care workforce had to have an *equal* voice to play a powerful role in changing aging services. The evidence and logic you presented provided the basis for a new argument that the women who made up the majority of the paid workforce in aging services brought unique cognitive and psychosocial skills to their work. This was transformative to how management saw them, and how they saw each other. Your work identified strengths upon which culture change advocates could build new, person-centered cultures of care through the use of adult-focused models of education that involved active learning, problem solving to create work places where social construction of knowledge built communities of practice (Ronch, 2003).

Our goal at the Erickson School is to promote developmental (vs. declinist) aging using models of collaboration that take advantage of what you termed "constructive interdependence."

> There are some collaborations across generations in which the younger collaborative partners have skills and backgrounds which are complementary to that of their mentors...They occupy a dual role, that of learners as well as that of equals within the partnership. (p.174)

We recently completed a project with freshmen students and elders who co-produced digital video stories about their life transitions and the wisdom to be gleaned from them. I am also working with colleagues to examine the critical role that language plays in the psychosocial experiences of elders and their caregivers.

My work has stressed that person-centered, strengths-based care of elders requires that the elders are collaborators with staff and families, because "productive interdependence is a critical resource for expanding the self throughout the life span" (p.191). Elders are not merely passive recipients of care services. That is how the highest quality of life and highest quality of care are sustained. They co-create meaning in their collective lives.

In our last conversation, when I knew that you were pleased with what I had accomplished, I asked you why you admitted me to graduate school. I imagined you would say something about a latent talent you saw back then. You replied to my question by saying sweetly: "I couldn't bear to see you get drafted." Thanks for embracing me, and for starting me on a pilgrimage of identity that allowed me to make a difference in the lives of my students and those elders I cared for as a clinician (and I do remember that you were opposed to us going down that road). Thank you for allowing me to carry forward your partnership with me. Your magic circle—and mine—continues to grow as my students set out on their respective pilgrimages.

Your life is a powerful testament to your own statement that the self expands throughout the life span. Know that you have my most heartfelt gratitude for your singular collaboration in my pilgrimage of identity, and profound respect for your body of work. I am so fortunate to have you in my magic circle.

An embrace over the many years and miles,
Judah

JUDAH L. RONCH, Ph.D., is Dean and Professor at the Erickson School of Aging Studies at the University of Maryland, Baltimore County. His major areas of professional activity are clinical geropsychology and mental wellness in aging, dementia care, culture change in long-term care of the aging, the role of language in aging services organizations, and worker empowerment in aging services.

REFERENCES

John-Steiner, V. (2000). *Creative collaboration.* New York: Oxford University Press.

Ronch, J., & Goldfield, J. (Eds.). (2003). *Mental wellness in aging: Strengths-based approaches.* Baltimore: Health Professions Press.

Whyte, D. (2002). *Crossing the unknown sea: Work as a pilgrimage of identity.* New York: Riverhead Books.

LETTER FORTY-SIX

The Schools Have Failed the Poor

Carolyn Panofsky

The "behavioral consequences of living in poverty cannot be adequately studied without reliance upon a *generalized theory of the social environment.*" (John, 1971, p. 64)

Dearest Vera,

I almost cannot believe that it's been 30 years since we first met! It was the summer of 1982 and I was newly admitted to the Ph.D. program then known as Educational Foundations at UNM. I had discovered your work a few years earlier and hoped that you would be willing to be my advisor. Margaret Vasquez-Geffroy had given me a copy of your monograph, written with Helgi Osterreich, "Learning Styles among Pueblo Children," and I felt that for the first time I was finding the kind of work that could help answer the questions I had been struggling with as a teacher of writing and reading to students from historically under-served groups.

That summer of 1982, I signed up to take a course at the Santa Fe Graduate Center and discovered that you were the Director there. So, as the saying goes, I "screwed up my courage" and made an appointment to meet with you. I recall being very nervous, worried that I would fail to persuade you to be my advisor. My recollection of that first meeting, however, is that the meeting was nothing like what I expected. You seemed genuinely interested in talking to me about my work and in being my advisor. I was a bit mystified and also elated. After our conversation, I felt too excited to go to the uninspiring computer class I was taking; of course I went but had trouble concentrating in class that afternoon!

I set out to read whatever else I could find of your writing. Two early discoveries, along with the study of Pueblo children, were your chapter in Eleanor Burke Leacock's volume, *The Culture of Poverty: A Critique* ("Language and Educability," John, 1971), and your co-authored piece in *Harvard Educational Review*, "An Interactionist Approach to Advancing Literacy" (Elsasser & John-Steiner, 1977). It's disheartening to say that your opening line of the piece in the Leacock volume could still be said today. You wrote:

> Although the children of the poor are the focus of much public and academic attention, they are still but gross statistics to most university scholars. The statistics most often emphasized in the press as well as in research applications and reports relate to the dropout rate among minority youth, the "achievement gap," youth unemployment, and the much discussed "family instability" syndrome. (p. 63)

It's now forty years since you wrote that, and these are still things we hear about all the time. You argued in that piece that the "behavioral consequences of living in poverty cannot be adequately studied without reliance upon a *generalized theory of the social environment*," and you suggested that research to that time, even when acknowledging the crucial significance of the social environment, had either used the flawed approach of facile comparisons across classes, based on middle class norms, or of using "deprivation" as an explanatory variable. You commented that such attempts "can best be characterized as post-hoc explanations of statistical findings. They are not theories" (p. 64). Today, one might be less polite and characterize such work as biased, ethnocentric, and racist, but probably such words would not have been used at the time, especially in print. Your article hinted that social class, like culture, cannot be treated simply as a "variable"; I found this thought particularly intriguing, and your suggestion was probably way ahead of its time!

In that piece, you addressed various ways that the language of poor children was misinterpreted, devalued, denigrated, and suppressed. At one point you proclaimed with understated force: "The message that emerges is: *the schools have failed the poor*" (p. 72). Again, words written forty years ago, but sadly true today. While in some ways the educational discourse has changed since then, it's not hard to argue that in most ways the conditions of inequality remain the same or have grown worse, despite much wonderful and creative work by great scholars and activists both in and out of the cultural-historical community.

In that piece you did something else that I continue to find memorable. You referred to the linguistic power and eloquence of "spokesmen of the poor": Cesar Chavez, Reies Tijerina, Fannie Lou Hamer, Malcolm X, and along that line you quoted at length from Facundo Valdez, who had been the head Office of Economic Opportunity in northern New Mexico and whom I had met at Highlands University, where I had also taught. The intermingling in that piece of voices from across domains, what Bakhtin would call heteroglossia, was striking, though I could not have explained it then.

At the time that I discovered this piece, I remember the excitement of discovering ways of naming phenomena I "knew" from experience but had no language for. I was beginning on a journey that was finally leading me to the kinds of knowledge I had been seeking on my earlier rather meandering path of graduate study.

I had also found a mentor. But really more than a mentor, for (compared to "mentors" I used to hear about from other doctoral students) you were a mentor of exceptional generosity. And I'm not referring to all the lunches you treated me to—though those were wonderful, too! Significantly, you were especially generous as a scholar involving an aspiring new-comer in the practice of scholarship, providing the opportunity for true apprenticeship in the sense of Lave's definition of learning as "increasing participation in a community of practice" (1996). Sometimes the participation was even more than I "wanted" at the time, as when you offered this second author to give the conference talk at a BU child language conference: I didn't feel "ready" to do that, but also knew that I never would feel ready! And your generosity extended to first-authorship in publishing with many of your students: how rare that is in the academy!

But the most important part of those collaborations was undoubtedly the dialogue. We have had so many wonderful talks over the years, sometimes recorded, as we worked out the ideas, the examples, the metaphors, the argument of a piece. As Vygotsky would surely agree, that kind of free-wheeling, speculative, exploratory, not-always-goal-oriented discourse is most important in creating a context for learning and for generating new ideas. And something else, too: such contexts may be an ideal space for giving the gift of confidence. Long before the time that you (and Holbrook Mahn) were writing about the "gift of confidence" (Mahn & John-Steiner, 2002), you were ever so generous in giving such gifts.

I continue to be inspired by the need for a "generalized theory of the environment": it is the theme that guides all my work. And I continue to be inspired by all that I learned from you, whether about Vygotsky or creativity, cognitive pluralism or collaboration. But you have also been a source of inspiration beyond knowledge: your generosity as mentor and your gifts of confidence are a model for any teaching. Although it may seem to some that your later work on creativity is far from your early studies of learners in poverty, the threads of connection are clear to those who know you and your work: you have always been working against deficit views, and against nativist and individualistic theories, to build increasingly powerful understandings of the workings of the social environment and the profound interactions between culture and nature. All your work has helped to highlight differences between what is and what could be for all learners in schools, for the importance of all learners and all modes of expression, for the possibilities of truly meaningful learning and personal transformation.

I look forward to many more great times and great talks when we find ways to cross paths in New Mexico or Massachusetts or other points in the world!

With love and affection,
Carolyn

CAROLYN P. PANOFSKY is Professor of Educational Studies at Rhode Island College. She has taught in the areas of social and cultural foundations of education, teacher research, and qualitative research methodologies for 25 years drawing on scholarship on various issues of language, literacy, power, and schooling using a socio-cultural framework.

REFERENCES

Elsasser, N., & John-Steiner, V. (1977). An interactionist approach to advancing literacy. *Harvard Educational Review*, 47(3), 355–369.

John, V. (1971). Language and educability. In E. B. Leacock (Ed.), *The culture of poverty: A critique* (pp. 63–80). New York: Simon & Schuster.

John-Steiner, V., & Osterreich, H. (1975). *Learning styles among Pueblo children*. Final Report to the National Institute of Education. Albuquerque: University of New Mexico, College of Education.

Mahn, H., & John-Steiner, V. (2002). The gift of confidence: A Vygotskian view of emotions. In G. Wells & G. Claxton (Eds.), *Learning for life in the 21st century: Sociocultural perspectives on the future of education*. Oxford, UK: Blackwell.

Lave, J. (1996). Teaching, as learning, in practice. *Mind, Culture and Activity, 3*(3), 149–164.

LETTER FORTY-SEVEN

My Noble Quest

Annalisa Aguilar

"Some books are part of one's life for many, many years." (John-Steiner, 1997, *Notebooks of the Mind*).

Dearest Vera,

It has been a while now that I shared with you my first encounter with *Notebooks of the Mind*. It was in 1987. I was in my 20's and looking to find my way in the world. I had purchased your book from a used bookstore on the street where I grew up in San Francisco. I paid $12, which was a lot of money for me at the time. It was in pristine condition and I even remember where I saw it on the bookshelf. Its cover had that lovely deep turquoise blue. I did read it, but admit that it was difficult for me because it was in academic language. I couldn't understand all of it, but knew someday I would. Despite that difficulty, I remember feeling something in my heart, that there was a great truth woven in the words, and if I could just sit with it I would receive it. Magical thinking, I know, yet there was some effect like that. Your book planted the smallest seed: Specific forms of creativity were not innate things, but general creativity was. If one could be in a hospitable environment, with teachers and mentors, if *I* wanted to be creative, there was certainly a chance for me, as for anyone. The sadness that came with this new view on creativity was the realization that growing up, I had not had mentors or teachers who had developed my creativity in the way that you vividly described in the lives of all the wonderful "experienced thinkers" in *Notebooks*. My own creativity was invisible to me.

Before that, I had attended the University of California at San Diego, and majored in Pure Mathematics. We were in a recession and everyone was worried about finding a job after graduation. My parents had not gone to college and there was no one to tell me what to expect, how to study, or what to prioritize. At Revelle College, my peers were declared chemistry, pre-med, electrical engineering, physics, or some other science majors. I had a part-time job, and the intensity of studying, with which my peers were deeply committed, was extremely intimidating. I couldn't sit in the library until midnight, as they did.

An acquaintance, a physics major, had gotten her final exam back and she told me she received a 92 of 100. That was a B+. It gives a sense of what the curve was at UCSD. I didn't understand. Doesn't one go to university *to learn?* If one did well on the test, then one got a good grade, but this other system seemed to say nothing about learning. It was required for someone to accept a C, even if we all did equally well. By that time, I felt I was treading water. I must not be smart enough to play the game. Given that I am not a competitive person, if I was to put myself through such a painful experience, I wanted to know what it was going to be for. I had asked around, "What can one do with a Bachelor's in Pure Math?" I had met only one woman with my major, so I there weren't many peers to clue me in. I didn't want to be a Math teacher, and my grades wouldn't be good enough to become an academic. The only other thing anyone could tell me was that I could do statistics. Well, that person might as well said I could feed elephants, I did not know what it meant. What was a day in the life of a statistician? I never did find an answer.

So to be practical, I decided to drop out and go to fashion school. People would always need clothing, and it was creative, but in a practical way. That was my thinking at the time. I certainly used math, and dealing with vectors and curves and the sliced geometric shapes that I studied at UCSD I suppose helped me become a decent patternmaker. Strange that. It was at that time I purchased your book. I had just finished getting my certificate in Fashion Design, and I was working my real first job for a dress manufacturer as a fabric use analyst. After about two years, I became disillusioned by that industry for its exploitation of women, on many different levels. Then, I worked a short time as a porcelain doll designer for a Taiwanese gift company. I went to Taipei on a design trip and witnessed the poor conditions that the workers there experienced. Not long after, I traveled to New York City to the Gift Show and was dismayed by the sheer amount of meaningless objects that companies were selling as gifts. On the flight back to California, I recall looking out the plane window thinking about the consequences of these two scenarios. The workers in Taiwan would make all these tchotchkes that would be in gift stores in a few months, in someone's garage sale in a few years, and in landfill in a decade. I was contributing to that.

I began my search for something more noble.

In hindsight, it was your book that helped me gain the courage to apply to art school. I attended the San Francisco Art Institute and studied fine art photography. As your book promised, I saw myself develop a sophisticated eye because of the creative culture in which I was immersed. I learned to see. I thrived in an environment where we were occupied with solving problems that have no right answers, something that was foreign in my experience at UCSD. With mixed feelings, I can say that I received a good education there, but to be a working artist, I did not possess the connections nor the political nose to get into galleries. Having grown up working class, I could not even begin to fly with wealthy art patrons and their sybaritic ways, nor did I want to. When I graduated, I was closer, but still had not found the noble thing for which I was searching.

I was fortunate to land a job for a British software company. I was hired merely to answer the phone in the California time zone. It became uncomfortable not to be able to answer the questions that were asked of me about a very sophisticated software tool. I pummeled my boss with my own questions and finally came to learn the product. I wrote press releases and white papers, went on business lunches with movers and shakers, and came to fully grasp that computers were changing everything. What was far more important, looking back, is that I spent hours teaching myself to use the office Macintosh. It was the only unrestricted access I had ever had to a computer.

Eighteen months later, the company went belly up. I sequestered that office computer and I taught myself HTML. Startups were everywhere. The dot-com boom was in full swing. I built some websites. It was an exciting time and no one knew what lay in store with the Internet. After working in a few more startups, even one that sold a device to send smell over the Internet, I became disillusioned with the world of technology. I was tired of the layoffs, the newness at every turn, the hype that this would be a better world all because of the computer. I was not convinced. The world was becoming more fragmented as people became alienated by their gadgets. I still hadn't found what was noble. By this time, I had a better idea that I wanted to live a simpler life than I had witnessed in the ebb and flow of the Internet gold rush.

In an existential crisis, I went to India for a few months, and I witnessed an amazing culture. I saw that people with nothing could be happy. Things were made by hand. I saw that values had helped to shape who I was, and that I needed to understand better what I valued. I moved to Albuquerque hoping to slow down, to get distance from so much technology. For four years I tried my luck in a stenography program. I did not get anywhere with it. I desperately decided to duck into a graduate study program. This is how, and why, I ended up at the University of New Mexico in the Organizational Learning and Instructional Technology program. Slowly, my interest in technology became alive again because I discovered how I might leverage technology as a means to help others learn whatever it was they wanted to learn. But none of this so far is the clinching part of my story.

It must have been the Spring of 2009, I was walking into Hokona Hall, and I spied a flyer that looked just like the cover of *Notebooks of the Mind*. I stopped in my tracks. It was the flyer for your Creativity Seminar. I recall I said out loud to myself, "Oh! She's HERE!" *Notebooks* was still a treasured book. I made a mental note that I must take that class and meet you. I was dismayed not to find anything taught that Fall, yet near the end of that term, there it was, your flyer for the Vygotsky Seminar posted on the same pillar as the other one had been. It wasn't the Creativity Seminar, but something told me I had better take this class. That winter break before the spring class started, I re-read *Notebooks* and it was as though I had returned from where I began when I read it the very first time so many years before.

Vygotsky Seminar was a wonderful class. It was life-altering. Your knowing eyes would always catch someone's smile, which would trigger the phrase from you, "You're smiling." This would invite the most quiet among us to comment and to contribute.

Reading Vygotsky with you was a scholarly experience I will never ever forget. The longing that I had, the hunger for intellectual pursuit was made whole. I may not have had the society growing up, which Vygotsky so emphasized as key to development; however, my yearning for discourse was not misplaced, it was a basic human need. My search was not misguided, but a desire for society and interaction that was motivated by curiosity, by compassion, by consciousness. Certainly, I could mourn the lost opportunities, but I could now abandon the belief that I was indigent from wanting to live a life of the mind and to share that life with others. It was good and right to want those things.

It was not only those resplendent class seminars, but the generous time you spent with me at office hours, the occasional luncheon, the phone conversations, the e-mails you wrote after reading revisions of my thesis. It was your investment of time that was the essential ingredient to foster my own confidence. You found my ideas worthwhile and you let me push with my questions and my doubts.

You listened with your eyes.

At the end of every rendezvous, you would always craft the most marvelously shaped thoughts, which I would carry home, clutching them close to my chest. As I would go to sleep that night, I would admire their glittering beauty in the darkness.

Your shining insights helped me to realize that all the things I had done, all the things we all do, was in response to one's history, culture, society, and environment: It was the love of books that my mother instilled in me, from a childhood of going to the public library, that allowed me to find you. It was my distrust that test scores mattered or that competition was productive, as well as the lack of guidance, that impelled me to leave university, and from that I could come to know your own caring mentoring and value for collaboration. It was my resistance to participate in the manufacture of want and desire in objects of vanity, that led me to witness your efforts to foster confidence in my peers and that made me unashamed in my desire to do well by others. It was my disappointment in the economy of art and my doubts about the mythology that the artist is born not made, that carried me to your seminars where I learned that creativity is not an innately objectified noun, but a socially developed verb. It was my suspicion about the substance of the dot-com bubble, that prepared me for our talks concerning technology and the ways that tools mediate mind. All of these apparently disappointing life experiences that spurred me on, helped me find you, and it was you, my beloved teacher who helped me uncover the true meaning within those life experiences. There is a comforting symmetry to this, the symmetry of a circle. By a kind of grace, before I ever knew you, for many, many years your book inspired my search for what is noble. This must have been you.

> I'm so glad it was you.
> Brimming in paedeia,
> Shining in gratitude,
> Kindling for the future,
> Thank you.
> *Annalisa Aguilar*

ANNALISA AGUILAR is a determined advocate for friendly, useful technology who seeks to integrate cognitive science theories into technology design. While walking on the beach, Annalisa frequently imagines conversations between Vera John-Steiner and Lev Vygotsky.

LETTER FORTY-EIGHT

Grateful Recollections from Your Zone of Proximal Development

Kathryn (Kate) J. Miller

"The process of growth requires resolution of the contradictory tensions between the social embeddedness of learning and the creative individual's drive toward a personal voice. When a young artist or scientist begins upon a unique path by declaring his or her identity…he or she needs the assistance of others to overcome the limitations of a single view and to face public criticism or rejection. The demands of solitary work are coupled with those of participation with others in their creative fields through the lifespan of gifted individuals." (John-Steiner, 1997, p. 208)

Dear Vera,

I am deeply honored to be writing this letter to you, as our relationship has been transformational in my life. When I first met you, I had this sense you were likely to change my life and there would be both challenge and reward in the process.

Before we met, your students spoke of you with awe. Many said, "You'll fall in love with Vera—students fall in love with her all the time." It is no wonder, you brought such a generosity of spirit and wisdom—a kindness matched by high standards which were a stretch, ones for which I am grateful. Even when I did not feel like an insider in the academic environment, you showed me a vista that helped create my way and keep the long view in sight.

I found a note I had written in my copy of *Notebooks of the Mind*, "Remember Vera's image of '…being a guest in the house of academics.'" You fit so gracefully and practiced your art and craft beautifully. You looked so at home in the academic landscape and deeply invested in new knowledge and research into areas at the edges of new thinking—creative collaboration is but one example. I was fortunate to be one of your students and I knew it then and even more clearly now. Your understanding of what to say at just the right time in this environment (e.g., "I have always been a visitor") helped me in seeing I could also discover my place. Your insights facilitated my finding direction and focus; stretching my sense of who I was and who I could be in a land that felt unfamiliar—yet some part of me knew academia was not my permanent place of residence. I felt your partnership, collaboration, and a practiced nimbleness as you guided me along my way.

You gave me room to be myself and added generously to my thinking, nudging me to broaden my own, helping me tease apart my own concepts. Our conversations brought me fresh points of view—I was often challenged by your abilities and never doubted how much you cared. You helped me see I might have something of value to say and consistently urged me on. With you I learned the value of care along with challenge.

Vera, over time I learned about the power of language through your eyes and I hope I have used that learning well, learning to use a client's language in order to aid their new process of thinking and development.

Since I completed my doctoral work, I have often worked with technical and scientific individuals in private industry—a primary focus of mine as an organization development practitioner and Executive Coach. Some of these senior leaders have made their own transitions from academics to corporate environments—pulled by the possibility of having a greater impact and increased possibilities in their fields of expertise.

The demands on these individuals can be challenging. The challenge for the individuals who work for them can be equally as demanding as the lesser experienced leader develops his or her leadership voice. My own lessons learned with your mentoring regarding narrative structure, zone of proximal development, collaboration have served me to take a necessary step back and again see, feel and hear the long view speaking. It is unlikely one individual scientist will create a cure alone for a deadly disease, however with collaboration these talented individuals can create breakthroughs as they work with other scientists on their teams—all of them differently remarkable and all very necessary to reaching their ultimate goals.

With you, Vera, I learned to pursue lines of thinking that allowed my partnership with clients who were experts in their fields and needed to gain skills in leading an organization while creating connections with the people they were hired to lead. I have learned to see creativity in the light of spontaneity, connection—holding the light as well as holding the space for their scientific passions to gain new footing in their worlds. Although these individuals were not novices in their field, at least not as I have known them, I at times have asked them to bring a beginner's mind to our work together. As working through others is uniquely different than depending on self and expertise to move to where you want to go independently.

As you so generously engaged me in deep conversations, I bring the concept of care along with challenge to my clients. I have seen academics move from significant university settings and research centers into private industry that drives for results and has jarring time frames. Yet that transfer of knowledge is critical and the willingness to learn in the new environment—a new culture—may be even more difficult when one has been acknowledged and admired for their expertise over years. Again, the issue of care and challenge; to learn to hold the light, yet not lower the bar, and to remind these individuals "yes it is possible" and "you may be the only one that can do this". Yes, I learned this with you.

The concepts you and I have discussed have opened new and valuable avenues of thinking with these experienced scientists. What would an experienced leader or distant teachers advise? This thoughtful reflection can and often does give additional vitality to the research and work in process. Even a distant or deceased teacher still gives support even when they no longer can be a present directly as mentor—providing a useful scaffolding to build upon. You have written about this in *Notebooks of the Mind*.

In the need to discover their own teachers from the past, there is recognition that work of another evokes a special resonance in them. Once such a bond is established, the learner explores those valued works with an absorption which is the hallmark of creative individuals. In this way, they stretch, deepen, and refresh their craft and nourish their intelligence, not only during their early years of apprenticeship, but repeatedly throughout many cycles of their work-lives. (John-Steiner, 1997, p. 54)

Your insight here was accurate then and speaks so clearly now.

As I have looked back over our relationship I realize your finely tuned expertise as mentor created a unique smoothness in your approach. I did not recognize how you were teaching me about "zone of proximal development" almost from the first moment we met. And when I began talking about how zone of proximal development had application with adults you smiled and nodded knowingly. You were consummately gracious and graceful with this "beginner". I am grateful for that patience and persistence.

As I worked with you as you developed the original Q-sort for your book on collaboration I saw stunning examples of creativity and perseverance. It has been fun to read back through those words and realize how many of them were descriptive of how you behaved with me as my chair for my dissertation. Examples include:

When you didn't think I was experienced enough in some area, you were cautious in the way you challenged my ideas. You definitely spurred me on to complete my project. It felt at times I was able to talk with you at the speed of thinking. Even when I wasn't able to keep up with your thinking, you always made room for me. The talks we had together did add enthusiasm to my work. I felt I had autonomy and freedom as we worked together.

It was a unique to know what these examples meant to research and education since I had experienced them in real time. I use these concepts regularly and make my attempts to model what you so beautifully modeled for me.

Although I have always had an active inner life, Vera, you helped me punctuate that inner landscape with valuable external experiences pressing me to deepen my thinking, helping me find questions that "itched" my life, and discover the value of the questions themselves. I often thought both to myself in my inner dialogues and with you in our discussions, "Where do questions come from?" Those thorny questions were an integral part of my learning with you. It was certainly your patient and reflective conversations with me that opened doors and windows, allowing new thinking to flow through.

Thank you for your scholarship and belief in the value of collaboration—something our world needs so badly in these days—you were at the cutting edge of that understanding. Thank you for your friendship. So many thanks for the significant contribution you have made in my life and in the life of so many other students who have benefited from your scholarship and gracefulness. Thank you for the knowledge you have added to our world and for your care and challenge along the way.

With love and appreciation,
Kathryn (Kate) J. Miller

KATHRYN J. MILLER, Ph.D., PCC, is a Senior Partner with the Design Training Collaborative and serves as an Executive Coach and Organization Development Practitioner to corporations, not for profits, and schools. She teaches with the Academy of Coaching and Neuro-Linguistic Programming.

LETTER FORTY-NINE

Vera and the Gift of Confidence

Holbrook Mahn

Vygotsky emphasizes a theoretical approach, and consequently a methodology, that telescopes change. His effort in charting developmental change is, in part, to show the psychological implications of the fact that humans are active, vigorous participants in their own existence and that at each stage of development children acquire the means by which they can completely affect their world and themselves. (John-Steiner & Souberman, 1978, p. 123)

Dear Vera,

Over the two decades of our collaboration, I have had the privilege to learn from you in a number of different capacities: as a doctoral student, a research collaborator, a mentee, a co-author, a co-teacher, and as a friend. As a graduate student in your classes at the University of New Mexico, I would sit in wonder as you clearly expressed complex thoughts by constructing equally complex sentences, which reached Joycean proportions as clause built upon clause, yet syntactical integrity was always maintained. Like my fellow doctoral students, I found myself having to choose between trying to take notes to capture your thoughts and risking losing the train of thought or eschewing notes and trying to following the train of thought and risk missing key points. As our collaboration developed, I was able to accompany you on our joint flights of thought that engaged complex topics with equally complex sentences. However, you also had the knack of conveying a lesson in the shortest of sentences. Three particular instances come to mind.

The first was during our first writing collaboration, a book review of Cziksentmihalyi's *The Evolving Self*, for the *American Journal of Psychology*. While I appreciated his book, *Flow*, I found his prescriptions for social change laid out in *Evolving Self* to be naïve, especially since I had spent two decades before embarking on my doctoral studies at UNM working full-time in movements for social change. Much of the writing that I did during that time was polemical and that style carried over into the draft of our book review. You indicated that you agreed with the critique, but added, "But he's my friend." This was an important lesson for me about the nature of academic discourse, and also underscored the collegiality that has marked your entire career.

The second instance was in our next writing endeavor, the article "Sociocultural Approaches to Learning and Development: A Vygotskian Framework," which appeared in *Educational Psychologist* (1996). As we were going over a section on methodology for which I had responsibility, you commented on a sentence I had written about "the mind reflecting reality" by saying, "I don't think that we need to introduce Lenin's theory of reflection." Because I was so surprised at hearing this statement from a professor in the College of Education and because I did not have Lenin's statement in mind when writing that sentence, I remember just nodding in agreement as I found myself speechless. We had not talked much about our individual political backgrounds, but there was a common appreciation of Marx and Engels' influence on Vygotsky's work. As I reflected on your statement, I learned two important lessons. First, was the need for precision in the language used to describe mental processes. This attention to the precise meanings of words, especially in relationship to language and thinking, has been central to my work as I have explored with you the meanings of the Russian words Vygotsky uses to explain his central concepts, particularly *znachenieslova*—meaning through the use of language—and *perezhivanie*—the way in which experiences are emotionally perceived, appropriated, and understood. The second lesson your comment on Lenin drove home to me was the danger of taking the writings of a great thinker and applying them willy-nilly to a different discipline. In describing the relationship between Vygotsky's theoretical frameworks and that of Marx and Engels, there is a tendency within sociocultural theory to apply Marx and Engels' writings on economics and the laws of motion behind human social formations to the study of the human psyche.

From the beginning of our collaboration, you have emphasized the importance that Vygotsky placed on developing methodological clarity. In doing so, he relied heavily on the methodological approach developed by Marx and Engels, but he cautioned that one could not just take the specific method that Marx and Engels used to analyze human social formations and apply it to the study of the human psyche. He critiques this approach in *The Historical Meaning of the Crisis in Psychology: A Methodological Investigation* when discussing the way that "Marxist" psychologists attempted to find a methodology "ready-made in the haphazard psychological statements of the founders of Marxism" (1997, p. 312). Adding that this approach of taking phrases out of context and using them polemically to bolster an argument yields nothing "more than a pile of more or less accidental citations and their Talmudic interpretation. But citations, even when they have been well ordered, never yield systems" (1997a, p. 313). I always appreciated the emphasis you placed on using a systems approach to analysis.

The third instance of a lesson learned through a short sentence of yours occurred after we had been collaborating for a number of years, when you gave me a draft to review of a chapter to appear in *Creative Collaboration*. After I had read it and made marginal annotations, we had a meeting to discuss the chapter. I went through my comments and questions and after about 10 minutes, you stopped me and said, "But did you like it?" I think that was the most embarrassing moment I have had in our collaboration. As a writing teacher of second language students, I always made it a practice to begin my written or oral comments to students with praise. And as a professor I have always emphasized in my teacher education courses on second language writing the importance of finding something concrete in students' writing to praise. However, I forgot this important advice when discussing your chapter with you. It drove home the need we all have, whether students struggling to write in a second language or an internationally renowned scholar, to hear authentic praise. I still use this anecdote in my writing classes to underscore the importance of praise.

This incident also underscored the importance that you place on the influence of emotions in human cognitive development and in social interaction. I came to appreciate this in the course of writing the chapter "The Gift of Confidence" together where we drew from Vygotsky's work on emotions and then applied it to second language writers. Beyond the intellectual emphasis on emotions, you bring the ethos of care to all of your relationships, whether it is with students, colleagues, friends, or family. I have been fortunate over the last two decades to be a recipient of this ethos of care and have learned from you what it means to be a thoughtful, caring human being. We used a quote of Elkonin's about Vygotsky to introduce our "Gift of Confidence" chapter, which I invoke to conclude this letter, because I feel it equally applies to you.

Lev Semonovich possessed an extraordinary ability to give support. I have probably never met a single person who was so little interested in proclaiming his own authorship as Lev Semonovich. It was the extraordinary generosity and scope of ideas of the kind of person who gave everything to everyone. (Elkonin in Vygodskaya & Lifanova, 1999, p. 37)

HOLBROOK MAHN, Ph.D., is Associate Professor in the Department of Language, Literacy, and Sociocultural Studies at the University of New Mexico. He currently directs the Academic Literacy for All Project to enhance the content literacy of middle and high school students.

REFERENCES

John-Steiner, V., & Mahn, H. (1996). Sociocultural approaches to learning and development: A Vygotskian framework. *Educational Psychologist, 31*(3/4), 191–206.

Mahn, H., & John-Steiner, V. (1996). Psychological uses of complexity theory. Csikszentmihalyi's *Evolving Self. American Journal of Psychology, 109*(3), 465–475.

Mahn, H., & John-Steiner, V. (2002). The gift of confidence: A Vygotskian view of emotions. In G. Wells & G. Claxton (Eds.), *Learning for life in the 21ˢᵗ century: Sociocultural perspectives on the future of education* (pp. 46–58). Cambridge: Blackwell.

Vygodskaya, G. L., & Lifanova, T. M. (1999). Part 2: Through the eyes of others. *Journal of Russian and East European Psychology, 37*(3), 32–90.

Vygotsky, L. S. (1987). *Problems of the theory and history of psychology. The collected works of L. S. Vygotsky* (Vol. 3). New York: Plenum Press.

LETTER FIFTY

Vera
My Inspiration for Discovering the 'Invisibilities' in the Activity-Theoretical Studies of Innovation

Mervi Hasu

"A crucial advantage of collaboration is the strength it provides to overcome one's socialization into a discipline and a thought community. Ludwik Fleck wrote that knowledge is constructed among a 'community of persons mutually exchanging ideas and maintaining intellectual interaction.' In joining such a group, the new member must appropriate its governing ideas. These ideas become part of the belief system of the participant. When faced with new facts, it is difficult, sometimes wrenching, to loosen the hold of these concepts and frameworks." (John-Steiner, 2000, p. 119).

"The very effort to work together, to risk an undertaking that is so different from the norm, is a creative act." (John-Steiner, 2000, p. 204)

Dear Vera,

In an important phase of my professional life, you, Vera, gave me a social gift, a "sign" of confidence in more strongly expressing myself as a researcher. You showed me the way, and gave me the strength, to become a researcher who does not deny her subjectivity, her gender in particular, in her research work among the scholars of the cultural historical activity theory tradition. This social gift has not only benefitted my own personal and work life, but also that of the close female colleagues with whom I interacted while I was reinventing my identity.

Life is full of surprises, and introduces us to people that we never expect to meet. Even a short or infrequent interaction may become significant in a particular moment of a person's life, for instance when she or he is in a reflective mode, in search of something new or different to what is already familiar. My own search for "something different" led me to you, Vera, a meeting that turned out to be very significant for me.

Our paths met almost accidentally; as a by-product of other, more intentional interactions between you and my close colleague Eveliina Saari. The 'triad' comprised you, a distinguished Professor of Linguistics, and my colleague and me, Finnish doctoral students in the same professional situation. In a way, this triad was the kind of (extended) dyadic partnership you discuss in your works.

I have not met you many times in person; perhaps ten times or less. Still you are among the people to have had the greatest influence on my work as a researcher, and definitely among the ones to influence my most significant scholarly re-orientations.

THE INTERSECTING TRAJECTORIES OF OUR LIVES

Our first common denominator is Professor Yrjö Engeström for whom I wrote my Master's Thesis at the University of Helsinki, and the prominent founder of the Helsinki group of activity theory. The Helsinki group emerged gradually in the late 1980s, made up of a group of friends and colleagues. It drew particularly from Leontiev's thinking and Engeström and his colleagues' theorizing and modeling of the activity system and expansive learning (Engeström, 1987). When the Ministry of Education and the Academy of Finland first started funding for doctoral graduate schools in Finland in 1995, Professor Engeström, at that time acting professor of Communication at the University of San Diego and associate professor of Adult Education at the University of Helsinki, applied for and was granted four-year full-time funding for ten doctoral students. This achievement was noticed and praised in the international scientific community, and it boosted the identity and expansion of the group.

I was among the ten students who successfully applied for a doctoral student's position and funding, and who witnessed—but did not quite understand as yet—the significance of the coming together of international researchers in Helsinki during the first years of the graduate school. It was all very new then: reading texts in English and discussing them with doctoral students in San Diego via e-mail. I'm sure your name was mentioned but I did not recognize you then, during the very first years of the Helsinki school. Later you visited us.

You were part of the already established scientific community of cultural historical research, and I assume that you knew Professor Engeström at least somehow, probably through Michael Cole, the common contact between you and Yrjö. I can imagine now that you and others in the established cultural historical community were curiously interested in the newly born Helsinki group. You must have looked at it, through a participant or eye-witness' eyes, as part of the emerging variations of applications of Russian psychology. You had "been there" yourself, developing this research tradition you had seen how it had spread and taken on various nuances. This is something which I hardly understood then: how the variations of the cultural historical school were *alive*. To a doctoral student in Helsinki in the mid-1990s, the roots of the cultural historical school were mostly relics: badly translated cryptic texts. Variations of the cultural historical tradition were not actively taught; they were often seen as different generations of activity theory.

It was through Yrjö Engeström's guidance that first my colleague, and myself soon after, came across your influence in New Mexico, Albuquerque. When we met I was a third-year doctoral student in the first group (class of '95) of doctoral students of the Helsinki graduate school. My colleague had the opportunity to stay in New Mexico for several months, while I was only able to stay two months, to conduct ethnographic fieldwork as part of our PhD theses. Spending the summer of 1997 together in New Mexico was a unique experience for me and my colleague, and it created a mutual interdependence (an important concept in your works) and trust between us, which continues today. We had the opportunity to meet you at the University of New Mexico, and later in your adobe home in Santa Fe in 1997.

I like to think now that from your point of view we were two examples of the kind of intellectual and collaborative spirit of the relatively new and expansive Helsinki group. If that was indeed the case, we did not see it. We were puzzled by everything around us. Somehow we did not quite know how to deal with your generosity when you invited us to celebrate your birthday party in your beautiful home in Santa Fe. We discussed at length whether we should really accept your invitation. We were almost afraid to come and meet your friends, and had great difficulty in finding our way to your home. However we somehow managed to drive to Camino Rancheros. We brought a large salad bowl as a gift, and the ingredients for a salad, which we prepared in your small kitchen. It was my favorite salad and I still remember exactly what the ingredients were. The memory of the almost spiritual atmosphere of the evening is still vivid. We listened—not able to contribute much because of the language and social barriers—to the sparkling intellectual conversations between you and your friends and colleagues. We felt like two aliens dropped into the middle of an intellectual wonderland! Looking back now, our hesitation seems ridiculous and pitiful. But I am happy that we took the risk and joined in the interaction, despite our limited capacities.

I wonder if already then you looked at us—the two precarious female PhD students from Finland—with a curious and empathic eye, interested in our development as individuals and as part of the Helsinki group. After all, you, Vera, Veruschka, had also once been in our situation, with English that was not so fluent. I remember you expressing your admiration for us because we had been able to negotiate (because our written English was quite good) our way to conduct extensive ethnographic field work in the US. You said to your colleague: "The Finns are well-organized." We felt your support although you did not underline it in so many words.

To two learners of academic discourse, you represented something very special, a true intellectual of the 'old times'. Your calm and humble self-confidence impressed me. There was something distant, queen-like in your behavior on the one hand, but something very ordinary on the other: for instance you gave us detailed instructions for our *Thelma and Louise* road trips south of Albuquerque. I felt then that when you spoke, it could have been printed text, it sounded so clear and structured. More important, you represented a connection to another—perhaps more nuanced—way of viewing cultural-historical theory.

MY MENTOR AND SUPPORTER OF SCHOLARLY TRANSITION: DEVELOPING THE NOTION OF 'SENSITIVE ETHNOGRAPHY OF CHANGE'

I did not really familiarize myself with your ideas during my visit to Albuquerque, since I was occupied with my hands-on ethnographic fieldwork in the VA Hospital. I dwelled deeply in the view of the materially (instrumental, tool/artifact) mediated activity framework that was taught to us in the graduate school in the mid-1990s. The Helsinki school of activity theory introduced us to the extensive list of founding 'fathers' of socio-cultural theories, I found the situation very peculiar. There were no founding 'mothers' presented to us, no independent women role models for the female doctoral students who formed the majority of doctoral students.

Apprenticeship is a license to learn with and from a more advanced peer at first, and then later, to take an independent builder path and move forward. Doctoral candidates and supervisors are not in an equal relationship in terms of collaboration. Inherently, at its best, the relationship forms a powerful, creative tension: in many ways, two different worlds collide. A wise supervisor may gently nudge the apprentice to make the move forward and challenge or even oppose what has been previously taught.

So when Yrjö Engeström asked me in the spring of 2001 to review your new book *Creative Collaboration* for the *Trends in Cognitive Sciences* journal, it marked a turning point in my apprenticeship and began the process of reinventing my identity. I assume that the journal had first asked him to write the review. I do not know if it was a coincidence that he asked me to do it, but I like to think that he believed I was the right person for the job. I took it willingly and delved into your text. There I discovered a different world of cultural historical tradition at play. I realized that I had found a founding 'mother', who labeled many matters with names, which I felt had been lacking. The emphasis on semiotic as well as relational and emotional signs in mediation, the focus on relationships and dyads, and elaborations on subjectivity, experience and interdependence in creative endeavors (with a feminist flavor), written in such a fascinating manner, watered the drying land into which I had entered. I felt as though you were talking directly to me through your book. Consequently, I entitled my review "The Power of Interdependence", thus recognizing both the empowering as well as the suppressing potential of interdependence. The review was published in the August 2001 issue (Vol. 5, No. 8) of *Trends in Cognitive Sciences*.

After carefully reading your book, I started to see my own application of cultural historical activity theory with new eyes. I began to reinterpret some of my data analysis and critically reflect upon my former voice and ways of writing as a researcher and ethnographer. I was inspired to parallel my subjective experience in the expansive, male-dominated research group with the experiences of the women users of complex technology that I had witnessed in my ethnographic fieldwork. I developed a methodological re-orientation for activity-theoretical analysis, called 'sensitive ethnography of change'. It is inspired by your thinking of the socio-cultural and feminist theories. My article was published in *Mind, Culture and Activity* in 2005. The appreciation of an ethnographer's 'hands on' practice, not only as a data-producing machine, but also as a theory-builder started to gain ground among the research group. A stronger practice of ethnographic authorship began to spread among my colleagues. Work along these lines still goes on today.

THE CASE OF THE WHITE LINEN TROUSER SUIT (ANECDOTE)

One of our interactions has a very special meaning for me. You were invited to Helsinki to act as an opponent for Eveliina Saari's public PhD defense in the late spring of 2003. I had the pleasure to be your host the day after the event and celebrations. We had lunch together and discussed the future prospects of the Helsinki group, which seemed to be at a crossroads, in a critical transitional phase. I had already finished my own PhD and I opened up to you about how I was worried about the future of my career in the group. I am afraid I was not in a very cheerful mood. We went out to do some shopping together. I assisted you in buying a raincoat in Helsinki's best department store, Stockmann. As we were trying to find the raincoats, you stepped aside to look at a collection of women's outfits. I thought you were looking for something for yourself, but you quickly picked out an outfit and asked me to try it on. It was an expensive white linen designer trouser suit, the color of apple blossom. I tried it on but did not intend to buy it. You looked at the suit on me and insisted I buy it, saying: "You look gorgeous. You will regret it if you don't take it." I ended up buying the suit although I couldn't really afford it. Your well-developed sense of style had picked me out a timeless outfit.

Almost ten years later, I still use the white linen trouser suit in the summer-time. The last time I wore the suit I gave a speech to an audience that comprised "work-pairs of organization and business developers," namely, top executive managers and second-rank managers in charge of the development function in their organizations. My speech was about creative dyads, and I drew from your thinking. I amused myself thinking that every piece was in place in the presentation; even the outfit of the presenter was chosen by the scholar whose work was cited. I felt confident when I got dressed and left home that morning. What made me feel comfortable and confident was not just the beautiful suit itself. It was the social gift that I received when you encouraged me to buy it. When I wear my white linen trouser suit I always think of you, and the gift of confidence that you gave me.

Mervi

DR. MERVI HASU is Specialized Researcher at the Finnish Institute of Occupational Health (FIOH). Her research is focused on social innovation in various private and public sector service contexts, employee-driven innovation and well-being in innovation implemented in various industrial and business contexts ranging from the traditional machinery industry, subcontractor networks, science-based spin-off firms, and user communities.

REFERENCES

Engeström, Y. (1987). *Learning by expanding: An activity-theoretical approach to developmental research.* Helsinki, Finland: Orienta-Konsultit.

John-Steiner, V. (2000). *Creative collaboration.* Oxford, UK: Oxford University Press

LETTER FIFTY-ONE

Finding Myself in Vera and Finding Vera in Me

Linney Wix

"In their need to discover teachers from the past, there is recognition of the importance of an intense and personal kinship that results when the work of another evokes a special resonance in them"(John-Steiner, 1997, p. 54) Autumn into Winter, 2011

Dear Vera,

As you know, I visited your homeland this year. I traversed bridges spanning the Danube; traipsed around Buda Hill visiting the National Gallery, the palace, the churches, even the underground labyrinth. I toured the Jewish Quarter and the synagogues, found museums both large and small, and took a bath. Over and over again I imagined you as a young girl at home in your city. It was easy for me to see you making your way from Buda to Pest or ambulating along the river's edge with a friend. You pervaded my thoughts as I wandered the streets of your city, and I loved imagining you in a time before war tore apart your world. Having caught a glimpse of your early years in my imagination, I marvel at all you have done and been for so many in the years between then and now.

While I laud your mighty contributions to sociocultural theory and practice and your passionate thinking and writing on creativity and collaboration, it is our multi-faceted relationship that has stretched me beyond who I knew myself to be. In my professional and personal life, you have served and continue to serve as mentor, teacher, colleague, co-author, and occasional lunch companion. In every role, besides being brilliant, you have been thoughtful and kind, deeply influencing me in my own roles as mentor, teacher, author, and world citizen.

When I came to your 1998 Thought and Language course, perhaps oddly, I arrived a tenured faculty member amid losing the art therapy program, the reason I was at the University of New Mexico. The course had me, an artist, sitting among vociferous thinkers in a small room in the education building that no longer exists. I was intimidated by merely thinking of studying thought and language yet adored your eloquent lectures and your sharp remarks in response to over-zealous students. The idea of inner speech captured my imagination and became central to my final work involving painting and poetry. Both informed my understanding of thought and language as I practiced painting as a way of thinking and poetic language as congruent with my ways of knowing.

Inspired by your vast and deep knowledge, I persevered, taking one course after another through Psychology of Creativity and Psychology of Women. Entering each with trepidation, as I moved into and through the coursework, you and your teaching informed me in ways I hadn't known in my educational career. In each course you validated me as an artist and a thinker—you an astonishing and respected scholar—confirming my attempts to understand myself in an educational system that didn't seem to work yet in which I both taught and studied. Influential in each course was your mid-term peer exam, which I tend to call a peer pondering process.

In Psychology of Women you suggested two classmates with whom to sit for the exam. My peer partners, Po and Sarah, were straight talkers who meshed and wove their words with mine. Our required visits became conversations in which we responded to one another rather than trying to out-talk each other. We were down to earth, attuned to the feminine, not just feminist but rather deeply feminine in our ways of knowing and being together in our thought community.

We ended up painting together—making ours a painting and thinking community. I'm not sure how it happened, but every Friday morning for an entire semester, usually at Sarah's huge glass dining room table, we painted while we talked and talked while we painted. Our words mixed easily as we pushed paint around on cardboard. Our relationships with each other and with myriad matters and ways of knowing deepened as we gave form with art materials to ourselves, to each other and to mutual caring. Besides painting, we enacted our evolving relationships: I remember a morning when I wrapped and covered my partners in sun-soaked sheets. Ours was the ultimate co-laboring, a definitive "mutual connecting" (John-Steiner, 2000, p. 200). This experience of inter-dependence and building relationship through painting and talking was a pinnacle in my education—the experience was transformative: the three of us held each other, took each other into ourselves. While regular meetings provided the container for the essence of the experience, we could not have done it, could not have held each other in the ways we did without being held by you. You held us while we moved farther into relationship with one another, contained individually and as a group by you. There was something deep and pure in the tenderness among us—and the "us" included you.

In ways like this your teaching affected who I became as a student and continue to become all these years later as a professor. The relationship between you and me in the teaching and learning contexts you created support me in becoming the person and teacher I strive to be: committed, tenacious, hopeful. Psychological roots that underlie your teaching and thinking and mine provide shared ground. Perhaps this is part of what is transformative in my learning from you: the heart of your teaching, and mine too, is psychological manifestation in and of human relationships. This relational heart appears in our work together: in your teaching me, yes, but also in our writing. It's natural to me that we wrote about your peer exam. It's natural because of the exam's deep relational roots. Its focus on co-constructing knowledge through dialogical peer inquiry (and art) processes is core to the work of making sense of the psyche and thus for me has to do with psychological self-knowledge. Too few in education understand this, and too many fear it.

Recently you and I discussed problems with the peer exam, how some students misconstrue the intended experience. Perhaps the problems reflect a continued denial of "the long-neglected role of peers in constructing knowledge" (Wix & John-Steiner, 2008, p. 218) and an outdated reliance on producing for a teacher. Performance-based education has pervaded too many students, whose concentration is limited to a grade. Students thus pervaded seem unable to engage in processes that examine their ways of knowing in relational learning contexts. Other students, like "Sasha" in our article, come to know the experience as deeply meaningful in co-constructing self-knowledge. For me, "Sasha" captured the core of the peer experience when she wrote,

> Reciprocal relationships were everywhere, so obviously interconnected.... These relationships expanded within me and created space; the more full I felt, the more space opened up: space for image, for points of view, and for being. (Wix & John-Steiner, 2008, p. 223)

Based on our conversation on problems encountered in the peer process, I hope in the future to better craft my words to encourage students to open to the engagement with others, to experience the process as psychologically expansive in the ways "Sasha" did.

As meaningful as studying and writing with you have been, I remain ultimately moved by your writing for *Through a Narrow Window: Friedl Dicker-Brandeis and Her Terezín Students*. In the foreword you weave your scholarship into a fresh context when you write that in learning about Dicker-Brandeis's teaching of art to children in a concentration camp,

> ...we experience the power of creative engagement in a unique way, by viewing and witnessing paintings created under life-threatening conditions.... To create is to go beyond restrictions of habit, pain, terror, and the known. It requires a continuity of concern, an absorption in shaping experience in a novel and moving manner. (John-Steiner in Wix, 2010, p. ix)

You note Dicker-Brandeis's aim to encourage "her students to work collaboratively, a process that prompted them to rely upon each other as sources of strength and community" (p. x) and say that "Dicker-Brandeis achieved the delicate balance between interdependency and individual expression" (p. xi). With these words you connect the work done by Friedl Dicker-Brandeis to yours and ultimately to mine. I love that you built inter-relationships with Friedl and with me.

Themes core to your life work—creativity and collaboration, relationships and their reciprocities—characterize our work together. You entered my life at a time when I was vulnerable and have since steadfastly served as teacher and mentor. Your ideas on creativity and peer processes of collaboration directly affect my teaching and scholarship. The cups of lentil soup I offer these days are small gifts for all I have received from you.

Years ago, you introduced me to Bakhtin's words, "I cannot do without the other...I must find myself in the other, finding the other in me." The years of building and savoring our relationship have given me occasion to find a part of myself in you and a part of you in me. I treasure what we share.

With gratitude and love,
Linney

LINNEY WIX, Ph.D., is an art therapist and professor in the Educational Specialties Department at the University of New Mexico. An artist, curator, and writer, Dr. Wix investigates the role of art and peer processes in the social construction of the self.

REFERENCES

Bakhtin, M. (1981). *The dialogic imagination: Four essays.* Austin: University of Austin Press.

John-Steiner, V. (2000). *Creative collaboration.* Oxford, UK: Oxford University Press.

John-Steiner, V. (1997). *Notebooks of the mind.* Oxford, UK: Oxford University Press.

Wix, L. (2010). *Through a narrow window.* Albuquerque: University of New Mexico Press.

LETTER FIFTY-TWO

Creative Transformation through Mentorship and Intergenerational Collaboration

Sara Abercrombie

"Collaboration across generations reveals some of the most important features of human interdependence. It is built on mutual attraction and the establishment of effective emotional bonds, and on the realization that both learners and mentors can meet their goals and hopes together more fully than by solo activities." (John-Steiner, 2000, pp. 184–185)

"Through collaboration we can transcend the constraints of biology, of time, of habit, and achieve a fuller self, beyond the limitations and the talents of the isolated individual." (John-Steiner, 2000, p. 188)

Dear Vera,

As a graduate student at the University of New Mexico, I had a keen sense of anticipation when I enrolled in the first course I took with you, *The Life and Works of L.S. Vygotsky*. When, a few weeks into the course, it became apparent that we were both commuting over sixty miles one-way from Albuquerque to Santa Fe, and I was asked to join your carpool, I was excited and more than a little nervous at the chance to interact with you in a more intimate setting. I think it was during our many long rides up and down La Bajada that you became a great mentor, teacher, and friend. As the miles slipped behind us, I found my initial unease was unfounded in light of your generosity, kindness, and willingness to listen to my young ideas. Like the forces that shape the desert surrounding us, I began to learn from you how to tune in to the subtle processes shaping the landscape of our minds.

In *Creative Collaboration*, you described the ways in which collaboration across generations is mutually beneficial for the both the mentor and the younger collaborator:

> Collaboration across generations is an expression of hope. For the senior participants, who mentor and work with their younger students and colleagues, it provides continuity, a new embodiment of their knowledge. It also stimulates them to reach for transformative ideas with the help of energetic and questioning young colleagues. For younger part-

> ners, the advantages of intergenerational collaboration include a guided entry into the complex worlds of human achievement and the opportunity to closely observe an experienced thinker, indeed to witness that person's modes of thought. Young collaborators may learn from multiple mentors and distant teachers, using processes which are usually intricate—a mixture of admiration, of hard and, at times, repetitive work, and of rebellion. As well, they have the opportunity to appropriate what they have witnessed and been taught. (John-Steiner, 2000, p. 151)

As a new scholar, just beginning my academic career, your description of mentorship resonates deeply with me. As I write this, I am wrapping up my first semester out of graduate school as an assistant professor. Since my graduate training, I have paused to remember your words even more, and the words of the other great teachers in my life, as I navigate the complexities of the educational research community and find my voice as an independent researcher. Both my career path and my thinking have been strongly influenced by what you have taught me about the importance of research method. In *Notebooks of the Mind*, you demonstrate how focusing on the tools of the creative process, such as tentative ideas, initial sketches and analogies, journals, and notes, plus descriptive personal accounts can enrich our understanding of creativity as a construct and a human activity. In a broader sense, your research models the many ways in which we can deepen our understanding of the mind and human activity by choosing appropriate methodological approaches.

Your emphasis on the centrality of method in your teaching and research echoes and expounds upon the critical role method plays in Vygotsky's works; *"The search for method becomes one of the most important problems of the entire enterprise of understanding the uniquely human forms of psychological activity. In this case, the method is simultaneously prerequisite and product, the tool and the result of the study"* (Vygotsky, 1978, p. 65). Indeed, by focusing greater attention on the dynamic processes of learning, we might not only more keenly grasp how learning occurs, but develop forms of scientific inquiry more closely aligned to the complexity of the subject matter itself.

Your methodological approaches at once help us gain access to and develop a better understanding of the processes of the mind, and help demonstrate Vygotsky's concept of the dialectic method (John-Steiner & Mahn, 1996; Vygotsky, 1978). In this way, your theoretical framework, research, and teaching model an elegant, unified research program. In *Creative Collaboration*, through numerous interviews with artists, scientists, and other creative individuals, you documented how early experiences play a particularly salient role helping people develop passion and creativity (John-Steiner, 2000). These experiences include family rituals focusing around books and conversation; celebration of nature through walks, gardening, and other immersive experiences; and joyful and playful experiments in creating food, sketches, letters, and other objects. In many of our long car rides together, you would ask me about my own family, and how they might have influenced my own interests and creative goals. At times, I felt as if I was one of your interviewees, an experience that at once helped me reflect on my own childhood experiences, and illustrated for me the dynamic nature of interview research—since through sharing and discussing my experiences with me, you were teaching me about my own thinking and about the research process.

The creative process is, from a cultural-historical perspective, necessarily collaborative, since creativity is dependent upon synthesizing existing knowledge from diverse influences (John-Steiner, 2000). Intergenerational collaboration most clearly illustrates the centrality of collaboration as a human endeavor, since it marks the historical transformation of knowledge from parent to child, from teacher to student, from mentor to mentee, while simultaneously transforming the knowledge of the more senior collaborator. As such, intergenerational collaboration is indeed an expression of hope (John-Steiner, 2000), not simply that one's legacy will live on, but that through creative transformation of the thought landscape, we help move and expand the social mind through joint effort. Therefore, the study of the processes of creative collaboration across generations becomes a mapping of where we have been and where we are going, shedding insight into our history and guiding future generations.

The current volume is also an expression of hope as much as it is a celebration of your scholarship and the transformation you created with your "magic circle of family, friends, collaborators, and students" (John-Steiner, 2000). No doubt, you are and will be a distant teacher to many more not recognized in this volume. I feel very lucky to count you as one of my mentors, whose influence on my learning is still emerging. I know that if I am able to translate even a small part of what you have helped me learn to my own students, I will count my efforts a great success.

With love, gratitude, and hope,
Sara

DR. SARA ABERCROMBIE is Assistant Professor in the School of Educational Foundations, Leadership and Policy at Bowling Green State University in Ohio. Her research interests include multicultural teacher education, inquiry-based learning, and the relationship between cognition and assessment with a focus on formative assessment for higher-order thinking and transfer.

REFERENCES

John-Steiner, V. (2000). *Creative collaboration*. Oxford, UK: Oxford University Press.

John-Steiner, V. (1997). *Notebooks of the mind: Explorations of thinking* (rev. ed.). New York: Oxford University Press.

John-Steiner, V., & Mahn, H. (1996). Sociocultural approaches to learning and development: A Vygotskian framework. *Educational Psychologist, 31,* 191–206.

Vygotsky, L. S. (1978). *Mind in society: The development of higher psychological processes.* Cambridge, MA: Harvard University Press.

LETTER FIFTY-THREE

Enacting What We Sought to Understand
Michele Minnis

"Generative ideas emerge from joint thinking, from significant conversations, and from sustained, shared struggles to achieve new insights by partners in thought." (John-Steiner, 200, p. 3)

Dear Vera,

Although I have been writing solo six years now, and in a field remote from that of socio-cultural theory, my work continues to reflect your influence. For countless hours—over a full quarter century!—we collaborated. We thought out loud, planned research, and wrote papers together. The audiotapes of our meetings remind me of how we worked and what challenged and puzzled us. Here are bright memories of those times.

We met in autumn, 1981, when I was new in town and, in a career sense, adrift. My recently earned Ph.D. in behavioral psychology did not fit what I wanted to study: the interaction of thinking and writing processes. Someone who had read *Mind in Society* (Vygotsky, 1987) suggested that you might offer me direction. I wrote to you, we met over coffee, and you reached out. You suggested readings, invited me to your seminar course, and, when I said I would like to teach expository writing, suggested that I "check out the law school."

Before long I was teaching writing at the UNM School of Law. I was also deep into *Thought and Language* (Vygotsky, 1962) and other writings by, and inspired by, Lev Vygotsky. His emphasis on the socio-cultural context of learning struck home, as I was scrambling to learn the assumptions, vocabulary and pedagogy of legal education.

After sitting in on law classes, reading appellate court opinions, working with law students, and consulting their professors, I began to grasp the genres and standards of legal writing. Eventually, I developed a writing program for first-year law students. Having so recently felt myself a foreigner in the law school community, I was able to recognize in others a foreigner's discomfort. Many first-year minority students, for example, having grown up in rural or tribal communities, were unprepared for the individualistic, impersonal, and competitive law school culture. Expected to divine the rules of the road on their own, some of them were at sea—or, at least, behind the curve of their more broadly experienced and rigorously schooled classmates.

Shortly after the release of *Notebooks of the Mind* (John-Steiner, 1997) you and Carolyn Panofsky and Larry Smith created a book on socio-cultural approaches to language and literacy. You asked that I contribute a chapter on legal education, legal writing, and socio-cultural theory (Minnis, 1994). Here was a chance to discuss the socialization of lawyers, while also exploring the Vygotskian idea of the *zone of proximal development (ZPD)*. Coaxing me through many a false start on this assignment, you deftly demonstrated how a more experienced learner can scaffold a less experienced one across that zone.

Within year or so, we were working together regularly. Still at the law school and intrigued by cross-disciplinary exchange, I had joined the staff of Natural Resources Center (NRC), the research and public service arm of the school's *Natural Resources Journal*. Both institutions, the NRC and the *NRJ*, were multidisciplinary in character. At that time, the NRC was spearheading the establishment at UNM of a multidisciplinary master's program. It would address the manifold responsibilities of 21st century water managers.

Twenty-five faculty members from nine academic units and three research centers designed the *Water Resources Program*. Its curriculum centered on three courses taught by faculty teams. Team members were drawn from various schools and departments; for example, law, engineering, public administration, community planning, and earth & planetary, biological, and social sciences. The core courses were called *interdisciplinary*, as their aim was to help students *integrate learning* across the kinds of knowledge represented within the teaching team. How would that integration occur? Could one observe a *ZPD* from multi-disciplinarity to interdisciplinarity? These became burning questions for me, the communications instructor in all three courses.

Conversations with you, Vera, had sensitized me to the blinkering effect of disciplinary paradigms. It seemed to us that cross-disciplinary groups *could be* ideal for surfacing original insights about complex problems. You were well along in writing *Creative Collaboration* (John-Steiner, 2000) which inquired about human interaction that produced 'the new' (as against transmitting 'the known'). My contribution to this inquiry was a preoccupation with defining 'interdisciplinarity' in practical terms. As we later put it, "'[I]nterdisciplinary collaboration' is an idea in search of a concrete, instructive exemplar.(Minnis& John-Steiner 1993).

In the late 1980s, the AIDS pandemic and market globalization moved us to determine that we would observe sustained collaboration focused on consequential, cross-disciplinary problems such as these. An opportunity materialized when the NRC organized a research-design team to study the effects of global warming on the Rio Grande basin. The six team members—an ecologist, a lawyer, an economist, an engineer, a geographer, and me, representing the NRC—were released from teaching responsibilities for six months to concentrate on the task. Audiotapes of the team discussions produced a database, which inspired the two of us to seek a research grant to analyze the team's development.

That grant proposal, our first, taught us how to write together. I would be researcher and scribe; you would be expert reader and guide. This arrangement suited me fine. Between us, you were the scholar, and I had discovered that my best entrée into new disciplinary terrains was to write my way into understanding.

As mentor, you are the best. You listen. You direct, but gently. Most important, you persevere. We two have met to review a draft at least a hundred times. I am sure of it. You were there in the snow, when the streets were icy, when the postmark deadline loomed and we lacked the required signatures on our submission—proposal, conference presentation, book review, or journal article. Once, as we were scurrying to make a deadline, you fell ill with the flu. But you showed up anyway. Your daughter Suki delivered you to my office with a box of tissues and instructions about taking the pills she had packed. Never did you beg off, come unprepared, or fail to attend totally to the task at hand.

Later, when National Science Foundation funded "Collaborations: Values, Roles and Working Methods," we delved into theoretical questions. Attempting to 'scale up,' as the bioscientists say, we looked at collaboration both psychologically and sociologically, at the scale of the individual and at the scale of the group. We attempted to interweave Vygotskian theory and the sociology of science, especially, Giddens' (1986) theory of structuration.

How did we keep it all straight? Looking back, as in the following snippet from one of our tapes, both theories seem impossibly layered and folded.

VJS: [referring to a draft of our paper] Now, why are these paradoxical axioms?

MM: They are talking about something that is two things at once: it is a means and an end; it is a tool and the thing created by the tool. Seems to me that's paradoxical, because we tend to think of those things as separate.

VJS: In a way, they are and they aren't. First of all, I'm a little bit more comfortable with 'assumptions' rather than 'axioms.'

MM: 'Axioms' sounds a little bit more formal and fixed.

VJS: And axioms rely upon traditional logic; we are using a more dialectical logic. Let me just say very briefly that semi-stable systems, like the individual, are thought of as co-constructed relationships, so that, what has traditionally been a dichotomy, the individual and the social, is thought of as...one could say "are rooted in dynamic assumptions," perhaps..."In socio-cultural theory the assumption has been expressed as follows...," And we can quote Wertsch. [reading from draft] "The structural properties of systems are both the medium and the outcome of the practices that constitute those systems." That sounds very clear to me. So the dynamic assumptions, in a way, deal with...the structuration one with medium and outcome; and the socio-cultural deals with individual and social. *Both of them are dynamic assumptions, because they talk about the interpenetration of things that are traditionally dichotomized.* [emphasis added]

Through the NSF project we examined reported mutual suspicion between practitioners of the "soft" and the "hard" sciences. With Robert Weber, we wrote an article on collaboration (1998). Finally, through your synthesis, we produced "The Wheel," a model of relationships we had identified in collaborative groups. As a graphic, The Wheel is a set of nested circles, each of which represents a collaborative pattern. The continuum from the outermost to the innermost circle is one of increasing integration of knowledge. The whole figure is cut radially, from the 'hub' to 'rim' across the collaborative patterns, by 'wedges' representing our variables: values, roles, and working methods.

In the succeeding stage of our own collaboration we again attempted to connect theory to lived experience. This time, we were spurred by our (2001) essay review of *Perspectives on Activity Theory*, a compilation of contemporary research and theoretical writings inspired by the work of Vygotsky protégé A. N. Leontyev and by my co-directing three-week field trips to Honduras with the water program students.

For five summers in a row, groups of WRP students camped in mountain villages along the Honduran north coast and helped the villagers build on-site water delivery systems. Students and community members prepared and ate meals together. They played soccer together. Working side-by-side, they constructed small dams and concrete water tanks, and laid steel pipes to connect the two. *Through these activities*, it appeared, the students achieved interdisciplinary integration.

As explicated by Yrjö Engeström, one of the co-editors of *Perspectives*, cultural-historical activity theory offered a framework for discussing the integration of learning evident in the Honduran field trip experiences. It also motivated us to write conference presentations and journal articles, one of which is reprinted in *Issues in Integrative Studies* (Minnis & John-Steiner, 2006).

What a ride, Vera. You led me into and through this marvelous adventure. But so lightly did you lead that I never felt behind. Thank you! Un abrazofuerte.

Michele Minnis

DR. MICHELE MINNIS is a psychologist, professor, and writer who has worked in hydrosciences. An interdisciplinary scholar, she has brought her expertise in psychology, communications, and collaboration to the study and conservation of water.

REFERENCES

Engeström, Y. (1987). *Learning by expanding: An activity-theoretical approach to developmental research.* Helsinki, Finland: Oriental KonsultitOy.

Giddens, A. (1986). *Constitution of society: Outline of the theory of structuration.* Berkeley: University of California Press.

John-Steiner, V. (1985). *Notebooks of the mind: Explorations of thinking.* Albuquerque: University of New Mexico Press.

John-Steiner, V. (1989). Beyond the transmission of knowledge: a Vygotskian perspective on creativity. In R. Bjornson & M. R. Waldman, (Eds.), *Rethinking patterns of knowledge* (pp. 51–68). Papers in comparative studies 6, Center for Comparative Studies in the Humanities. Columbus, OH: The Ohio State University.

John-Steiner, V., Weber, R. J., & Minnis, M. (1998). The challenge of studying collaboration, *American Educational Research Journal*, 35(4), 773–783.

John-Steiner, V. (1998). University of New Mexico Annual Research Lecture.

John-Steiner, V. (2000). *Creative collaboration* Oxford, UK: Oxford University Press.

Minnis, M. (1994). Toward a definition of law school readiness, in V. John-Steiner, C. Panofsky, & L. Smith (Eds.), *Sociocultural approaches to language and literacy: An interactionist perspective* (pp. 347–390) New York: Cambridge University Press.

Minnis, M., & John-Steiner, V. (1993). Analysis of interdisciplinary collaboration in a global-change research team. Unpublished grant proposal submitted to the [U.S.] National Science Foundation, Science, Society, and Technology Studies Program, Ethics and Values Studies.

Minnis, M., & John–Steiner, V. (2001) Are we ready for a single, integrated theory? An essay review of *Perspectives on Activity Theory* by Yrjö Engeström, Reijo Miettinen and Raija-Leena Punamäki, *Human Development* 44, 296–310.

Minnis, M. & John-Steiner, V. (2004). *Interdisciplinarity in action: Integrated and experiential learning.* Presentation at the 25–26th Annual Conference of the Association for Integrative Studies, Johnson C. Smith University, Charlotte, North Carolina, October 13–17.

Minnis, M., & John-Steiner, V. (2005). The challenge of integration in interdisciplinary education. *New Directions for Teaching & Learning*, 102, 45–61

Minnis, M., & John-Steiner, V. (2005) . *Researchers and subjects as collaborators in interdisciplinary inquiry.* Presentation at First ISCAR (International Society for Cultural and Activity Research) Congress, Seville, Spain, Sept. 20–24.

Minnis, M., & John-Steiner, V. (2006). Interdisciplinary integration in professional education: Tools and analysis from cultural historical activity theory. *Issues in Integrative Studies*, 24, 32–88.

Vygotsky, L. S. (1978). *Mind in society: The development of higher psychological processes*. Cambridge, MA: Harvard University Press.

LETTER FIFTY-FOUR

Being Community
Engaging Struggles, Constructing Academic Lives, and Effecting Social Change

Lois M. Meyer

"So much was going on during those decades, especially in the 1960s, that in some ways it took our practice to lead us into our theory. History was happening intensely all around us, requiring a different understanding of human consciousness." (Vera John Steiner, Researchers' Dialogue with Courtney Cazden, held at the College of Education, University of New Mexico, 2004)

Dear Vera:

Time and its passage are very much on my mind as I write this letter. Only a few weeks ago, the year 2011 sheepishly slinked to its close, leaving many in this country and beyond unemployed, disappointed, despairing. Now a new year has announced itself. I wonder: Will 2012 really be new? How will it differ, other than its date, from the tired, old one? Is there really hope of change, profound transformation, in the year ahead? Or, despite the Arab Spring and the Occupy Movement, will this country and this society relentlessly reproduce its current barrage of foreign wars, political posturing, and yawning economic disparities, all in the name of democracy and national security? Will we continue to claim in vain that defeat and devastation are really "victory" and that a flutter of stars and stripes can conceal broken promises and missing limbs and deeply wounded spirits?

More personally, I wonder, "How will I, and my students, define ourselves, both professionally and personally, within the uncertainties, frustrations and foment of this time in which we live? Will we find the strength and the personal courage not only to observe or investigate the struggles of our time, but to join in, shoulder to shoulder, to create change?

It seems quite appropriate, Vera, to take time here to reflect on time and its passage, as I know that history and the importance of places, peoples, cultures and societies *in their historical contexts*, are of central significance in your life and your work, as they were in Vygotsky's.

Almost eight years ago, in March 2004, you and Courtney Cazden participated in a very special event at the University of New Mexico (UNM), a researchers' dialogue in which together you reflected on your now classic collaborative publication with Dell Hymes, *Functions of Language in the Classroom* (1972), and the historical and sociocultural context that generated that ground-breaking book. In your dialogue, each of you delineated the creative trajectories of your individual lives before and especially since you joined forces on that book's publication. In preparation for writing this letter, I revisited the DVD of that fascinating dialogue, reflecting anew on the inspiring interwoven yet distinct biographies and collaborations that have formed you and Courtney as professionals, collaborators, and also caring friends across these many years.

Additionally, last week my colleague, Tryphenia Peele-Eady, and I asked our students in a doctoral seminar which we co-teach, to view and reflect in writing on the DVD of your 2004 dialogue with Courtney. My comments in this letter are sparked primarily, but not solely, by the reflections that you and Courtney generously offered to UNM graduate students and faculty during that very special collaborative conversation in 2004. In recent weeks you graciously expanded some of those comments for me by e-mail. I also draw here on the thoughtful, often moving, responses written by our doctoral students only days ago, students who have witnessed now in 2012 a dialogue conducted in 2004 about a book published forty years ago in 1972. Time, as well as historical and sociocultural contexts, gently seep and flow in and out of this letter to you, at times starkly delineating contextual differences across eras , and at other times hopelessly merging and blurring them.

Biographies record and interpret the events that compose lives across time. Reliving your dialogue, I was struck by the fact that the professional biographies you and Courtney recounted were and are so profoundly marked by the developing and enveloping events of the decades you have lived, decades of epochal changes in this country and the world. Significantly, neither of you remained passive or distant from the turmoil of your time, nor did you contemplate from an academic's so-called "objective" distance the societal convulsions you were witnessing. Instead, you participated actively and passionately in momentous changes as they overtook and impacted your lives. In your dialogue, each of you related life experiences that channeled your passions and defined your life work.

In your case, Vera, there was the early history you lived in Hungary before and during World War II, the school you organized at age 14 while you were interned in a Nazi death camp, and your consuming desire to understand both the strength of the women in the camp and the psyche of those who would inflict such horrific genocide on fellow human beings. These profound experiences pointed you toward the study of psychology. But after immigrating to the U.S., you encountered the discipline of psychology at its Skinnerian apex, unable and unwilling to contemplate your questions. Instead, you comment in the dialogue, it was your *collaborative practices*, rather than either Skinnerian or later Chomskyan thought, that influenced and molded your theorizing. You recounted rich and diverse practices along your path: participating in the establishment of a preschool in high rise, low income black communities in Rochester, NY, in the early 1960s, an effort which was a precursor of the federal Head Start program; teaching in the amazing thought community that was Yeshiva University later in that decade; and your move to the Southwest where you worked closely with community-based education in local Hispanic and Native American communities, especially at Rough Rock on the Navajo Nation. Participating in these deeply collaborative, culturally based communities of practice convinced you that "culture was not a slogan, not an academic word. Culture was the daily reality of what it was to be human." Enmeshed in these collaborative communities of practice, you came to realize, you told us in 2004, that understanding culture, rather than merely learning language, was central to your work, and to human learning.

Courtney's trajectory was different but equally passionate and engaged. Both of you have acted within the circumstances of your lives, and your research has been courageously porous to all you experienced, mirroring but also reciprocally helping to mold the thinking and scholarship of your time, and ours.

Your primary concern during those early years, you e-mailed me, was "racism in schools and in academia."

The courage, commitment, and rhetorical power of the leaders and participants of the Civil Rights movement provided the historical setting for opposing racism in academia. Some aspects of the scholarly literature in psychology, linguistics, and anthropology provided an intellectual foundation for our work fighting discrimination, but we needed a broader theoretical framework to link our practice to a historically situated learning science (John-Steiner, personal communication). Then you added, "Vygotsky provided that basis for me." With the arrival from Russia of two new manuscripts which eventually were combined into *Mind in Society*, "it became clear little by little that the study of human consciousness and language development could be approached from a profoundly historical, social and cultural perspective" (ibid).

Last week, the students in our seminar were struck by your words, *little by little*. The fact that you would admit that your personal journey toward understanding Vygotsky has been a *slow, incremental process*, surprised, even astonished, them. They also found it deeply significant that teaching Vygotsky is one way you continue to learn about Vygotsky. As you explained in the dialogue, the give-and-take with students in the classroom gives you "the opportunity to explore more fully the implications of his theory," and in so doing, you learn and deepen your understanding of Vygotsky, even as you teach his works to others.

Our discussion in class returned over and over to the genesis of your own groundbreaking thinking. Your comment in 2004 that your developing consciousness of the depths and impact of Vygotsky's sociohistorical theory was a product of many years of committed, collaborative participation in the real-world struggles for justice of a diversity of communities.

> It slowly became clear that the overriding conception of using the individual as the unit of analysis, and looking at what it means to be human solely from the independent, isolated human self, was in stark contradiction to what was happening all around us—the Civil Rights movement, the anti-war movement, the women's movement. All of these developments were based on people doing things *together*, being profoundly, humanly connected in their attempts to change their reality. (Cazden & John-Steiner, 2004)

These comments sparked deep reflection among all of us, doctoral students and faculty alike: Is it possible to live lives such as yours and Courtney's in academia today, and if so, how? Can we imagine, and then create, lives that embrace the struggles for justice in *our* moment in history, lives that are collectivized and collaborative, rather than individually and competitively focused on "making it" in academia? In a recent e-mail you commented that you see even sharper tensions between individualistic and social theories than at the time of the interview in 2004. It felt as though all of us in that seminar room were quietly assessing our personal strength and courage to break out of the egotistical academic mold in order to be community with each other and with others who struggle.

You closed your 2004 conversation with a final warning and challenge to the faculty and graduate students present:

> Qualitative methods and field methods are under attack today. We would not know what we know about classroom culture, or about language acquisition, or most of what we know about cognition, were it not for studies that are long-term, both qualitative and quantitative studies, in naturalistic settings. Among the many things that we have to fight for, and the list grows longer every day, we have to make sure that the accomplishments of these ways of learning about human learning are protected. (ibid.)

Yours is a call to collective academic action. We must fight to conduct long-term studies, in naturalistic settings, where the accumulation of our observations and collective practices over time, recorded in the notebooks of our own minds, little by little help us understand, in community, about consciousness and what it means to be human. According to the poet Rilke, "verses that are good" come only when a lifetime of experiences and memories "have turned to blood within us, to glance and gesture, nameless and no longer to be distinguished from ourselves." Vera, I believe you are telling us, and teaching us by example, that it is our active engagement in communities of struggle across our lifetimes that can, "in a most rare hour" the poet says, give birth to scholarship, and academic lives, that truly matter.

DR. LOIS MEYER is Professor of Bilingual and ESL Education at the University of New Mexico. A former classroom teacher, program coordinator, and curriculum specialist, her research encompasses teacher preparation and curriculum development for linguistically and culturally diverse classrooms, language policy in Mexico and the U.S., and the ethnography of indigenous bilingual education in Oaxaca, Mexico.

REFERENCES

Rilke, R. M. (1968/1974). *For the sake of a single verse: From the notebook of Malte Laurids Brigge.* New York: Clarkson N. Potter.

LETTER FIFTY-FIVE

Bridges Beyond Budapest
The Work of Vera John-Steiner

Valerie Clement

Dear Vera,

You've crossed bridges and you've built them. You've used the bridge as a metaphor yourself at times and are fond of the image of the Széchenyi Chain Bridge. And like the Széchenyi Bridge, you have constructed connections throughout your life as scholar and mentor and teacher, creating unity and community like Buda to Pest.

The bridge is an appropriate metaphor for your work because it illustrates many aspects of your lifelong underlying vision of connecting us, making visible the truth that is the foundation of human accomplishment—that we live and work and create and grow not in isolation and independence, but in relation and interdependence. We live our lives in collaboration. And it is through this inner to outer to inner flow

ERIKA CHOUNG, *SZÉCHENYI CHAIN BRIDGE BY NIGHT*, 2007.
Reprinted by permission of the artist. All rights reserved.

of experience that we grow beyond the limits of our singular isolated potential. (You have said this better yourself, as readers will see in your quotes throughout this volume.) Your commitment to the work of making connections is extraordinary. You have spent a lifetime supporting others and sharing tools for exploration. Linking, joining, supporting, collaborating. This is why the image of a bridge suits you particularly well.

> Bridges connect us.
> They link one place (or idea) to another.
> They bring people together.
> They provide a means of crossing over obstacles.
> Bridges are testaments to visible, as well as hidden, means of support.
> Bridge building requires collaboration—integrating the various skills and talent of specialists "joined by a shared vision."
> All of these functions apply to your work spanning time and place and cultures.

So, dear Vera,
> Thank you for encouraging explorations in thinking.

Thank you for making the hidden visible.
Thank you for being a supporting pillar, a truss, a beam.
Thank you for expanding horizons of understanding.
Thank you for building bridges
> between disciplines
> among students and colleagues
> across generations

linking previously separate ideas, fields of knowledge, academic departments and bringing us together, creating interdisciplinary communities from which new ideas are visualized and constructed, providing scaffolding for the future.

Thank you for helping this student find a path to herself and connection to others.

With gratitude,
Valerie Clement

VALERIE CLEMENT, M.A., is a freelance editor, instructional designer, and project manager. An assistant to Dr. John-Steiner for 12 years, she helped establish the Arts-in-Medicine program at the University of New Mexico Hospital where community artists bring creative encounters to patients and medical professionals to restore health.

PART FIVE

Expanding the Community of Thought

LETTER FIFTY-SIX

A Blueprint for an Architecture of Accomplishment

M. Cathrene Connery and Robert Lake

Dear Colleagues, Collaborators, and Friends:

At the start of this book, we invited you into the heart of the three nested circles that organize our text. In the first circle, you became familiar with the extraordinary resilience, intellectual talent, and diverse roles Dr. Vera John-Steiner has demonstrated across her career. Within the second circle, you gained access into the sphere of thought represented in Vera's scholarship. Letters from this second sphere also established the personal salience and professional significance of Vera's effort to shed light on the creative, collaborative life of the mind. We encourage you to review her companion volume, *The Selected Works of Vera John-Steiner*, for additional explorations and discoveries. In reading the correspondence of the third ring, you gained entrance into a circle of learning and development through the *perezhivanija* or lived experience of Vera's students, mentees, and collaborators.

From this vantage point, we would now like to ask you to reflect on what it means to be a scholar, a teacher, a mentor, a colleague, and collaborator. In transacting beyond the multi-modal, diverse voices expressed in these letters, what can we learn from this collective text? What might we take away? Why did Vera's students, mentees, collaborators, and colleagues respond to their task in such a powerful manner? What lies at the core of their reverence, respect, and loyalty? A measured, scientific analysis of the collective body of letters establishes a series of emergent themes from which we might draw instruction, inspiration, and hope. In the text below, we share these observations with you.

THE WOMAN: A TRAILBLAZER AHEAD OF HER TIME

The collective correspondence describes this scholar, teacher, and mentor as a woman of beauty and presence. In her lifetime, Vera has called Budapest, Geneva, New York City, Rough Rock, and Santa Fe her home. After a childhood interrupted by war, the warmth and support of secondary school mentors in Switzerland nurtured her belief in the healing force of knowledge. This principle has inspired Vera's life-long journey in learning beside resilient peoples that have included Rochester's African-American community and the Diné tribal council on the Navajo Nation. Having served as a full-time or visiting faculty member at a host of institutions including Hawaii, Columbia, Yeshiva, Helsinki, and the University of New Mexico, upon retirement, Vera once remarked that academia had always been her country. Those individuals closest to her describe the scholar as an "example of unfailing pure kindness", possessing "a deep interest in trying to understand what the universe is all about" accompanied by "an unbreakable commitment to trying to make this a better world" (Hersh, 2012). Meyer (2012) recounts how Vera's engagement within these rich and diverse communities provided a springboard for her to be an active agent in the world, "understanding culture, rather than merely learning language…[as] central to human learning".

In this service, Smagorinsky's (2012) letter establishes Vera as a trailblazer ahead of her time. He places the intellectual and woman in historical context, calling attention to the sociocultural challenges and choices that shaped both the venue and body of Vera's academic work. Smagorinsky reminds us, "Not only did she go against orthodoxy…she did so as one of the few women to work on a doctorate in the 1950s, as a Jew at a time when Jews were held to quotas in many universities and other institutions and were associated with communism through questionable attributions of the Bolshevik Revolution to Jewish leadership, and as an immigrant during a period of post-war xenophobia fueled by the anti-Semitism". Brice-Heath's (2012) correspondence further confirms Vera's avant-garde stance, noting "identifying as a psychologist, she came from a field that centered on the individual as learner. The era in which she received her training was full of 'individual' pioneers, inventors, artists, corporate leaders, adventurers, and statesmen (with few women acclaimed as individuals in any of these areas of achievement). Yet she looked around her and pushed back against what others all around her proclaimed".

Several letters pointed out parallels between Vera and L.S. Vygotsky, another pioneer in the social sciences. Stetsenko (2012) muses that both the scholar and her distant mentor came of age in the turmoil preceding world wars where "the most valued human activity was developing and working with ideas, engaging in impassioned conversations about the great achievements and traditions of human knowledge". Unlike many individuals impacted by social discrimination, personal tragedy, and cultural destruction, Vera and Vygotsky are both well known for their "generosity of spirit and wisdom—a kindness matched by high standards" (Miller, 2012). Just as Vygotsky provided a positive, transformational influence to his many students and colleagues, Spolsky (2012) describes Vera as "a role model of intellectual rigor and social responsibility". A student of many years, Shonerd (2012) characterizes Vera's teaching and mentorship by elaborating, "Your nurture and challenge, face to face and through your writing, has been fundamental to what I think and do in the world. To a world of mindless power, you have spoken the power of ideas. I take those ideas very personally. They save me every day from alienation and despair. To connect that living, breathing person to those powerful ideas gives hope, energy, and commitment". Let us now move to examine why the letter writers of this text experienced Vera's scholarship in such a profound way.

THE SCHOLARSHIP OF VERA JOHN-STEINER: FROM THOUGHT AND LANGUAGE TO CREATIVITY AND COLLABORATION

A COMMITMENT TO SOCIAL JUSTICE

Vera's scholarship is hallmarked by its historical-political origins, intellectual rigor, and methodological accessibility. Inspired by the courage and example of individuals engaged in the civil rights movement, the corpus of her work is founded on a commitment to equity and social justice. Cole's (2012) letter describes the historical context in the field of psychology where "issues of cultural differences in cognitive ability" were being discussed during the late 50s and early 60s. He notes, "This tangle of issues around the role of culture and socio-environmental factors in bringing about the 'achievement gap' present when *Brown vs. Board* became law, provided an important arena" for what Panofsky (2012) portrays as the impetus to challenge and correct "biased, ethnocentric, and racist" policies and perspectives by a novel generation of social scientists.

The fight against poverty and oppression both from and within academia necessitated an epic, paradigmatic shift. In an early publication, Vera asserted the "behavioral consequences of living in poverty cannot be adequately studied without reliance upon a generalized theory of the social environment" (John, 1971, p. 64). Gratefully, she found her muse in the genius of Vygotsky. As one of four co-editors to introduce Vygotsky's sociocultural theory to the West, Blunden's (2012) letter points out that the publication of *Mind in Society* during the late 1970s provided the theoretical scaffold to revolutionize the social sciences as so many individuals in Vera's thought community strive to achieve to this day.

Vera's second muse was found in the pedagogy of the Brazilian educationist, Paulo Freire. When viewed as an integrated whole, the writings of these distant mentors provided Vera with an ideological framework to challenge the status quo. With Vygotsky's and Freire's praxis at each elbow, Vera and others engaged in the long-term, intensive task of paradigm change by dismissing universal, ahistorical theories that have traditionally isolated human beings and entrenched discriminatory bias in the academic literature. By placing culture at the heart of our lives, development, and learning, Vera and others recast learners as active, engaged agents, which redefined "learning as the fulfillment of human potential rather than the transmission of knowledge and the training of skills" and the role of education as an "essential, liberating" endeavor (John-Steiner, 2010, n.p.). Because Vygotsky and Freire emphasized the role of physical and psychological tools as artifacts capable of transforming cognition, Vera was able to stand on the shoulders of these giants to find her niche in researching "the full development and use of language and communication as part of empowerment" on behalf of self, community, and society (John-Steiner, 2010, n.p.).

The sociolinguist Bernard Spolsky (2012) observed in his letter that Vera's "choice of a Russian and a Brazilian as intellectual gurus, account for [her] early publications encouraging bilingual education of children" at a time when such a pluralistic stance was considered radical, if not unpatriotic. Indeed, in a collaborative writing venture during 1978, Elsasser and John-Steiner maintained, "Vygotsky and Freire shared approaches that emphasized the crucial intertwining of social and educational change. While Vygotsky focuses on the psychological dynamics, Freire concentrated on developing appropriate pedagogical strategies" (p. 362). Spolsky's letter suggests that, as a trailblazer who recognized "that the brain was not naturally monolingual, a common assumption among U.S. psychologists who conducted research on white monolingual first year students...[Vera was] able to explore the burgeoning multilingualism of New York and the established multilingualism of New Mexico, going beyond the Texan approach in which 'bilingual' was a polite word for Mexican". As additionally noted in her *Selected Works*, Vera's family background, personal motivation, and distant mentors shaped the sociocultural, historical-political foundations of her scholarship in the cause for social justice.

RIGOROUS, INCLUSIVE INTERDISCIPLINARITY

From her earliest book on bilingual education (John-Steiner, 1971) to the inner life of mathematicians (Hersh & John-Steiner, 2010), the intellectual rigor of Vera's scholarship has been distinguished by a complex, balanced, inclusive interdisciplinarity. Several letter writers evidenced the thinker's ability to deeply tap and cross-reference multiple wells from the research literature as a distinctive feature of her scholarship. Spolsky (2012) recalls how Vera's penchant for interdisciplinarity provided leadership at the University of New Mexico supporting faculty attempts to integrate "theoretical findings of a number of related approaches to the study of language and literacy (anthropological, linguistic, educational, sociological, psychological) with the practical task of dealing with educational problems of the disenfranchised as well as the majority student, and appropriate localization of international learning".

This interdisciplinary approach not only added walls to the framework Vera had been developing based on Vygotsky's and Freire's conceptual plans, but eventually provided the scholar with the theoretical, methodological, and pedagogical tools to pursue a life-long quest to answer, "What sustains creative and intellectual endeavors?" (John-Steiner, 1985, p. xiv).

Additional correspondents elaborated on the balanced, inclusive treatment of subject matter in Vera's lectures, presentations, and texts. In calling attention to the equal treatment of emotion and intellect, Smagorinsky (2012) portrayed Vera's scholarship as a "radical departure from the clinical approaches to skull-bound cognition". Indeed, numerous writers described her even-handed attention to thought and feeling while drawing on the work of both female and male thinkers as decidedly feminist in orientation. Vera's expansion of Vygotskian theory with the help of feminist concepts is further evidence of her measured treatment of and commitment to dispelling dichotomous myths in psychology. As Snyder (2012) warns us, "Thought is never separate from feeling. They are seamless. In recent decades, we have learned more about how much our brain is 'hard-wired' to attune empathically to the embodied meaning of what the other is communicating. To reflect thought accurately without reflecting feeling is not only virtually impossible, but is a violation of the richness and complexity of human meaning-making which is grounded in living".

METHODOLOGICAL ACCESSIBILITY

Such a balanced, inclusive interdisciplinarity was constructed using radical, sophisticated yet accessible communicative tools. A host of writers, including Richard-Amato (2012) and Putney and Wink (2012) credited Vera's translations and elaborations of Vygotskian theory to be essential to their understanding. Indeed, Rychly's (2012) first reading of Vygotsky's *Thought and Language* "felt like trying to pry open a locked box." However, Vera's "clear and insightful explications" offered the novice scholar a missing key. The aesthetic experience of listening to or reading Vera's scholarship proved to be equally paramount for several correspondents. Many contributors relate a parallel experience to Danberg's (2012) "Heschel test" whereby readers are able to randomly open one of Vera's texts only to locate "beautiful, memorable prose that expresses something you otherwise knew but could not say".

Perhaps Oppenheimer (2012) best captures the sense of emotional connection Vera forges between herself and her readers, sharing "I can still remember the visceral rush of reading [your] words in great long gulps of astonishment and inspiration. Here was someone who could eloquently explain what I had thought". Such affective resonance is an additional reflection of the rich balance of sources Vera taps for her data including interviews, biographical material, primary source materials, sketches, notebooks, short character studies, observations, and three-dimensional prototypes. De Santis (2012) astutely points out that the scholar "went directly to [your] sources, creative human beings, especially those living, to explicate the dynamics, the power of self-awareness, of intuition, imagination and boldness." While highly academic in nature, Goncu (2012) additionally characterizes Vera's writing through its resonant use of meaningful examples as "powerful evidence presented in a fluid and warm narrative...illustrating how one can defy dry disciplinary boundaries in the effort to remain loyal to human existence".

At the same time, Pléh and Boross (2012) remark that Vera's approach is both novel and international in scope, noting, "Vera's methods in a way precede and foresee the new network theories of human relations and knowledge dissemination. There certainly is a growing new network theory around the social sciences at large (Borgatti, Mehra, Brass, & Labianca, 2009)". As Sawyer (2012) concludes, Vera's trademark is her "ability to draw on profound and substantial theories to gain insight and to aid in... interpretations, but then to communicate...findings clearly and reach a broad audience". Myer's (2012) letter reminds us that the methodologies Vera actively employs cannot be taken for granted: "We would not know what we know about classroom culture, or about language acquisition, or most of what we know about cognition, were it not for studies that are long-term, both qualitative and quantitative studies, in naturalistic settings...we have to make sure that the accomplishments of these ways of learning about human learning are protected".

MEDIATION AND SOCIOCULTURAL CONCEPTS

Many letter writers reveal how Vera's scholarship provided meaning and connection to their personal and professional lives. Their testimonies relate how Vera's articulation and elaboration of Vygotskian theory offered stepping stones to significant academic, pedagogical, and performative pursuits. Following in her footsteps, Vera's students, mentees, and collaborators discovered how Vygotskian theory validates the complexities of dialectical development that occur as a result of the interplay between natural life forces and human agency. As the letters attest, thinkers from a variety of disciplines abandoned previously constructed notions from the literature, to recast notions about themselves, others, and children as "active, vigorous participants in their own existence...[who] at each stage of development...acquire the means by which they can completely affect their world and themselves" (John-Steiner & Souberman, 1978, p. 123). Toward this end, Vygotsky, Vera, and other sociocultural theorists offer alternative definitions of mind, meaning, and meaning making by placing motion, resilience, and choice at the heart of human development. Indeed, St. John's (2012) epistle calls our attention to the novel language that allows socioculturalists to validate and express complicated intricacies between relationship, development, and learning: "Consideration of the dynamic interplay of exchanges in the ZPD [zone of proximal development] has resulted in such terms as *distributed, interactive, contextual*, and the result of the *learners' participation in a community of practice*. These imply rich and divergent environments...and *mutual appropriation* [whereby] children manipulate ideas as they offer and receive contributions, moving from imitation to mastery".

McCafferty (2012) highlights the same dynamisms as they relate to the site and source of learning and development. Drawing inspiration from Vera's work, he asserts, "Contexts and orientation should never be ignored, something that has not always been at all kept in mind in the mainstream approach [to second language acquisition], in which 'subjects' are often treated as objects and orientation to the task is sidelined along with individual differences". Indeed, the role of context has been especially significant in McCafferty's explorations of private speech and language development. Crediting Vera's emphasis on Vygotsky's development of consciousness, his letter underscores "how critical the intertwining of thought and language is, forming a new modality that becomes central not only to cognition / affect, but to ontology as well as in relation to culture".

The success of Elsasser's (2012) *Books for Bluefield* project offers a pedagogical example of what Vera often refers to as the complex interlacing of thought and language within meaningful contexts. In Elsasser's description of an activist approach to literacy development, she explains that the appropriation of literacy proficiencies was girded by "the inextricable interactions between internal cognitive development and external social context". In her project, Nuevo Mexicano middle schoolers and Nicaraguan school children were engaged in a series of powerful dialectical transactions between the two populations and their larger society, facilitating both literacy development and social empowerment. While Vygotsky humanized psychology by highlighting the role of culture in experience, Vera's scholarship maintains his legacy by expanding on the importance of context. In turn, her work has endowed theoreticians, researchers, and practitioners with a conceptual and pragmatic inheritance that emphasizes the role of authentic learning within realistic, dignified, and humane environments.

Additional writers spotlight Vera's contributions to their understandings of sociocultural theory. For example, Putney and Wink (2012) explain how the scholar's extensive work on spontaneous / everyday and scientific / academic concepts assisted them in representing concept development as "a complex process that moves from *heaps* of things that the child thinks belongs together, proceeds into *complexes* in which the connections between the items are functional, and then evolves into *conceptual thinking* that requires and demonstrates a generalized understanding". Putney and Wink (2012) go on to characterize that "this progression of conceptualizing happens in relation to problem solving actions on the part of more experienced others who scaffold the process". Vera's own writing calls attention to the sociocultural, historical-political nature of this process whereby, "the meaning of a fully developed concept involves cultural and intergenerational transmission, verbal thinking, and practical application" (John-Steiner, 2007, p. 138).

Other thinkers credit Vera's Vygotskian scholarship as the source of a methodological blueprint for the examination of complex, interdisciplinary processes including the "simultaneous consideration of both a fully developed system and a system in the process of development" (John-Steiner et al., 1998). Meehan's (2012) correspondence describes the intricacy and precision of the functional system's approach which afforded her "the opportunity to study the dynamic internal and external processes of dyadic interaction while embedded within the sociocultural context of substance using mothers". With Vera's mediation of meaning through Vygotsky and Luria's sociocultural concepts, Meehan was able to analyze "various processes within the system...but only as they relate to the other interdependent functions (John-Steiner & Meehan, 2000)".

FROM THOUGHT AND LANGUAGE TO CREATIVITY

Vera's early scholarship into Vygotsky's notions regarding the relationship between thought and language eventually provided a springboard into what many of her correspondents consider her greatest contribution. As Spolsky (2012) outlined, she began "to look at non-linguistic aspects of brain activity and coding, such as the 'languages' of mathematicians and artists and choreographers, and move beyond the cramping simplistic Whorfian hypothesis of thought constrained by a language to exploring creativity itself, and beyond the limitation to single minds to the understanding of the nature and possibilities of creative collaboration". Vera's sophisticated yet lucid development of the concept of cognitive pluralism proved to be a pivotal point for her career and psychology as a whole. Her ground-breaking notion validated Vygotskian perspectives on inner speech, while extending Vygotsky's legacy into the realm of multimodal meaning-making.

In his letter, Smagorinsky (2012) depicts cognitive pluralism as the processes whereby "people think symbolically and construct textual worlds through which they make their lives meaningful". For example, Kellogg's (2012) letter juxtaposes visual and verbal language through a dynamic reading of two paintings, highlighting the relationship between signs and perception, attention, and memory. He additionally points out parallels between Vera's early work on bilingualism, sociocultural theory, and cognitive pluralism observing that "Verbalized perception, verbalized attention, and verbalized memory are not, of course, separate skills like pronunciation or handwriting. On the contrary, it is almost as if each psychological function has a lower end which interfaces with the environment (like a spoon, a knife and a fork) and which therefore differs from all the others, and then a higher end which interfaces with volition, where the functions are all the same, or at least very similar." Pléh and Boross' (2012) letter targets the utility of cognitive pluralism asserting, "She has elaborated the 'mediation' into modern theory about the role of external mediating media.... The important point is that in her version of mediation, theory mediating notes not only regulate behavior but also help to create novel ideas."

Multiple contributors write of the epic impact *Notebooks of the Mind* had on their understanding of themselves, their students, and their respective place in the world. As an artist, Sowell-Lovejoy's (2012) first introduction to the concept of cognitive pluralism was a transformational event: "That is when I discovered *Notebooks of the Mind*. That book changed my life. Not only did it offer directions for my artwork, but it also influenced my teaching style." Cotter's (2012) case studies further attest to the power and potential of cognitive pluralism when viewed as a theoretical and pedagogical tool. Her letter highlights the essence of this sophisticated concept, while issuing an urgent call to cultivate the multimodal thinking processes of young children and adolescents. The pedagogist offers a variety of ways in which the languages of the mind can replace the "rigidity of thought" that pervades K–12 schooling, calling for schools to serve as an ideological refuge for diverse thinkers while implementing an engaged, enriched, and equitable education (John-Steiner, 1997, p. 86).

Across the course of many years, the seed of cognitive pluralism blossomed into Vera's mature scholarship on human innovation and ingenuity. Her scholarship removed the study of creativity from the attic and ivory tower, placing it back into the sunny, cluttered windows of the studio, lab, and everyday spaces where we engage in multi-modal problem solving. Sawyer (2012) describes her novel definition of creativity as "a rich, active, collaborative, conversational, and embodied complexity". Usher's (2012) letter spotlights Vera's talents in providing accessibility to these complicated intricacies, noting her appreciation for the scholar's "rich and textured stories of creativity and collaboration" that permit "us all [to] think through how the mind works, and examine the genesis of how people grow into their passions".

Feldman's (2012) correspondence recounts the dual imprint Vera's scholarship has made to and on the field of creativity studies as a whole. A member of an elite group of scholars charged with charting new directions for the discipline, he relates the struggles his committee encountered in redefining ingenuity in developmental, domain-specific, and large-scale cultural terms. After engaging in much dissention, "Vera's remarkable effort to capture and describe a major shift in the field of creativity studies as involving the formation of a thought community" allowed the group to reorganize, reassess, and persevere, through her efforts to contribute, model, and co-construct a dynamic essential to the group's success. In addition to crediting Vera with the introduction of Vygotskian theory to creativity studies, Feldman observes, "I see that she actually contributed to the effort to give it clarity and became a member of that very thought community itself".

Such a unique contribution and productive redirection could only be facilitated by Vera's profound understanding and elaboration of Vygotsky's notions of inner speech. As Snyder's letter (2012) points out, Vera's discussion of verbal thinking in *Notebooks of the Mind* calls attention to the fact that language and thought are neither the same nor mutually exclusive processes. As a poet, Snyder validates Vera's understanding of the creative process typified in the quote, "It is through making explicit not only what is new inside one's mind, but also what is the implicit background of ideas, knowledge, and beliefs that novelty and insight arises" (John-Steiner, 1985, p. 139)". Snyder explains, "There is a process of 'dissolving' language into its felt meaning as we turn inward thought outward.... Thus it is that great poetry can at times appear to be not only the preferred way to express a truth, but the only way". Wix (2012) additionally found inspiration in Vera's revisioning of thought and language relating: "The idea of inner speech captured my imagination and became central to my final work involving painting and poetry. Both informed my understanding of thought and language as I practiced painting as a way of thinking and poetic language as congruent with my ways of knowing". Lake's (2012) epistle also corroborates the "fusion of self speech, inner speech, and outward expression in communication" as a transformative bridge leading to cognitive-affective movement. As an educator and doctoral student, he had been in search of a means "to connect the inner processes of incubated thinking and meditation with curriculum and pedagogy". But like so many correspondents moved by Vera's books, cognitive pluralism and creative collaboration "instilled me with a greater sense of personal agency by providing me with a language that allowed me to make sense of my own experiences."

Several correspondents recall their first experience of reading Vera's scholarship on creativity employing terms related to sustenance and renewal. Connery has previously noted the painful experiences many innovators have weathered including social marginalization, discrimination, and other forms of oppression. She describes the experience of encountering realistic, authentic, and positive understandings about creative individuals within the legitimacy of the formal literature to that of the experience of a wanderer discovering water in an existential desert. Vera's readers often needed time to integrate the significance of her contribution before personal transformation was precipitated. After reading *Notebooks of the Mind*, Aguilar (2012) explains: "The sadness that came with this new view on creativity was the realization that growing up, I had not had mentors or teachers who had developed my creativity in the way...vividly described in the lives of all".

An additional contribution of Vera's scholarship on creativity included a shift away from the representation of innovative thinkers as the proverbial 'tortured soul' or drug-addicted eccentric. This distorted, sometimes pathological view was replaced by a more accurate portrayal of imaginative thinkers engaged in a holistic quest for meaning, relevance, and connection as a part of a larger process of personal healing and professional achievement. As an administrator and music educator, Usher (2012) underscores the value of a balanced view regarding "the role of personal loss and illness in the lives of creative thinkers. Pointing out that a creative life is bound to include setbacks and struggles in addition to the joy of discovery underscore the rich complexity of being human and can be well used by young scholars in the contemporary era". Indeed, after years of marginalization by and within institutions, several letter writers noted that Vera's scholarship had girded and advanced their personal and professional work. As Brice-Heath (2012) attests, "the ideas of John-Steiner have taken me to a micro-view of human interactions around symbol systems ranging from language to musical notation to the codes within graffiti arts. Head nods, eye gazes, overlaps and interruptions in conversation, and simultaneous talking and sketching stand out as some of the most obvious ways in which individuals communicate and create as they talk about ideas not immediately present in objects, models, actions, or representations. In these instances, the joint work of imagining what is not seen relies on mutual tuning of attention to mental sketching and collectively imagining". Methaney (2012) highlights both the generative content and powerful example of Vera's scholarship confiding, "I've used your work with Vygotsky and creativity so many times to pull myself from the despair that threatened to engulf me and my research, my writing, and my life".

COLLABORATION AS THE ESSENTIAL PLAIT

In reviewing a lifetime of scholarship, Vera's emphasis on human collaboration can be described as the essential plait around which her many research interests have been interwoven. After a career spanning five decades, her commitment to social justice, human agency, and a balanced, inclusive interdisciplinarity is evident in the passage: "Through collaboration, we can transcend the constraints of biology, of time, of habit, and achieve a fuller self, beyond the limitations and the talents of the isolated individual" (John-Steiner, 2000, p. 188). Interestingly, this specific quote was repeatedly cited in her correspondents' letters as a means of highlighting both Vera's scholarship on collaboration as well as her willingness to engage in the collective dynamic.

Vera's study of collaboration spans all levels of structure, from micro to macro dimensions of human relationships and our larger society. Blunden (2012) reminds us of Vera's unique contribution as "the only person who has made a genuinely deep study of collaboration, while in my opinion, collaboration is the archetypal human relationship and ought to be at the centre of *all* social and psychological research". In calling attention to her typology of distributed, complementary, family, and integrative collaborations in his letter, Blunden asserts the *"collaborative project* is the essential unit of human, social life" and through her research and writing, Vera has "given us the first anatomy of human life adequate to understanding the modern world" (John-Steiner, 2000, pp. 196–204).

Like many other students, the noted second language pedagogist Richard-Amato (2012) credits Vera with introducing her to the concept of the zone of proximal development. Convinced by the efficacy of mutually assistive, collaboratively constructed learning opportunities from her work with adults in the field, Richard-Amato went on to build seminal bridges linking cognitive and sociocultural theories in the field of second language acquisition. At a micro level, Parker-Rees' (2012) letter calls attention to Vera's insights into the role gender plays in collaboration. From a feminist perspective, Vera once asserted that traditional "male-type autonomy is only possible when scaffolded by caregivers and partners—often women—who support the man's questing for fulfillment" (John-Steiner, 2000, pp. 106). Parker-Rees' letter highlights Vera's informed understanding that "gender distinction between autonomy and caregiving is socially constructed, not biologically inevitable...emphasiz[ing] the functional advantage which comes from the flow of ideas between people who each have their own, complementary ways of thinking". At the macro level, the need to resolve large-scale, complex issues in a cross-disciplinary manner served as an impetus for Vera's collaborations with both Minnis and Meehan. Meehan's (2012) epistle relates the challenges in moving problem solvers from multidisciplinary thinking to a state of interdisciplinarity through the integration of knowledge.

In summarizing her contributions to the academic literature, Panofsky (2012) aptly notes that the common thread across Vera's scholarship—from thought and language to creativity and collaboration—has been her challenge "against deficit views, and against nativist and individualistic theories, to build increasingly powerful understandings of the workings of the social environment and the profound interactions between culture and nature". Like the metaphor of researcher as onion peeler presented in Moran's (2012) letter, Ervin-Tripp (2012) underscores the significance of Vera's scholarship is "not to find final answers and put issues away, but to open new issues and make extremely rich observations that will lead to new research on mental processes". Brice-Heath's (2012) discussion of the new brain research prompts us to consider the importance, profundity, and magnitude of Vera's contribution: "No individual can live, think, know, or create except in interdependence with others.... Almost daily, researchers in the neurosciences discover ways in which divergent populations of neurons collaborate to generate reciprocities.... John-Steiner made us see the integration of patterning in relations—among humans, in works of art, and behind science experiments and ventures of discovery. She must certainly have done so knowing that others would someday find this kind of integration in new kinds of evidence from developing fields and disciplines".

Perhaps the value of any corpus of research is determined not only by the questions it attempts to answer or the inquiries it leads us to, but its potential to combat human suffering. In repeatedly returning to the question, "What sustains creative and intellectual endeavor?", Panofsky (2012) notes Vera's scholarship "has helped to highlight differences between what is and what could be for all learners in schools, for the importance of all learners and all modes of expression, for the possibilities of truly meaningful learning and personal transformation".

SCHOLARSHIP AND RELATIONSHIP: PRAXIS IN TEACHING, MENTORING, & COLLABORATING

In her letter to Vera, Brice-Heath (2012) reminds us that "the Western world's celebration of individualism and separate disciplines since the Renaissance has led to the mistaken idea that the end point of identity is *autarkeia*, independence from external factors as the optimal goal of each subject. Human history points decidedly toward oppositional narratives". But it is the rare individual who enacts a truly egalitarian, collaborative dynamic in their professional relationships. Within the ivory towers of academia, such a practice is especially uncommon. Perhaps what makes Vera so unique is her willingness to live her findings: like her distant mentor Vygotsky, Vera's research simultaneously became her method. Stated in another manner, the theoretical and research gains Vera has developed through her scholarship additionally provide the venue by which she achieves praxis in her teaching, mentoring, and collaborations.

Indeed, the collective body of letters points to a scholar who not only talks the talk, but walks the walk along a continuum of professional relationships ranging from teacher and mentor, to colleague and collaborator. Usher (2012) draws our attention through her admiration for Vera's "profound dedication to [your] students and the ways in which [you /she] mentored them as emerging scholars and encouraged their early professional opportunities and growth." In launching the careers of multiple individuals from diverse disciplines both inside and outside academia, we encounter an academic who has risen above petty, departmental wars over student pawns and the professorial guru who attempts to reproduce replicates of themselves.

The systematic analysis of letters in this volume revealed that the same themes that distinguished Vera's scholarship were found to characterize her teaching, mentoring, and collaborations. In the movement from scholarship to relationship, Vera's correspondents validate her commitment to equity and social justice, intellectual rigor, and methodological accessibility. They relate the intentional, measured, and pragmatic application of understandings regarding the nature of thought and language, as well as the cultivation of creativity and collaboration. In her capacity as teacher, mentor, colleague, and collaborator, and through what Brice-Heath (2012) terms "the integration of patterning in relations", we observe Vera's active construction of a thought community, one learner at a time.

In Vera's example, we witness an ethical professional with a willingness to walk beside and with the learner until both teacher and student are collaborating together. Wix (2012) describes this continuum as a "multi-faceted relationship that has stretched me beyond who I knew myself to be. In my professional and personal life, you have served and continue to serve as mentor, teacher, colleague, co-author, and occasional lunch companion". Panofsky (2012) employs Lave's (1996) definition for this experience as "increasing participation in a community of practice" in which the easing of asymmetrical power relations is earned by the novice over time, and access to resources available within collaborative interactions undergo their own developmental transformations. For many of Vera's correspondents, this process began by walking into one of her graduate classes.

VERA'S TEACHING: ORGANIZING THE SOCIAL LEARNING EXPERIENCE

The collective epistolary indicates that taking a course from Vera was often a unique and transformative experience. Angermeier (2012) employs visual and verbal modes in her epistle to capture what it felt like to walk into one of Vera's classes. Her graphic letter admonishes readers: "Prepare to be SEEN". A hushed silence usually fell after a first session together, as students considered the profundity of the instructional session and the professor herself. It was obvious to anyone sitting in her class that we had enrolled in a course delivered a brilliant, gentle, and great mind. Without saying very much and in her own quiet way, Vera communicated care and high expectations for students before, during, and after our sessions together. As Ronch (2012) recalls, Vera's "poise, warmth, humanism and genuine interest in me felt like the welcoming embrace of family. In [your/her] calm, assertive way [you/she] became for many...students the strongest creative and moral force in our education."

The instructional context was unusual in that knowledge was enacted as a social experience. Each student's funds of knowledge were publicly recognized as a collective resource to expand and extend within the course. This practice was often a surprise to new students who were not used to Vera's abrupt departures to target someone's specific expertise or interested body language. As Moran's (2012) letter confides, the "teaching methods were unlike any I'd encountered before. The emphasis…placed on interlacing personal experience with conceptual knowledge (both your own and students), the focus on meanings not just findings, and the fluidity of conversations became standards against which I judged later courses I took or taught". Sowell-Lovejoy (2012) further attests, "The pedagogical structure of the class provided a collaborative experience, perception and support for myself, a young artist who fit the description 'beset with anxiety'.… Your class, knowledge, books and insights provided…support".

From seminars on Language Acquisition to the Psychology of Women, Vera's course content was intensely complicated, dense, and rigorous. Interdisciplinarity of thought and practice was modeled as a distinct means of collaboration within disciplines and between fields. As Shank (2012) recollects, "lectures were thought-provoking, packed with information, terminology and ideas, plus she always seemed to elegantly integrate the themes and topics from the assignment reading into her prepared comments, observations, and reflections…with her experience and knowledge in the domains of language, cognition, psychology, bilingualism, and of course Vygotskian theories and their application".

Several writers referenced Vera's distinct discourse style in which she executes dense, yet elegant thought-syntheses while scanning the top of the ceiling for the visual references in her mind. Richard-Amato (2012) describes how Vera "spoke in cogent paragraphs, complete with parallel structures and transitions—almost as though…writing a book in the air with…every word". The experience of listening in class often encompassed being transfixed and frustrated at the same time: several correspondents reported the difficulty of capturing complex information in cryptic notes mediated through the most graceful of aesthetics. In keeping with Danberg's (2012) "Hershel Test", it was often tricky to decide whether to focus on the meaning or the beauty of words as they were presented. Perhaps Aguilar's (2012) letter best depicts the experience many students had of being in class with Vera who "would always craft the most marvelously shaped thoughts, which I would carry home, clutching them close to my chest. As I would go to sleep that night, I would admire their glittering beauty in the darkness…[their] shining insights helped me to realize that all the things I had done, all the things we all do, was in response to one's history, culture, society, and environment".

At the same time, Minnis (2012) points out that the mediation of such complex information was "about producing the new instead of transmitting the known". Shank (2012) notes the content in Vera's classes was "usually created an environment of inquiry, robust dialogue, and discussion between Vera and her audience. It was within this resulting dynamic, as Vera worked to guide us through the complexity of the assigned literature and subject matter, where I feel she made one of the most indelible impressions upon me as a student and teacher". Indeed, Aguilar (2012) recalls, "Reading Vygotsky with [you / Vera] was a scholarly experience I will never ever forget. The longing that I had, the hunger for intellectual pursuit was made whole. I may not have had the society growing up, which Vygotsky so emphasized as key to development, however, my yearning for discourse was not misplaced; it was a basic human need. My search was not misguided, but a desire for society and interaction that was motivated by curiosity, by compassion, by consciousness". In class, the artist and educator Sowell-Lovejoy (2012) acquired essential understandings for her own larger goals, sharing: "I theorized that if I could make art that specifically communicated through various processing modalities then I could expand my own intellectual understandings of society, language and thought. Throughout the course of the semester, I learned how various people think, construct knowledge and how they creatively process that information into cultural artifacts. Not only did I learn about famous individuals, but also about my fellow classmates".

A seriousness of purpose pervaded each class session. In being true to the integrity of the content and seriousness of her scholarly mission, Wix's letter (2012) recalls Vera's "sharp remarks in response to over-zealous students". Language was carefully used as a tool to communicate concepts and co-construct the containers in which thoughts lie. Similar to Rychly's (2012) "receptive discourse" where teachers engage in dually directed meaning-making with their students, the goal of Vera's linguistic faculties was to validate the communicative intent and inner voices of her students and thereby nurture the confidence and capacities of emerging scholars.

Shank (2012), a linguist himself, aptly describes Vera's intentional and pedagogic construction of the zone of proximal development where,

> regardless of either the nature, formulation, phrasing or even relevance of a student's question or comment, Vera always, without fail or noticeable hesitation, seemed to effortlessly and adroitly find the relevant or germane element and relate it back to the topic under discussion. The net result was that Vera was almost always able to smoothly validate both the content of the question and the legitimacy of the questioner and thus maintain the speaker's sense of face and confidence and the larger atmosphere of risk-taking and inquiry in the classroom.

Danberg (2012) describes this form of teaching in his letter whereby we "learn the commentary and teach it. The…class itself is the commentary, each member, the time we take, the work we do, our perceptions, efforts and the rhythms of return that compromise our movement from beginning to end, all are the commentary we learn". Shank (2012) validates the efficacy of this practice in its potential to "create and sustain a very positive classroom and discourse environment for the students even when faced with the insecurity associated with dense or complicated reading assignments". The collective result of these practices "maintains a classroom atmosphere of congeniality, respect, risk-taking, and inquiry", eventually leading to the co-construction of a thought community over time (Shank, 2012).

Course assignments additionally supported collegial, collaborative, inter- and cross-disciplinary explorations. Methaney (2012) characterizes Vera's mid-term or "peer exam", as "sociocultural historical pedagogy made manifest in an evaluative teaching tool". Otto-Diniz's (2012) letter describes the peer exam as a "seemingly simple assignment [that] addressed a complex array of elements at the heart of Vygotskian theories of creativity and education while simultaneously and seamlessly interweaving Vera's own scholarship, teaching, and mentorship". This task required students to meet with a colleague outside of class to discuss a topic of interest or importance to them. After a series of meetings, each dyad helped to shape research questions for each other. On the day of the exam, peers would orally present the findings their investigations had yielded to their partner. This conversation was then tape-recorded, transcribed, and further developed by the student to eventually submit to Vera as a written exam.

In her epistle, Wix (2012) draws attention to "the exam's deep relational roots. Its focus on co-constructing knowledge through dialogical peer inquiry (and art) processes is core to the work of making sense of the psyche and…has to do with psychological self-knowledge. Too few in education understand this, and too many fear it". Her letter provides an account of the interpersonal and intrapersonal reciprocity structured by the peer exam, and its transformative potential to construct intimacy in relationships between the self and others. Otto-Diniz's letter (2012) describes the long-lasting impact of the exam, affirming "the lived experience of that assignment of 13 years ago—particularly the experience of problem-finding as negotiated with a partner, the delay in closure on defining the problem, and the power of choice to foster intrinsic motivation—continues to reverberate through my current practice as a museum educator". Her letter describes how the features of the assignment and its resulting impact echo and reverberate in the collaborative interpretation of art works with museum visitors, placing curiosity, intrigue, and joint meaning-making at the heart of the social learning experience.

FROM TEACHING TO MENTORING & COLLABORATION

In her writing and courses, Vera often emphasized that "an individual learns, creates, and achieves mastery in and through his or her relationships with other individuals. Ideas, tools, and processes that emerge from joint activity are appropriated, or internalized, by the individual and become the basis of the individual's subsequent development" (John-Steiner, 2000, *Creative Collaboration*, p. 5). Prior to this collection of letters, perhaps few have known the extent to which Vera engages in facilitating such development. This collective correspondence sheds light on her remarkable efforts in intellectual midwifery and the construction of a thought community through extended mentorships and long-term collaborations.

COMING INTO BEING: RELATIONSHIP AS REQUISITE FOR SELF-REALIZATION

Moran's letter expounds on one of Vera's principles of human development, reminding us that "we not only create artifacts and tools for each other to use, we create each other.... Perhaps our greatest creative achievements are the kinds of people we develop through interaction and role-modeling". Suki John (2012) portrays her life-long relationship with her mother as a vibrant celebration of self-discovery, a disciplined, hopeful, yet honest realization of abilities, and the cultivation of a fierce dedication to the life of the mind. The professional dancer, writer, and academic relates in her letter that Vera "has helped me to make sense of everything from Balanchine to Bakhtin, at the same time helping me to make sense of myself."

As a former student, Ronch (2102) employs similar terms to describe the mentoring he received, crediting Vera's "generous spirit and profound influence…with the basic tools to undertake the journey to 'come into being' wherever it took me" (John-Steiner, 2000, p. 187). The willingness to co-construct the essential conditions and dynamics leading to another's transformation ensures the success of the teaching-learning experience. By championing and assisting her students to "come into being", Vera's mentorship can be described as an active and open-ended form of 'people-shaping' and creative collaboration.

Multiple correspondents verify that the acquisition of personal knowledge within their relationships with Vera proved to be essential to their own self-realization: Wiltshire's (2012) letter emphasizes the role of mentoring as a relational requisite to her own professional transformation. She points to Vera's insight that "the process of growth requires resolution of the contradictory tensions between the social embeddedness of learning and the creative individual's drive toward a personal voice. When a young artist or scientist begins upon a unique path by declaring his or her identity… he or she needs the assistance of others to overcome the limitations of a single view and to face public criticism or rejection" (John-Steiner, 1997, p. 208). While observing, "The inner work is solitary, because it is internal, requiring careful and constant observation of the mind so as to understand how it works", Wilshire stresses that "the effort to arrive at this point of self-recognition requires the help and support of many people and appropriate conditions". As a mentor, Vera's provision of physical, mental, and emotional resources allowed Wiltshire and others the opportunity to engage in "joint thinking...significant conversations, and...sustained, shared struggles to achieve new insights", affirming that "productive interdependence is a critical resource for expanding the self through the life span" (John-Steiner, 2000, p. 191).

WITHIN THE ZPD: VALUES, COMMITMENTS, AND COLLABORATION

In establishing that human learning, growth, and transformation are dependent on positive, healthy, and professional relationships, this collection of letters demonstrates how Vera based the construction of a thought community on this principle. However, as Moran (2012) stresses,

> co-construction comes not from simply throwing people together.... Co-construction in 'thought communities' requires a mindset to influence and be influenced by the other, to accept a process of emotional as well as cognitive engagement, and to commit to our interdependence as constructors of knowledge and possibility.

Whether serving as a mentor-guide across a foreign landscape or a collaborator-companion walking at an equal pace, Vera's example confirms that successful mentoring and collaborations are founded on the values of open mindedness, shared power, emotional sensitivity, and a respect for the developmental process. She then enacts these values as commitments to form the very structures of her professional relationships.

In parallel with her scholarship and teaching, Vera's mentees and collaborators point to her long-standing commitment to diversity, manifested through her dual attention to inclusiveness and interdisciplinarity. Several epistles recount measured, intentional moments where she pulled individuals traditionally excluded 'outside' the periphery of academic circles into her thought community. By tapping thinkers with multiple funds of knowledge from a variety of disciplines, both the scholar and her learners benefitted from a dialectical approach to learning and relationship, to apply the notion: "In creative work, opposition and dynamic tension often yield new understanding" (John-Steiner, 2000, p. 52).

The collection of letters also portrays a constellation of key commitments present within zones of proximal development across several historical periods. For example, Aguilar (2012) shares that Vera's commitment of time "was the essential ingredient to foster my own confidence. You found my ideas worthwhile and you let me push with my questions and my doubts". Vera's allegiance in providing access to resources otherwise unavailable allowed Abercrombie (2012) "the opportunity to closely observe an experienced thinker...to witness that person's modes of thought" (John-Steiner, 2000, p. 151). Sharing informal car pool conversation with her professor permitted Abercrombie the chance to see the world through the eyes of a unique other, as Abercrombie shares: "Like the forces that shape the desert surrounding us, I began to learn from you how to tune in to the subtle processes shaping the landscape of our minds". Many correspondents indicate such access not only ensures the acquisition of theoretical knowledge, but allows for the appropriation of paradigmatic or meaning-making structures unreachable without an experiential platform. Abercrombie describes the process of internalizing the subtle, nuanced processes of intergenerational collaborations in her appreciation of Vera's "finely tuned expertise as mentor created a unique smoothness in approach. I did not recognize how you [Vera] were teaching me about zone of proximal development from almost the first moment we met".

On the other hand, Hersh (2012) identifies the value of Vera's "psychological insight,...sympathetic imagination [and] willingness to speculate about people's minds and hearts" as the cornerstone of her commitment to cultivating her mentees and collaborators' unique ontologies. This compassion for the human condition, coupled by an uncanny ability to assess the developmental strengths and challenges of individuals, underpins Vera's commitment to assist people in recognizing and pursuing exactly what they next need to grow. The gift of this vision made all the difference to several writers. As Hersh (2012) affirms, "Writing another book was something I would never have undertaken, with my 80th year approaching. Yet we have succeeded. We produced something worthwhile". At the same time, the letters reflect Vera's deep respect for the individualistic integrity of the developmental process, including an unshakable belief that the agencies of her mentees and collaborators will be realized in their own time, space, and personal trajectories, noting "the realization of one's special talents and the best way to use them—does not necessarily follow a simple linear progression" (John-Steiner, 1985, p. 72). When coupled with the gift of confidence, Vera's commitment to ontological development allows her mentees and collaborators to nurture trust in their own selves and capacities for growth.

Mahn's (2012) letter stresses Vera's commitment to emotional sensitivity as evidence of the importance she places "on the influence of emotions in human cognitive development and in social interactions". By observing Vygotsky's notion that thought is preceded by emotion and concepts move from external to internal understandings, Vera's validation of personal and relational affect lays the foundation for success in both learning and labor. Miller (2012) relates how she experienced and appropriated a discourse of collaborative leadership modeled by her teacher and mentor. Today, Miller draws on Vera's cognitive-affective use of language to assist business professionals who additionally seek to scaffold dignity and discovery in the service of scientific progress. Her letter credits Vera's willingness and capacity to simultaneously offer both challenge and care, "to learn to hold the light, yet not lower the bar, and to remind [the learner] 'yes it is possible' and 'you may be the only one who can do this'.

Still other mentees describe Vera's commitment to shared power within carefully calibrated, meaningful apprenticeships. Shank's (2012) moving letter outlines the benefits of challenge, uncertainty, and triumphs experienced through the struggle of collaborative achievement. While Vera offered the gift of confidence and academic shoes she knew Shank to be capable of growing into, the student and mentee recalls:

> It was intimidating to be given free artistic and analytical reign with Vera's source material and to engage her on an equal level given her clear seniority and considerably more experience, but at no time did she ever deviate from the role of collaborator. I felt both valued and an important contributor through the entire process.

As we read in his epiphanic account, in publicly acknowledging Shank's efforts and status as her collaborator, Vera's commitment to shared power allowed the emerging scholar the opportunity to co-construct his professional competencies, sense of efficacy, and future academic career.

In identifying this constellation of commitments, it is important to recognize that their implementation is mediated through a profound understanding of the power of language as an affective tool. Vera's correspondents report a rich continuum of informal and formal conversations held over lentil soup or within academic journals. From Panofsky's (2012) description of "free-wheeling, speculative, exploratory, not-always-goal-oriented discourse" to Mahn's (2012) insights regarding "the need we all have…to hear authentic praise", Vera's mindful, measured, intentional, and constructive use of honest language was repeatedly evidenced across the collection of letters. In some instances, correspondents report that Vera's discourse provided gentle direction to guide thought and action. In other situations, she issued overt, direct, and authoritative comments. In yet other circumstances, Vera engaged in non-verbal or the deliberate absence of messages, employing powerful communicative forms that occur only in the silence. A mode of expression often exercised by Vera's Diné friends and colleagues, De Santis (2012) recognizes her ability to "allow moments of silence to prevail over clatter. This is not the absence of human communication, but a gradual process of engaging others, forming friendships and eventually establishing a professional or personal relationship". Often, Vera participated in freeing her mentees' inner voices through coded means including extensive e-mail conversations, in alignment with her observation that "the need to reach somebody by words, written words, is important, as the young person frequently feels too tentative for self-expression in the presence of those he or she respects and loves" (John-Steiner, 1997, p. 50).

Regardless of the form, the mediational integrity of these communications lies in what Rychly (2012) describes as the "pedagogical possibility" of receptive discourse in which educators listen for learners' "thinking behind the words they use. Receiving and responding in this way maximizes the potential of classroom discourse to help students know themselves as agents of meaning construction…[to] develop persistence in the face of confusion or frustration."

Vera's exercise of receptive discourse is significant in that, beyond the propensity to externally direct thought and behavior, she enacts her commitment to employ professional speech that might potentially become internalized in the imagination, choices, and actions of her mentees and collaborators. Indeed, many of her correspondents report a common experience of having conversations with Vera in their heads or asking themselves, "What would Vera do?"

In addition to shedding light on the processes inherent in people-shaping and community-building, these letters signal the internalization of voice and identity while highlighting the powerful impact of an influential and constructive mentor. For many writers, this transformational experience was the first validation of gendered subjectivities within a lifetime of invisibility, disregard, or discrimination. Like a child accidently discovering the sweetest scent inside an elegantly carved perfume bottle, Hasu's (2012) letter captures Vera's essence as a female role model and the discovery a founding mother,

> who labeled many matters with names, which I felt had been lacking. The emphasis on semiotic as well as relational and emotional signs in mediation, the focus on relationships and dyads, and elaborations on subjectivity, experience and interdependence in creative endeavors (with a feminist flavor), written in such a fascinating manner, watered the drying land into which I had entered.

Through Vera's language, graciousness, and honored commitments, Hasu confirms, "You showed me the way, and gave me the strength to become a researcher who does not deny her subjectivity, her gender in particular, in her research".

A CREATIVITY OF HOPE

In reviewing Vera's scholarship, teaching, mentoring, and collaboration, we hear a call from the collective community to place creative collaboration and collaborative creation at the heart of initiatives related to human development and learning. In contrast to "the individual, social group, family, [or] state" Blunden's (2012) letter calls our attention to the fact that the "collaborative project" is *the* universal, normative, and essential mode of human activity. Stetsenko employs similar terms in her letter stressing: "Having now reread Vera's works, I think it is important to explicitly include creativity among these formative constituents of human nature, asserting that it is human nature to be creative and innovative." Vera's new definition of creativity is essential to many projects, including the advancement of understandings regarding the teaching-learning process, the implementation of educational reform at all levels, and the ongoing effort to achieve social justice in society. Methaney (2012) argues that creativity is a social requisite in contemporary times, pointing out, "In today's information, technological and innovation driven society, creativity has become more of a necessity for psychological health and life success. It can no longer be viewed as a luxury or marginal to 'the good life'; it is essential to society's ability to develop and work under conditions of fast-paced change". Yet, Cotter (2012) and many other correspondents lament the epic neglect many educational institutions have waged when it comes to validating, let alone nurturing, the qualities and contributions of creative thinkers.

On the contrary, Stetsenko (2012) asserts that creativity constitutes a fundamental aspect of that which defines and unites us as human beings. Following in the footsteps of Vera and her distant mentors, she argues on behalf of a sociocultural perspective which places creative collaboration and collaborative creation at its center, embracing the notion "that human development has to do with active and purposeful…collaborative activities and practices of transforming the world". In reflecting on Vera's work, Stetsenko maintains, "Many of her observations on creative individuals can be applied to elucidate the most generic ways of how humans develop and learn. The role of continuous seeking for varied directions and meanings, sustained commitment to queries and creative life, immersion and exploration, continuity of concern, perseverance, independence and flexibility, non-conformity…point to key dimensions of what it is we need to nurture and help our children to develop, including in educational settings". The individual and collective experience of contributors to this text affirms that it is not only possible, but necessary, to place creativity at the forefront of our personal and professional relationships. As Stetsenko proposes, "Putting emphasis on the notion that there is a creative genius in all of us might be the best way to fashion development and learning that indeed can set us on a path of true creativity" as learners, scholars, teachers, mentors, and collaborators.

In locating meaning, agency, and relationship at the center of innovation, Vera's example provides us with a creativity of hope. Her message, methodology, and instructional mode compel us to re-vision human beings and their potential as learners, teachers, mentors, and collaborators. In keeping with Blunden and Stetsenko, Vygotsky and Freire, her life-long professional commitments and praxis call on us to redefine the nature of humanity and the thought community as the source and site for humane and dignified learning.

STANDING AT THE CENTER: CO-CONSTRUCTING COMMUNITIES OF THOUGHT

At the start of this text, readers were invited into three nested circles by reading a series of letters that composed each sphere. In the first circle, you became familiar with the extraordinary resilience, intellectual talent, and diverse roles Dr. Vera John-Steiner has demonstrated across her career. Within the second circle, you gained access into the sphere of thought represented by Vera's scholarship. Letters from this second circle also established the personal salience and professional significance of her effort to shed light on the creative, collaborative life of the mind. In reading the correspondence associated with the third ring, you gained entrance into a circle of learning and development through the *perezhivanija* or lived experience of Vera's students, mentees, and collaborators.

Now that you are standing at the center of these nested circles, we once again ask you to turn and look outward. In doing so, you will witness a rare, breathtaking view of interconnectivity among an overlapping network of common and unique, individual and collective thinkers. This collective epistolary allows us to witness a professional life dedicated to achieving praxis and social justice while gaining essential insights into what it means to be both a learner and teacher at the heart of a thought community. From this exclusive vantage point, Vera's example offers insights into how we might initiate, cultivate, and sustain thought communities for individuals of all ages, based on a collaborative, creativity of hope.

Learner / Teacher as Dignified Human Beings: Findlay (2012) distinguishes Vera as a role model who understands that "educational theory begins with the fact that persons are not abstract, ideal entities, but flesh and blood people, who live in a real, particular social world". In our attempts "to understand and describe this dialectical process of mutual transformation", learners and teachers must approach each other with psychological insight, sympathetic imagination, and basic dignity. Because the dialectical nature of pedagogy is a reciprocal relationship between teaching and learning, Putney and Wink (2002, 2012) underscore that what we teach is as important as how we teach it to all parties involved.

Achievement Is a Cognitive-Affective Quest: As dignified learner-teachers and teacher-learners, personal and professional success is a cognitive-affective quest. Basteá (2012) highlighted that the need to achieve within thought communities is an aspect of a larger, intimate, cognitive-affective quest. In her letter, Basteá stresses: "We join these communities for the love of learning, of a good challenge, or of fulfilling a secret desire. We wish to connect again with a relative or friend, here or gone, who once inspired us…we strive to create a whole that is larger than the sum of parts, to be part of a community again, to contribute and receive, to learn and pass down information". We need to honor the multiplicity of motivations for travelers on our individual and collective journeys as we establish, implement, and reform communities of thought.

The Site Is the Source of Development: Because context serves as both the site and source of development, in order to facilitate development, thought communities must ensure that desired resources and structures are in place to successfully cultivate human and humane goals. If learners do not have access to target knowledge, skills, strategies, dispositions, mentors, artifacts, and / or other necessary sources, their absence often dictates a negative outcome. If we seek to nurture creative, intelligent, and resilient learners, we must arrange our instruction and institutions to provide access to those examples, artifacts, and activities that allow such qualities to flourish. Toward this end, Basteá (2012) encourages us to rethink the spaces in which learning and development might occur, urging us to consider the "borderless world of the internet" and other alternative platforms to co-construct community.

St. John (2012) offers us a window to view what our thought communities might look like. Her letter supplies us with a snapshot of the teaching-learning process in which the flow experience of young music-makers is encouraged, sustained, and transcended through the multimodal re-integration of signs and tools into scripts, artifacts, and cross-scripts. She highlights the dynamic potential of the ZPD as a framework whereby "finding a place to be, the child is free to discover competence through exploration and negotiation built on mutual trust. Participating in this kind of collaborative environment allows the community of learners to collectively experience the exhilaration of enabling each other to belong, to grow, and to learn". St. John notes that such contexts and conditions lead to a state of dignified interdependence.

Creativity and Collaboration Provide a Generative Focus: In our efforts to construct new spaces for growth and development, Basteá (2012) affirms that "learning is inherently creative and rooted in community". For thought communities to thrive, we need to continually focus on the efficacy of our efforts to creatively collaborate and collaboratively create. By concentrating our efforts on these common goals, we can move beyond the dichotomous criticism of competitive conflict to achieve a collegial, generative dialectic. Brice-Heath's (2012) letter identified the "foundational elements of collaborative creativity among young people" to be "complementarity of talents and channels of access to information, shared motivation to achieve, recognition of the need for productive failures, and mutual acceptance of both vertical and horizontal guidance". A focus on creative collaboration and collaborative creation eliminates the mythical "zero sum game" that prevents development, growth, and transformation. As Basteá affirms, "learning, like playing, is innate and self-generative. And that creativity needs to be continuously nurtured in order to thrive."

Proficiencies are Co-constructed in Active, Authentic Apprenticeships: Both individual proficiencies and thought communities are developed, sustained, and grow through meaningful apprenticeships where novices "immerse themselves in the work of their elders" as they "explore their inner resources...[and] varied invisible tools that help transform a gifted young person into a productive artist or scientist" (John-Steiner, 1997, p. 59). Elsasser's (2012) students appropriated essential knowledge, skills, strategies, and dispositions by "engaging in meaningful research, struggling with the conceptual challenges of artistic expression and participating in expanded social networks [which] profoundly changes how...students see themselves, and view the world". In targeting the internalization of essential knowledge and tools of craft, Minnis (2012) emphasizes that such proficiencies are developed*through* active and authentic problem solving complemented by joint productive activity and scaffolded instruction from multiple mentors. While Abercrombie (2012) stresses:

> Intergenerational collaboration most clearly illustrates the centrality of collaboration as a human endeavor, since it marks the historical transformation of knowledge from parent to child, from teacher to student, from mentor to mentee, while simultaneously transforming the knowledge of the more senior collaborator", access to multiple and distant mentors, through libraries, museums, and other collections remain just as essential to individual apprentices and the collective thought community.

Play Is Time Well Spent: As a nation, we have often failed to understand the requisite, generative properties of play for both children and adults. Berk's (2012) letter reminds us that children's formal learning is built upon the multiple, integrated foundations constructed in play. Vera's research affirms that, "The earliest sources that creative individuals draw upon are linked to childhood play to the many hours they have spent entranced by nature, the play of lights, or by a book" (John-Steiner, 1997, p. 37). A walk through the laboratories or studios of any institution of higher learning provides strong evidence of adults' need to engage in imaginative play.

Despite a wealth of international research on play across the life span, open-ended inquiry, innovation, and exploration have been stripped from American preK–18 classrooms with tragic consequences. As Berk (2012) relates:

> Underprivileged preschoolers and kindergartners are especially likely to be exposed to training in fragmented academic skills, and they are also the most harmed by it. Young children who spend much time filling in worksheets, as opposed to being actively engaged in play-based learning centers, show reduced motivation and developmental progress in motor, cognitive, language, and social domains. (Marcon, 1999; Stipek, Feiler, Daniels, & Milburn, 1995)

> These negative outcomes translate into poorer study habits and academic achievement during the elementary school years, with stronger effects for children from low-SES homes. (Stipek, 2004; Stipek & Byler, 1997)

In order to realize true educational reform, we must embed joyful, imaginative explorations that cultivate confidence and competencies within our curriculums, through successive approximations and multiple opportunities for success.

Göncü's (2012) letter explores the dynamics active in the garden of play where the thinker's inner teachers and audiences inhabit both sides of the psychological scene. Play is essential to development and innovation in that it frames an interior world where the imagination is free to weave meaning between self and society. He asserts, "When people are deprived of play opportunities, their growth and creativity are arrested". Because we re-create our identities, capacities, and futures through the intrapersonal and interpersonal dialectic of play, Göncü asserts, "taking play opportunities away from children should be questioned in research on social justice". Healthy learners and thought communities require the benefit of play.

Education Is a Process of Creating the Psychological Voice(s): If Lake and Oakeshott are correct, we do not inherit "an inquiry about ourselves and the world, nor of an accumulating body of information, but of a conversation" (1962, p. 490). Instead of viewing the primary role of education as the transmission of cultural capital, we need to reframe our notions about the learning process. Ultimately, the psychological voice is the most significant, lasting product of socialization and education. As a result, we need to place the languages of multi-modal meaning making, including a discourse of emotion, at the center of our pedagogies. Toward this end, Cotter (2012) urges us to consider how we are silencing children "by drowning our young minds in a deluge of information and requirements, suppressing their ability to make their own discoveries". We must unpack time-on-task mythologies, inquiring what learners ultimately gain from "the weight of repetitive and prescriptive homework" as a substitute for rich, sustained, and long-standing interactions and explorations.

Gallimore's (2012) description of natural or conversational teaching between parents / caregivers and children points to the need for teachers, mentors, and collaborators to employ "extended dialogues, leading questions, connections to a child's existing knowledge, more equitable turn distribution, collaborative inquiry over an extended period, and co-instructed text and event interpretations". By monitoring the discourse structures we employ, Gallimore advises we can engage in "interactions that nurture thinking and speaking...scaffolding, assistance in the zone of proximal development, or intellectual midwifery". When creating time, space, and opportunities that intentionally develop the inner voice, we must slow down and truly listen to engage in Rychly's (2012) receptive discourse. She argues that teachers, mentors, and collaborators can facilitate the developmental processes of learners by "listening for and responding to students' thinking....[as] a way to honor this responsibility."

Basteá (2012) also emphasizes that "schools need to focus on setting free the multiple voices of children in the spirit of learning, creating, and making for humans to thrive". Referring back to Cotter's (2012) example, we can provide ideological refuge from homogeneous "rigidity of thought" (John-Steiner, 1997, p. 86) by combining "language, sound, and movement to teach musical concepts...and integrated learning experience incorporating and combining the various languages of the mind".

We see from Wix (2012) and Otto-Diniz's (2012) letters that alternative assignments designed to scaffold, validate, and cultivate the inner voice(s), such as Vera's peer exam, have the potential to cultivate personal investment and place intellectual rigor in the accountability process, affording students with what Wix (2012) calls the opportunity to "examine their ways of knowing in relational learning contexts". Meyer (2012) and Shonerd (2012) point out such forms of assessment and research methods retain the potential value and obligation to shed light on human learning, development, and transformation to "help us understand, in community, about consciousness and what it means to be human" while offering and implementing "a humane narrative of learning and development".

AN ARCHITECTURE OF ACCOMPLISHMENT

At the start of this book, we invited you into the heart of our thought community. In the beginning of this chapter, we asked you to use Dr. Vera John-Steiner's example to reflect on what it means to be a scholar, a teacher, a mentor, and a collaborator. By reading diverse letters from nested circles related to her biography, scholarship, and professional relationships, we assert that the evidence is overwhelming: what we think about truly matters; the choices, language, behaviors, and actions we engage in have a direct impact on those around us; and a constructive, collaborative praxis is an achievable and worthwhile possibility. However, the collective correspondence of this volume also confirms that the ripple-in-the-pond phenomenon we may secretly aspire to does not rest on the efforts of a lone individual. Rather, as Gallimore (2012) reminds us, "It is a sociocultural phenomenon that arises when a small band of individuals set and share a common quest, commit to searching until they find a solution, develop and try out solutions, collect, share and reflect on results, and return to the old problem or turn to a new one. Their grail is better teaching and more learning, a search that makes meaningful progress but is never ending—in the best circumstances it becomes a career-long pursuit of continuous improvement".

But for now, we conclude with the reflections of Valerie Clement, who has served as a noted support and collaborator to Vera for many years. Clement's letter (2012) explores physical, psychological, and metaphorical bridges through a re-view of images, quotes, and genres to describe Vera's architecture of accomplishment. As editors of this text, it seemed especially appropriate to highlight this particular correspondent's insight into one of Vera's favorite symbols:

> The bridge is an appropriate metaphor because it illustrates many aspects of your lifelong (underlying) vision of connecting us: making visible the truth that is the foundation of human accomplishment—that we live and work and create and grow not in isolation and independence, but in relation and interdependence. We live our lives in collaboration. And

it is through this inner to outer to inner flow of experience that we grow beyond the limits of our singular isolated potential. This commitment to the work of making connections is extraordinary. You have spent a lifetime supporting others and sharing tools for exploration. Linking, joining, supporting, collaborating. (Clement, 2012)

As Lake's letter notes:

Bridges are only as valuable as the movement that takes place on them in bringing about connections. A bridge that is not traversed while connecting at least two specific points eventually gives way to the forces of entropy. But bridges that are traveled on become the means of reaching and embodying all that your scholarship embodies.

Therefore, we'd like to end with the image of multiple, sculptural bridges leading to a golden city where pillars of trust, kindness, democracy, and diversity are built upon a foundation committed to human potential. Drawing on the architecture of Vera's achievement, it has been our privilege to sketch out a basic blueprint for the thought community to which we welcome you, dear reader. What we will build now, depends on us.

REFERENCES

Elsasser, N., & John-Steiner, V. (1977). An interactionist approach to advancing literacy. *Harvard Educational Review*, 47(3), 355–369.

John, V. (1971). Language and educability. In E. B. Leacock (Ed.), *The culture of poverty: A critique* (pp. 63–80). New York: Simon & Schuster.

John-Steiner, V. (1971). *Early childhood bilingual education*. New York: Modern Language Association.

John-Steiner, V., & Souberman, E. (1978). Afterword. In Vygotsky, L. S. *Mind in society: The development of higher psychological processes*. (pp. 121–133). Cambridge, MA: Harvard University Press.

John-Steiner, V. (1985). The road to competence in an alien land: A Vygotskian perspective on bilingualism. In J. Wertsch (Ed.). *Culture, cognition, and communication* (pp. 348–372). Cambridge: Cambridge University Press.

John-Steiner, V. (1997). *Notebooks of the mind: Explorations of thinking*. Oxford, UK: Oxford University Press.

John-Steiner, V., Meehan, T. M., & Mahn, H. (1998). A functional systems approach to concept development. *Mind, Culture, and Activity*, 5, 127–134.

John-Steiner, V., Weber, R. J., & Minnis, M. (1998). The challenge of studying collaboration. *American Educational Research Journal*, 34(4), 773–784.

John-Steiner, V. (2000). *Creative collaboration*. Oxford, UK: Oxford University Press.

John-Steiner, V., & Meehan, T. M. (2000). Creativity and collaboration in knowledge construction. In C. D. Lee & P. Smagorinsky (Eds.), *Vygotskian perspectives on literacy research: Constructing meaning through collaborative inquiry*, (pp. 31–48). Cambridge, MA: Cambridge University Press.

John-Steiner, V. (2007). Vygotsky on thinking and speaking. In Daniels, H., Cole, M., Wertsch, J. V. (Eds.), *The Cambridge companion to Vygotsky*. New York: Cambridge University Press.

Oakeshott, M. (1962). The voice of poetry in the conversation of mankind. *Rationalism in politics and other essays* (pp. 197–247). London: Methuen.

Vygotsky, L. S. (1978). *Mind in society: The development of higher psychological processes.* Cambridge, MA: Harvard University Press.

www.ingramcontent.com/pod-product-compliance
Ingram Content Group UK Ltd.
Pitfield, Milton Keynes, MK11 3LW, UK
UKHW022238230426